Incentive relativity summarizes the early history of research on the effects of reward magnitude on animal behavior, emphasizing those studies that led to the recognition that rewards have relative, as well as absolute, effects. Recent research is presented in terms of three basic situations in which relativity effects occur: changing abruptly from an expected reward to a differently valued one (successive contrast); temporarily pairing two rewards of different value on a regular, daily basis (anticipatory contrast); and discrimination learning, during the course of which occurs behavioral contrast, which is viewed as a combination of the two more elementary contrast types. Each relativity effect is analyzed in terms of procedures, parameters, psychopharmacology, psychobiology, and theory. Potential extensions to relativity in human behavior are presented in the text, particularly in the prologue and the epilogue. An appendix summarizes the psychopharmacology of successive contrast and extinction, using four animal models of anxiety.

The book will be relevant for psychologists, behavioral neuroscientists, political scientists, and social scientists.

Incentive relativity

Problems in the Behavioural Sciences

Incentive relativity

Charles F. Flaherty

Rutgers University

CAMBRIDGE
UNIVERSITY PRESS

PUBLISHED BY THE PRESS SYNDICATE OF THE UNIVERSITY OF CAMBRIDGE
The Pitt Building, Trumpington Street, Cambridge CB2 1RP, United Kingdom

CAMBRIDGE UNIVERSITY PRESS
The Edinburgh Building, Cambridge CB2 2RU, United Kingdom
40 West 20th Street, New York, NY 10011-4211, USA
10 Stamford Road, Oakleigh, Melbourne 3166, Australia

First published 1996

Printed in the United States of America

Typeset in Times Roman

*A catalog record for this book is available from
the British Library*

Library of Congress Cataloging-in-Publication Data
Flaherty, Charles F.
Incentive relativity / Charles F. Flaherty
p.   cm.   – (Problems in the behavioral sciences : 15)
Includes bibliographical references and index.
ISBN 0-521-38118-5 (hc)
1. Reward (Psychology)   2. Incentive (Psychology)
3. Reinforcement (Psychology)   4. Psychology, Comparative.
I. Title.   II. Series.
BF505.R48F53   1996
156' .23224–dc20   95-37733
                                                                CIP

ISBN   0 521 38118 5 hardback

To:

George H. Collier

Michael R. D'Amato

John W. Davenport

Norman E. Spear

Contents

Preface

My academic interest in incentive motivation was probably first triggered as an undergraduate when I read Hull, Spence, and Kimble (on advice from two students of Spence, R. E. Clark, and Ralph Dusek, who were human factors psychologists at the U.S. Army Quartermaster Laboratories, where I worked part-time). In graduate school at Wisconsin, I encountered three more of Spence's students – John Davenport, Ken Goodrich, and Leonard Ross. My formal and informal instruction from the Hull/Spence perspective was intermixed with my own readings of Tolman, Mowrer, Amsel, Logan's *Incentive,* the Logan and Wagner book *Reward and Punishment,* Bolles, Neal Miller, and other contemporary books. A different perspective on motivation was provided by Harry Harlow both through seminars and in laboratory conversation; Harlow was no fan of Spence (nor of Skinner).

In addition to a general interest in learning, motivation, comparative psychology, and physiological psychology, my interests began to crystallize in part around the topic of contrast effects. No doubt everyone has experienced the sting of an unmet expectation or of a reward that is construed as unfair compared to what someone else received (as in the parable of the vineyard workers in the Bible). Actions influenced by relativity (that is, actions that occur when outcomes differ from expectations) probably contribute substantially to the variability and unpredictability of human behavior. The opportunity to go beyond folk psychology and experimentally study the topic of reward relativity was afforded by the contributions of early researchers in learning and those in perception, such as Helson and Bevan, who developed early conceptualizations of the problem and methods of study.

A move to Rutgers to be an assistant professor placed me among three very active learning psychologists, George Collier, Michael D'Amato, and Norman (Skip) Spear. These three created an atmosphere conducive to long hours in the laboratory, plus free and extensive discussion of the issues of the day. This environment, plus the 1968 reviews on contrast effects published by Black and by Dunham, further encouraged me to pursue the study of contrast (although one faculty member advised me in the early 1970s that the field was "mined out" and that I should study something else if I wanted tenure).

By the early 1990s it was clear that there were enough data and interesting theoretical issues to consider bringing the material together in one place so as to enhance its availability, encourage others to join the research, and perhaps stimulate the eventual discovery of answers to the variety of questions regarding the

ix

extensiveness of reward relativity, its adaptive value, neurobiology, genetics, and role in human behavior.

This book has been more difficult to write than I had imagined it would be, especially after all these years of conducting research on the topic. Even though incentive relativity is a restricted field, at least in terms of laboratory studies, it became clear that omissions would be necessary. One decision was to omit any extensive consideration of quantitative models. Thus, there is no treatment of the large literature generated by Herrnstein's matching law; no discussion of contrast in concurrent schedules (the context in which much of the matching-law research has been conducted); and no consideration of the DMOD model of Daly and Daly, which has applications to contrast in runway behavior, nor of the "equation for contrast" developed by Williams and Wixted. The omission of these topics was a decision based on what was appropriate for a book of this size and audience and is not a comment on the value of these quantitative approaches.

Many people have provided help and support during the course of this project. The advice and encouragement of Jeffrey Gray, the series editor for Cambridge, and of Abe Amsel is appreciated – as is the patience of Robin Smith of Cambridge.

I have benefitted not only from the research contributions of my graduate students but also from their informed discussions and suggestions. Their published papers are cited, but I would also like to acknowledge the intangible contributions of Howard Becker, Cynthia Coppotelli, Melissa Demetrikopoulos, Patricia Grigson Kennedy, Kathleen Krauss VanderGoot, Bruce Lombardi, Anne Brillhart Meinrath, Colin Mitchell, and Grace Rowan Szal. Cynthia and Colin had the bad luck to be in my laboratory while this book was in preparation and they have thus borne the burden (seemingly cheerfully) of reading drafts of the various chapters. I have also been fortunate in having many excellent undergraduates undertake research projects under my supervision. Many of these studies were eventually published; some functioned as pilot studies; some were "failures" that nevertheless provided useful information; some led nowhere. The assistance of the following recent undergraduates who have helped in the preparation of this book is especially appreciated: Sean Clarke, Anna Greenwood, David Hsu, Patricia Portugal, and Alba Rossi-George.

For much of the time that this book was in progress I have been chairman of the Psychology Department at Rutgers. I would like to thank the administrative staff, Carol Dixon, Donna Mignano, and Christine Seid, for functioning so efficiently that I was provided time for scholarly activities. All three also helped with some of the details of book preparation. Every department chair should be so lucky.

Special thanks are due to my wife, Mary, and daughter Jennifer for their help in reading drafts, for their patience, and, in Jennifer's case, for conducting some interesting contrast experiments in my laboratory.

Support for the preparation of this book was obtained from an NIMH grant (MH-48835) and from the Dean of Arts and Sciences, Rutgers University.

Prologue

If we rightly estimate what we call good and evil,
we shall find it lies much in comparison ...

– John Locke

We compare. Many of the pleasures and irritations of life are related to the match between an event and our expectancies – a comparison between what did happen and what "should have happened" based on past experience or vicarious knowledge. We compare meals, and components within a meal (wines with wines, salmon with salmon, bread with bread), we compare composers, presidents, books, performances, salaries, and many other events that have some interest or value. In the intellectual realm, a great deal of knowledge derives from comparison – comparative anatomy, comparative psychology, comparative literature, and so forth. Comparison is an automatic property of perception. Our judgments of brightness, hue, motion, depth, and so on, are strongly affected by the context in which stimuli occur – context being considered as other concurrently experienced stimuli and recently experienced stimuli. Complex judgments, such as the seriousness of a crime or desirability of a risky medical treatment, are also influenced by the context in which the judgments are considered (other crimes, alternative risks).

The passions are also affected by comparison and relativity. For example, a winner of nearly $800,000 in the New Jersey lottery said he "almost cried" when he found out that this was *all* he had won. He had expected 10 million dollars, but had to share the prize with 12 other winners (*Asbury Park Press*, 1983). Professional athletes paid large salaries in absolute terms are often unsatisfied because there are other athletes, perhaps viewed as comparable, who are paid more (*New York Times*, 1989). Labor unrest often follows periods of job reductions (see, for example, *New York Times*, 1984); even differential increases may lead to problems, as when New York police and firefighters threatened job actions because the pay raise they were offered was less than that which was awarded to transit workers. On occasion, reward loss leads to tragedy, such as when a professor, denied tenure, commits suicide (Associated Press, 1984) or when an executive loses his job and commits suicide (*New York Times*, 1987).

On occasion, some have found it tempting to relate global problems to psychological relativity. Klerman (1984) attributed a "current age of melancholia" to the "relative gap in rising hopes and the actual fulfillment of expectancies." It has

1

also been suggested that discrepancies between the material wealth possessed by two different groups or classes may precipitate unrest or social violence (for example, Abram, 1984; Feierabend, Feierabend & Nesvold, 1969). (An interesting question is that if this is the case, then why is such violence a relative rarity, given the pervasive discrepancies in material wealth.)

This book is not about the possible role of comparison and relativity in these complex personal and social issues. It is, instead, a beginning. It is about how rewards influence animal behavior when the animals are exposed to two or more levels of reward, compared to when they receive only a single level. Exposure to more than one level provides the opportunity for comparison. For example, one could ask how the maze behavior of rats rewarded with *either* 1 or 10 units of food differs from the performance of rats that are exposed to *both* 1 and 10 units of food. These differential rewards could be administered by training with one reward and then shifting to the other reward. Alternatively, animals could be trained in two mazes of comparable difficulty, but given a large reward in one maze and a small reward in a maze that is discernably different.

As it happens, the performance of animals is often substantially altered when they are exposed to multiple levels of reward, compared to when they are exposed to a single level of reward. The difference in behavior is the topic of this book.

Reward relativity was slow to be recognized – requiring some 50 years after the pioneering animal learning studies of Thorndike to be recognized as an issue, and requiring over 20 years after its demonstration to be fully appreciated. Another 40-plus years have elapsed since this time, and the mechanisms and functional significance of reward relativity are still only partially understood. The two-maze learning examples illustrate the two principal procedures in which reward relativity effects occur: (1) comparison of a current reward with the *memory* of a previously experienced reward; and (2) comparison of two rewards received more or less concurrently, but in different contexts.

Chapters 1–4 are concerned with relativity effects that occur when animals are shifted from one reward to another. The behavioral effects of such a shift are more robust when the shift is to a smaller reward, in which case behavior is often seriously, if transiently, disrupted. There are many interpretations of these behavioral changes, but it will be argued that a reward reduction, or loss, triggers a sequence of psychological processes that involve detection of a change, evaluation of the change, search for the missing substance, conflict (and emotion) if it is not obtainable, and eventual recovery. Neurobiological and neurochemical correlates of these behaviors will be considered. It will be hypothesized that this sequence is analogous, perhaps homologous, to what happens in humans following loss of a valued person or object, or perhaps following a simple disappointment. It will also be hypothesized that the effect is so pervasive, robust, and orderly, that the behaviors engendered by reward reduction must have been selected for through evolution because of their adaptive value – echoes of which may be seen in foraging behavior.

Reward relativity effects that occur when different contexts are correlated with different rewards are complex, but the literature reviewed in Chapters 5 and 6 suggests that there are two aspects to this type of relativity. First, exaggerations in responding occur just at the transition from a stimulus that signals one level of reward to a stimulus that signals a different level of reward. These effects are termed local contrast, and they may either energize or detract from ongoing behavior, depending on the direction of reward shift indicated by the relevant stimuli. In addition, there is an enduring change in behavior related to the anticipation of an impending reward. This anticipatory contrast develops slowly as the animal learns the sequence of rewards and/or the stimuli signalling the sequence. Anticipatory contrast may serve as a model of the manner in which the value of a current reward may be altered by learning that something better (or worse) will occur in the future. The anticipatory contrast procedure may serve as a way of studying time horizons in animal behavior – the temporal range over which the value of a current reward is influenced by an impending reward.

A general summary of empirical generalizations derived from contrast research is presented in Chapter 7. This final chapter also includes an epilogue that serves for further speculation regarding reward relativity effects in humans and lower animals. An appendix provides more detail on the material, presented in Chapter 4, that compares the psychopharmacological profile of reward reduction with profiles obtained in several animal models of anxiety. The comparison of such drug-effect profiles may permit inferences regarding commonalities of emotional states elicited by different animal models of emotion.

1 Brief history of reward magnitude research

Rats running the maze under the drive of hunger [learn] to
expect a specific reward rather than the mere satisfaction of
hunger.

> – M. H. Elliott, 1928

Incentive value is profitably viewed as proportional to the
distance between level of expectation ... and level of attainment.
...Amounts ... below the level of expectation ... [are] frustrating in proportion to the degree of negative deviation; ... amounts
above the level of expectation [are] elating in proportion to the
degree of positive deviation.

> – L. P. Crespi, 1942

The assumption that learning, at least trial and error learning, is based on the production of pleasure and elimination of displeasure was fundamental to the views
of Herbert Spencer (1870), Alexander Bain (1855), and Thorndike (1911; see
discussion in Boakes, 1984). This view, developing out of utilitarianism and
hedonism, and cast in a variety of forms, has been one of the enduring views of
learning and motivation (Bolles, 1967; 1991). If learning is supported by pleasure, then the question could be asked whether more or less pleasure supports
more or less learning – or, in behavioral terms, how does the amount of reinforcement affect learning and behavior. This would seem to have been a natural
question following the development of laboratory studies of learning in animals.

However, this seemingly natural topic did not lead to many studies. Perhaps
the answer to the question seemed obvious, or perhaps other questions regarding
the nature of learning and memory seemed to be of more importance. Indeed,
Thorndike (1911) barely mentioned the characteristics of the food he provided
the dogs, cats, and chickens in his learning experiments – he described it as a
few pieces of fish, in the case of the cats, or as an amount insufficient to sate the
animals even after a series of trials. Other early studies were concerned with the
comparison of pleasure and pain (food and shock) in their ability to support
learning, or with different levels of shock, or with different levels of hunger, or
with different degrees of delayed presentation of food (Cole, 1911; Dodson,
1917; Watson, 1917; Yerkes & Dodson, 1908).

Rietta Simmons (1924) was one of the first to specifically address the ques-

5

tion of the role of incentives in animal learning. She defined incentive as "the end which serves to arouse, to direct, and to bring to a conclusion some persistent activity" (p. 1). She compared qualitatively different incentives, substances such as milk and bread, sunflower seeds, opportunity to escape, opportunity for maternal behavior, and opportunity for sex, in regard to complex maze learning. Grindley (1929) chose the simpler problem of comparing different amounts of a single substance (grains of boiled rice), an approach that bypasses difficulties in scaling comparable amounts of qualitatively different substances (how much sex equals 2 grams of bread and milk?).

Grindley found that, by the end of training, the chicks with the larger amounts of rice ran faster; this finding was used by Hull (1943) to suggest that the amount of learning ("Habit Strength") increased with the amount of the reinforcing substance. Almost entirely on the basis of Grindley's experiment and a Pavlovian conditioning experiment by Gantt (1938), Hull went further to suggest that the form of this relationship was a positive growth function and also suggested that the reinforcement amount probably influenced the asymptote of learning, rather than the rate at which this asymptote was approached. Hull recognized that the data were not sufficient to confirm this suggestion. The actual paucity of data is indicated by Hull's citation of only two other studies, one by Wolfe and Kaplon (1941) in which chickens were reinforced in a runway with popcorn, and one by Fletcher (1940), who used pieces of banana to reinforce chimpanzees for retrieving objects against different degrees of resistance. These latter two studies also indicated better learning with larger reward, but the range of reinforcer values was not sufficient to determine if the same relationship to "Habit Strength" held in these studies as in the Gantt and Grindley experiments.

Hull did not cite two studies that varied reward quality, but that presaged the topic of this book – that rewards have relative as well as absolute effects on behavior. The first – a study by Tinklepaugh (1928) of delayed response learning in monkeys – reported how a monkey reacted when a piece of lettuce was substituted for the usual piece of banana located beneath the correct choice. The procedure of these experiments allowed the monkey to see the experimenter place the reward beneath one of two tin cups; there was then a delay during which the cups were out of view of the subject; finally, the animals were allowed to go to the cups and make a choice. The following reaction occurred when, unseen by the monkey, Tinklepaugh replaced the banana with lettuce:

She [the monkey Psyche] jumps down from the chair, rushes to the proper container and picks it up. She extends her hand to seize the food. But her hand drops to the floor without touching it. She looks at the lettuce, but (unless very hungry) does not touch it. She looks around the cup and behind the board. She stands up and looks under and around her. She picks the cup up and examines it thoroughly inside and out. She has on occasions turned toward observers present in the room and shrieked at them in apparent anger. After several seconds spent searching, she gives a glance toward the other cup, which she has been taught not to look into, and then walks off to a nearby window. (pp. 224-5)

Tinklepaugh noted that, under other conditions, the lettuce was appetizing to the monkey, but not after it had seen Tinklepaugh place banana under the correct cup. A second observer present in the room, Professor R. W. Miles of Stanford, verified Tinklepaugh's description of the events, and further wrote:

There was clear evidence in the animal's behavior that the preparatory state of having seen the banana had predisposed him [*sic*] to a certain expectancy which was frustrated on uncovering the lettuce. (p. 228)

In another demonstration, Tinklepaugh allowed three monkeys to observe him apparently place a piece of banana under one of three boxes but, in reality, Tinklepaugh had left a piece of carrot instead. When released, the monkeys raced for the boxes. Eva arrived first, grabbed the carrot and dashed off, with Psyche in pursuit. Eva outran her pursuer and then

climbed onto a perch and raised the carrot as though to put it in her mouth. When she looked at it her expression changed and she dropped it to the ground. Psyche gave up the pursuit abruptly. Pursued and pursuer quickly returned to the same box and renewed their search. They looked inside, under and around it. (p. 229)

After failing to obtain the banana, Psyche eventually ate the carrot. Tinklepaugh later tried a similar demonstration with children about 5 years old. Upon finding a piece of chocolate substituted for the preferred pink jelly bean, the children hesitated, exclaiming "That's different" and "You changed it" (p. 232). Tinklepaugh concluded that the monkeys and the boys behaved similarly in expressing "surprise" and "disappointment" (p. 233) and that both must have "retained some intraorganic cue which stood for the reward" (p. 234). Tinklepaugh also suggested that this behavior should be explained "on the basis of the simplest processes possible" (p. 234), in accordance with Morgan's canon (Morgan, 1894).

The second study reported on a similar, if less dramatic, experiment conducted at about the same time with rats. Elliott (1928) reported that rats ran faster and made fewer errors in a complex maze when fed a wet food mixture than when fed sunflower seeds. However, there was a substantial increase in both blind alley entries and time to traverse the maze when the wet food group was shifted to sunflower seeds – an increase that carried this group substantially above, in both time and errors, the group maintained on sunflower seeds. The change in performance was abrupt, occurring after a single trial with the substitute reward, and showed no sign of diminishing after 6 days of testing. Elliott's interpretation of these data was that the rats had learned to "expect a specific reward" (p. 29) and that the increase in errors and time was due to the animals' searching for the missing food. He thought that an explanation in terms of emotional processes was inadequate, because the behavior did not diminish after 6 days and emotional responses were generally thought to be temporary.

It was probably no coincidence that both of these experiments were conducted in the laboratory of E. C. Tolman at Berkeley.[1] Tolman's view of learning was quite different from other major figures of the time. Whereas Thorndike (1911) had argued that the food used in his studies served to strengthen stimulus–response connections, the food per se was not learned about. Rather, the food functioned as a catalyst (the term used by Rescorla, 1985) to promote the formation of an association, but it did not enter into the association. Tolman, however, argued that animals learned specifically about the goal object and that they also learned about "signs" that would guide them to that goal object. Whereas Watson (1913) and Hull (1943) argued that animals learned to make responses and that the food provided upon response completion served to strengthen this response learning, Tolman argued that animals learned expectancies, and the food items served to confirm or disconfirm these expectancies (see Tolman, 1932, 1959). From the perspective of Tolman's approach to learning, the term "reward" is appropriate to describe the food offered in the previously described experiments. The rice, banana, bread, and milk, opportunity for sex, and so forth, served to promote behavior. Once the animal learned of the availability of rewarding substances, the substance then functioned as a goal that the animal sought. The term "incentive" captures this meaning of the reward – it is an inducement that serves to pull the animal through the task in question.

However, from the perspective of Thorndike, Watson, Hull, and most other behaviorists, "reinforcement" was the preferred term. It captured Thorndike's view that the food objects used in his studies were not learned about or anticipated per se. Rather, they served to "stamp-in" or strengthen the connection between the stimulus and response relevant for learning in his puzzle boxes. For most behaviorists, reinforcement is the preferred term precisely because it does not carry the connotation that the animals are anticipating or expecting a particular outcome. In addition, reinforcement has certain advantages for describing behavior when aversive events, such as electric shock, are used to promote learning.[2]

The perspective we will adopt in this book is more closely allied to that of Tolman than to that of any of the other early theorists. Indeed, much of the recent research in animal learning has strongly suggested that lower animals do, in some sense, develop representations of the goal events used in learning and come to anticipate these goal events. Thus, we will tend to use "reward" and "incentive" as appropriate terms when discussing the experiments.

[1] A study at Yale by Cowles and Nissen (1937) also provided evidence that the effects of a food reward depended on the animals' previous experience, but the results were not as clear as in the above - cited studies.

[2] The issue of "reinforcement" or "reward" has received extensive consideration (see, for example, Berridge, 1996; MacCorquodale & Meehl, 1948). In recent history the two terms have often been used interchangeably. Alternatively, reinforcement is used either to refer to the act of giving a reward for a bit of behavior or to describe the change in performance that results from presenting a reward. Reward is then used to refer to the actual goal object (food, etc.). Black (1969) introduced the phrase "apparent reinforcement value" to refer to the strengthening effects of rewards. "Apparent" was used because, under some conditions, larger rewards lead to poorer performance than smaller rewards, leading to the impression that the smaller rewards are more reinforcing. That this is not the case is shown by reward reduction – when the large reward is decreased to the level of the small reward, performance declines.

Given that the early reward-shift studies of Tinklepaugh and Elliott were consistent with the view that animals develop representations of the goal object, it must be admitted that these studies had little impact and, in fact, were not even cited in Hull's *Principles of Behavior* (1943). One of the studies that Hull did cite, an experiment by Fletcher (1940) on the effects of reward amount on effort exerted by chimpanzees, clearly showed that the effects of a piece of banana of a given size depended upon the animals' experience with other sizes of banana pieces. Fletcher referred to these results as reflecting "relativity" and the presence of a reward expectation, but Hull did not consider this aspect of Fletcher's data. Instead, he referred only to the demonstrated effectiveness of absolute differences in amount of reward.

This failure to consider any of the data obtained by Elliott, Fletcher, or Tinklepaugh was unfortunate. Hull's theory had no provisions for reward relativity, an effect implied by the results of all three experiments. Furthermore, Hull's interpretations of associative learning, and the mechanism of reinforcement, precluded the occurrence of rapid changes in behavior following a reward shift. Instead, his theory predicted gradual changes in behavior to levels appropriate to the new reinforcement value (Hull, 1943, pp. 130–1). This prediction was specifically made in the case of upshifted rewards and was implied (but less specifically made) in the case of decreased rewards. Elliott's results clearly showed a rapid shift in behavior when reward quality was reduced, and Tinklepaugh's results showed that such changes in reward quality had an immediate impact on behavior.

A study by Crespi (1942) clearly showed that Hull's predictions regarding rapidity of behavior change following reward shift were incorrect and that relativity, which is not a component of Hull's theory, is indeed a factor to be reckoned with in the interpretation of reward/reinforcement mechanisms. Although the details of the experiment were somewhat complex, the basic results were clear: Rats for whom reward was abruptly changed – either increased or decreased – altered their behavior rapidly; this behavior did not simply adjust to levels appropriate for the new rewards, but instead went beyond these levels. Crespi had two conditions in the relevant parts of his experiment. In one of these, rats were trained in a straight runway at one trial per day. One group of rats was rewarded with a 16-unit incentive (each unit equaled one-fiftieth of a gram of Purina dog biscuit moistened with an atomizer). Two-thirds of the animals in this group were, after acquisition (20 trials), shifted to either 1 or 4 units of incentive and then shifted back again to the 16-unit value. The performance of these shifted animals was compared to the extrapolated running speeds of the unshifted 16-unit group. The results obtained are presented in Figure 1.1 – the upshifted animals reliably exceeded the extrapolated value of the 16-unit reward group in running speed.

In another experiment, Crespi shifted rats from 256 units or 64 units of incentive to the 16-unit value. In this case, the performance of the shifted animals was compared directly with an unshifted 16-unit control group. As illustrated in Figure 1.2, the shifted animals changed abruptly, with their running speed falling below that of the control group.

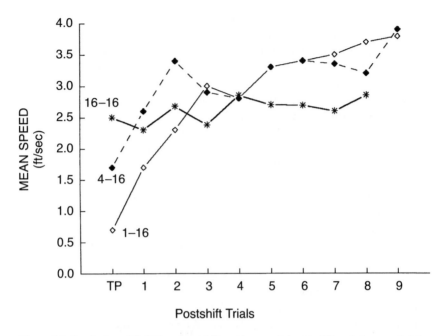

Figure 1.1 Terminal preshift (TP) and postshift running speeds in rats differentially rewarded during preshift (1, 4, or 16 units of food) and shifted to the same reward (16 units) postshift (trials 1–9). The animals for whom reward was increased ran faster than the control animals receiving the same reward level. This difference in performance was termed the "elation" effect by Crespi. (Adapted from Crespi, 1942.)

Thus, both of Crespi's experiments showed that, during the postshift period, the different groups of rats, all receiving the *same* reward (16 units), performed at different levels. Clearly, the effect of amount of reward on performance depended on the animals' prior experience with rewards of different values, as well as on the value of the currently available reward. These results define incentive relativity – that is, the effect of a given reward on behavior is, in part, relative to the animal's experience with rewards of different amounts or qualities.

What produced these relativity effects? Crespi (1942, 1944) was clear in his interpretation. He referred to the difference in running speed between the downshifted (256–16 and 64–16) and unshifted (16–16) groups as a "depression" effect and argued that it was caused by frustration due to the discrepancy between obtained and expected reward. Crespi's evidence for this interpretation was descriptive. He characterized the behavior of the rats for whom reward was decreased from 256 to 16 units as involving

general frantic peering, general delayed eating, repeated jumping-attempts to escape the food-box in three cases, and refusal to eat all or part of the incentive in three cases. Upon subsequent trials there was prolonged peering at the starting door, jerky hesitant locomotion, retracing, prolonged smelling and door biting. (Crespi, 1942, p. 510)

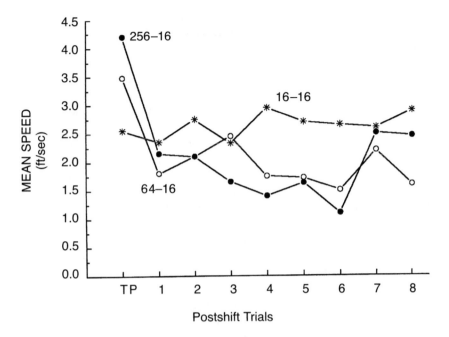

Figure 1.2 Terminal preshift and postshift running speeds in rats differentially rewarded during preshift (256, 64, or 16 units of food) shifted to the same reward (16 units) postshift (Trials 1–8). The rats for whom reward was decreased ran slower than the control group receiving the same reward (16 units). Crespi termed this difference the "depression" effect. (Adapted from Crespi, 1942.)

Lesser behaviors of the same type occurred following the shift from 64 to 16 units of food.

There were no obvious behavioral concomitants, other than the increased speed of running, in the animals for whom reward was increased from 1 or 4 units to 16 units. Nevertheless, Crespi labelled this outcome the "elation" effect, reflecting his view that it was due to a positive emotional experience.[3]

Thus, by 1942 there was substantial evidence that behavior changed abruptly when reward quantity or quality was shifted and that prior experience with rewards of different quantities or qualities affected the incentive value of a current reward. Neither of these effects was compatible with the all-encompassing theory offered by Hull (1943) or with other behaviorist approaches to animal learning. Yet, these data had little immediate influence. For example, Crespi's two papers were not cited in Hilgard's influential *Theories of Learning* (1948). The papers by Elliott and Tinklepaugh were cited as providing evidence favoring Tolman's view that animals develop an expectancy or "precognition" of the specific nature of the goal object, but the implications of this view for reward relativity were not developed. Hilgard, in his critique of Hull's theory, indicated a

---

[3] It should be noted that Tinklepaugh (1928) also included a condition in which his monkeys found a preferred piece of banana instead of lettuce that the monkey had been initially shown. As in Crespi's study, no ancillary behaviors other than the quick consumption of the banana were noted.

number of failings, particularly in Hull's conception of reinforcement and its role in learning, but did not mention the problems posed by Crespi's results for Hull's predictions regarding the effects of reward shifts.

In 1949, Zeaman replicated the essential aspects of Crespi's study in the context of investigating the effects of reward magnitude on behavior and the relationship of these effects to Hull's theory. Zeaman reported in a footnote that he had not been aware of Crespi's paper at the time that he conducted his studies. For our purposes, the relevant aspects of Zeaman's results were as follows. Two groups of rats rewarded with either 0.05 or 2.4 grams of cheese were given 19 acquisition trials at the rate of 1 trial per day (conditions that closely approximated those of Crespi), and then both groups were shifted to the alternative reward level. Zeaman used the extrapolated asymptotic values of latency scores after the 19 acquisition trials as control conditions to examine the effects of the reward shift.

Like Crespi, Zeaman found rapid changes in behavior following the reward shifts and both "elation" and "depression" effects. That is, the group for whom reward was increased from 0.05 to 2.4 grams showed a decrease in latency to a level below that of the extrapolated value of the 2.4-unit condition. The group for whom reward was decreased from 2.4 to 0.05 grams showed prolonged latencies – latencies longer than the extrapolated value from the 0.05 control condition. In Zeaman's study, the elation effect proved to be statistically reliable, but the depression effect was not reliable – an oddity, in view of the subsequent history of research on reward shifts.

Surprisingly, Zeaman interpreted the results of the increased reward to be generally "in accord with" Hull's theorizing, although he recognized "that large increments introduce contrast effects [which required] more elaborate explanation" (1949, p. 480). Zeaman's understatement is surprising because Hull specifically predicted that an upshift in reward would lead to a gradual increase in behavior appropriate to the new level of reward – he did not predict the rapid change and overshoot that necessitated a "more elaborate explanation."

Zeaman concluded that the depression effect from reward decrease suggested that there was a reduction in learning ("Habit Strength") following the downshift rather than an accumulation of inhibition that Hull proposed to explain extinction, which Zeaman interpreted as being closely related to the depression effect. Zeaman preferred to posit "drainage" of "Habit Strength" in part because the widely spaced trials of his experiment would not favor the accumulation of inhibition, at least not the type of inhibition based on effort that was favored by Hull.

In concluding his paper, Zeaman referred to the elation effect as a "positive contrast effect," and the depression effect as a "negative contrast effect," labels that have endured and will be used throughout this book. The term "contrast" was apparently borrowed from perceptual research, where it had been widely used to describe exaggerated responses (such as judgments of brightness or hue) to stimuli that were presented in close juxtaposition (see, for example, Woodworth, 1938; Woodworth & Schlosberg, 1954).[4]

The use of "contrast" in refering to the effects of reward shift did not suggest an emotional response, as the use of "elation" and "depression" clearly did. Zeaman was skeptical of Crespi's explanation in any case, because the contrast effects, particularly positive contrast, showed no indication of being temporary in either his experiment or Crespi's. Zeaman concluded that "a satisfactory theoretical account of the contrast effect remains to be given."

Thus, by 1949, the problem had been defined: Shifts in reward produced exaggerated changes in performance, changes showing that the effects of a given quantity or quality of reward depended on the animals' prior experience with other rewards, as well as on the physical characteristics of the new rewards. These reward-relativity effects suggested that animals have a representation of the rewards presented to them, both old and new – a suggestion consistent with Tolman's descriptive theory of behavior, but one that was not congruent with the mainstream behaviorist views (see also Lorge & Sells, 1936). Furthermore, there was no agreement on the causes of reward relativity, even at the descriptive level. Crespi and Tinklepaugh proposed an emotional root for the behavior, but Elliott explicitly rejected this explanation, instead favoring interference produced by exploration – an interpretation that was clearly limited to negative contrast. Zeaman was reluctant to accept an explanation in terms of emotional responses. He did not cite the work of Tinklepaugh, Elliott, or Lorge and Sells, which suggested searching behavior; instead, he favored an alteration in the asymptotes of learning. However, he recognized that there was no adequate explanation.

Still, the data had little impact. The Tinklepaugh and Zeaman papers were not mentioned in Brogden's 1951 review of animal learning. Crespi's 1942 paper was cited for its acquisition data, but not for the reward shift effects. Elliott's 1928 paper was described as showing that a shift from bran mash to sunflower seeds resulted in positive transfer of maze learning (an interpretation that is obscure, unless Brogden meant that the reward shift did not return the animal to its initial level of performance). Contrast effects were not described. Similarly, Hilgard's 1951 chapter on procedures used in the study of animal learning did not refer to any of the reward shift studies.

Spence (1951), however, did recognize that Crespi's demonstration of positive contrast (not referred to in these terms) presented problems for Hull's 1943 theory; he suggested that a motivational explanation in terms of heightened "Drive" might be useful to explain the data. The negative contrast effect was not considered. Spence did not refer to the Elliott, Tinklepaugh, or Zeaman papers.

Hull himself, in 1952, recognized the importance of Crespi's study. In his work *A Behavior System,* Hull modified his 1943 theory in part so that it could accommodate many of the phenomena explored in Tolman's laboratory. One of

---

[4] Skinner (1938, p.175) used the terms "negative contrast" and "positive contrast," but his use was quite different from that suggested by Zeaman and described effects quite different from those reported by Elliott, Tinklepaugh, Crespi, and Zeaman.

these modifications included a change in his conception of how reinforcement affected behavior. Whereas in 1943 Hull had postulated that the amount of reinforcement determined the asymptote of learning ("Habit Strength"), in 1952 he postulated that reinforcement played two roles: (1) A reinforced trial was necessary for the development of "Habit Strength," and (2) reinforcement also affected incentive motivation – the greater the reinforcement, the greater the incentive motivation. Incentive motivation was itself based on learning – rapid learning, Hull thought. Thus, with two types of learning now available in his formal theory – learning "how" to do something (habit learning) and learning to "want" to do something in a particular situation (incentive learning) – Hull was able to accommodate the rapid behavioral changes produced by reward shift.

However, Hull's concept of incentive motivation did not, in itself, account for incentive relativity as exemplified in Crespi's and Zeaman's contrast effects. That is, it did not account for the exaggeration in behavior produced by the reward shifts. On this score, Hull was content to state that the "excessive shift effect was an emotional response and therefore temporary" (Hull, 1952, p. 142), although he recognized that this had not yet been clearly demonstrated. Exactly how emotions affected behavior to produce the contrast effect was also not explained.

Spence (1956) provided an attempt to simplify contrast. He raised the possibility that the results obtained by Crespi and Zeaman may have been misleading in regard to positive contrast. His reasoning was that relatively few acquisition trials were given in both of these studies and, in Spence's laboratory, the performance of rats continued to improve well beyond the point at which Crespi and Zeaman shifted their animals. This suggested that performance levels extrapolated from the large-reward groups prior to the shift may not have been the appropriate control against which to measure the performance of upshifted rats. Spence reported that, in three experiments conducted in his laboratory, no positive contrast effects were obtained when acquisition training was continued for 48 trials prior to an upshift in reward value. However, in each case, a negative contrast effect was obtained. These results suggested that contrast was asymmetrical and that an explanation for negative contrast was all that was needed.

This suggestion was reinforced and amplified by Bower (1961), who used another training procedure and found negative contrast but no positive contrast. The procedure was differential conditioning – a group of rats was rewarded with eight pellets in a runway of one brightness and with a single pellet in a runway of different brightness. Eventually, these animals ran faster for the larger reward. Control groups received only the large or only the small reward in both runways. The noteworthy comparisons are between the behavior of these single-reward groups and the behavior of the differential-conditioning groups for equivalent rewards.

These comparisons, illustrated in Figure 1.3, showed that the differential group ran slower for the single pellet reward than did the single-pellet control group – a negative contrast effect. However, no positive contrast effect occurred. Instead, the differential group ran reliably slower for the eight-pellet reward than did the eight-pellet control group.

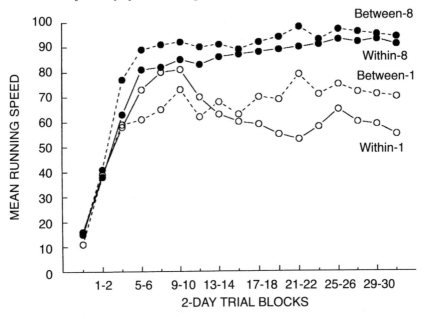

Figure 1.3 Mean runway speeds for three groups of rats in black and white runways. This study investigated the effects of magnitude of reward varied either within subjects or between subjects. The "Within" group received a reward of 8 pellets in one runway and 1 pellet in the alternative runway, thus experiencing both levels of reward. One "Between" group received 8 pellets in both runways and the other "Between" group received 1 pellet in both runways. Thus, the Between groups had no opportunity to compare rewards. The Within group ran slower for the 1-pellet reward than did the Between group. This difference was referred to as a simultaneous negative contrast effect. The Between and Within groups did not differ in running speed for the large reward. (Adapted from Bower, 1961.)

Bower's explanation of negative contrast followed the theme developed by Crespi, Hull (the 1952 version), and Spence, but with a new variation. The variation, derived from Amsel's explanation of the partial reinforcement extinction effect (Amsel, 1958, 1992), was that the small reward was "frustrating" for the group that sometimes also received the large reward; as a result of the conditioning of anticipatory frustration, a conflict developed between anticipation of reward and anticipation of frustration when the animals were placed in the small-reward context.[5] Implicit, but not stated, in Bower's explanation was that the conflict would involve responses that competed with approach to the goal, thus producing slower running. These competing responses could be imagined to be

[5] This interpretation was presented in the S–R terminology of conditioning model theory, as developed by Hull, Spence, and Amsel. The anticipation of reward was conceived of in terms of fractional anticipatory goal responses with stimulus accompaniments (r_g–s_g) that were elicited by conditioning apparatus stimuli and served to invigorate the instrumental response. A reduction of reward to less than that appropriate for a particular r_g (expectation) would engender frustration, which would also become anticipatory via conditioning (r_f–s_f). Anticipatory frustration would then compete with anticipatory reward, leading to conflict and, in the case of the contrast experiment, slower running. Hence, negative contrast.

exactly of the type described by Crespi. Bower, however, made no mention of such observations in his experiment.

Two other aspects of Bower's experiment are worthy of note. First, he suggested that frustration might be greatest during an intermediate stage of discrimination training, when generalization from the S^+ cue to the S^- cue might be high. This idea became the subject of substantial investigation in later studies of contrast in discrimination tasks. Second, he suggested that positive contrast might have failed to occur due to a "ceiling" effect. In order for a positive contrast effect to occur, the discrimination group would have to run faster for its large reward than would the control group. But if the latter group was at the limit for running speed under the conditions of the experiment, then it would not be possible to demonstrate positive contrast. This became a fundamental issue in future attempts to determine if positive contrast was, in fact, a reliable event. Ironically, the same interpretation could have been applied to Spence's 1956 study. That is, he failed to find positive contrast when he increased acquisition training to well beyond the point used by Crespi and Zeaman, but by doing so he could have introduced the ceiling problem, which was perhaps not present in the earlier studies.

In addition to the Bower and Spence studies, the 1956–1961 period saw the development of interest in varying the amount of reward provided in discrimination training studies with primates. Schrier (1958), working with rhesus monkeys, reported that object-quality discrimination learning was better with large reward than with small reward, but only if the monkeys were exposed to the range of rewards available (1,2, 4, or 8 units). There was no difference in the performance of separate groups of monkeys exposed to only one of the levels of reward. Although Schrier's results were not tested for in these terms, in graphical form they suggest the presence of a negative contrast effect, but no positive contrast effect. Another study from the same laboratory (Leary, 1958) reported similar effects; in this case, reliable negative and positive contrast effects in errors occurred in one of two tests where the effects could be measured. A similar finding – that the amount of reward affected errors in a discrimination task only when animals experienced both large and small rewards – was obtained at about the same time (Lawson, 1957) in a study conducted with rats. All these results suggest that contrast occurred in the form of exaggerated effects of amount of reward on error rate.

Schrier and Harlow (1956) conducted an experiment that suggested one possible mechanism for the occurrence of contrast in these studies. They varied amount of reinforcement between days (1, 2, or 4 units) in a series of discrimination tasks with Java monkeys. The monkeys in these experiments experienced the full range of rewards available, but received different values on different days. The interesting part of the results came from an examination of responses on the second trial of each 10-trial discrimination problem following a correct response on the first trial. In the case of the two larger rewards, there was a generally constant percentage of errors across the acquisition series. However, in the case of the smallest reward, errors on the second trial actually increased substantially across the acquisition period. Harlow (1959) described this effect by stating that "the monkeys actually 'learned' to perform below chance on trial 2, although they received no food reward for these response shift errors" (p. 525). In the light of the Tinklepaugh and Elliott studies, it would be reasonable to assume that these errors reflected a tendency for the monkeys to search for one of the larger rewards that they had experienced in some of the earlier trials – the more they learned about the occasional availability of larger rewards, the more likely they were to search after encountering a small reward for making the correct response on the first trial. Support for the error-inducing effect of within-subject variation in reward may be found in Leary's (1958) experiment, in which there was a greater overall rate of errors when monkeys experienced multiple levels of reward than when they experienced a single value of reward – either large or small. This outcome, like those obtained in the instrumental conditioning experiment of Spence and the differential conditioning experiment of Bower, also suggested an asymmetry in contrast – a greater effect of negative contrast than of positive contrast.

Thus, by the time that Bower's study was published in 1961 there was ample evidence that the effects of amount of reward on behavior were strongly influenced by the manner in which the rewards were presented. However, there was little evidence other than demonstrations of contrast. There had not been enough experiments to determine parameters of contrast or the effects of a multitude of variables that could conceivably be studied, and there was little in the way of systematic theoretical treatment of contrast. The Bower study stands close to the divide between the time when little research effort was devoted to contrast and the point at which experimental psychologists recognized that the problem had some interest and that there were many unanswered questions. This dividing line is exemplified by an examination of one of the major volumes on learning published this century – Volume 2 of Koch's series *Psychology: A Study of a Science*. This volume, published in 1959, was concerned with learning theory, yet there was no reference to the Crespi or Zeaman contrast studies. Elliott's shift study was also not cited; Tinklepaugh's study was mentioned in Neal Miller's (Miller, 1959) chapter but in the context of considering an animal's ability to anticipate specific rewards. Of the discrimination-learning studies, only the Schrier and Harlow paper was cited (by Harlow), and it was not described in terms of contrast. The Spence (1956) contrast studies were not considered, nor was Hull's attempt to include contrast in his 1952 theory.

After Bower's study there was an expanded interest in contrast – the conditions under which it occurred, its symmetry or asymmetry, psychological explanations, physiological correlates, and relevance for human behavior. There were two major reviews of contrast in animal experiments published in the late 1960s, four more in the mid-1970s, and two more in the early 1980s. In addition, there was substantial interest in contrast in the perceptual realm and its applicability to reward contrast. Also considered was the related issue of what contrast effects could contribute to the understanding of representational processes in animals (Mackintosh, 1974, 1983).

Summary and conclusions

Although the study of reward magnitude effects was slow to get underway following Thorndike's pioneering papers, the experiments of Tinklepaugh and Elliott in 1928 quickly established the fact that the behavioral effects of a given reward quality depended on an animal's prior experience with rewards of preferred quality. This finding was extended to quantitative variations by Crespi in 1942 and by Zeaman in 1949, both of whom found symmetrical positive and negative contrast effects resulting from abrupt increases or decreases in reward.

Other studies showed that providing animals the opportunity to experience more than one level of reward strongly influenced the outcome of a variety of tasks, from simple instrumental learning, to differential conditioning, to complex object-quality discrimination learning.

There was little agreement on what caused contrast. Suggestions ranged from emotional responses (Bower, Crespi, Hull, Spence, and Tinklepaugh), to exploration (Elliott, Lorge and Sells, and Tinklepaugh), to loss of "Habit Strength" (Zeaman).

Although these experiments had important implications for the major theories of the day, they were slow to be recognized. Hull and Spence did attempt to address theoretical changes forced by these data, but resultant modifications were far from adequate to address the questions raised by the early experiments. Major reviews of the era simply ignored the experiments and the issue of relativity.

2   Successive contrast: procedures and parameters

> It is ... not sufficient to have a rough acquaintance with the
> experimental evidence, but rather a deep and critical knowledge
> of many different types of evidence is required, since one
> never knows what type of fact is likely to give the game
> away.
>
> – Francis Crick
> *What Mad Pursuit* (1988*)*

What happens when a reward is suddenly changed? Crespi, Tinklepaugh, and Elliott all provided early examples of the substantial behavioral changes that occur following a reward reduction, and both Crespi and Tinklepaugh provided some data regarding the effects of an abrupt reward increase. Three chapters will be devoted to a further examination of this issue – behavioral parameters will be reviewed in this chapter, drug and lesion effects in Chapter 3, and theories in Chapter 4. The question of reward change attracts research interest for several reasons: (a) An animal's reaction to reward change provides information concerning the role of reward in learning – do they learn *about* the rewards (as Tinklepaugh's study suggested), or do rewards catalyze learning without themselves being part of that learning (as Thorndike conjectured)?; (b) changing rewards is one way of studying the process of comparison itself, a topic of increasing interest in learning theory (see, for example, Gibbon & Church, 1984; Gray, Whatly & Snape, 1991; Miller & Grahame, 1991); (c) an understanding of the psychology and neurobiology of reward loss in animals may illuminate the psychology of reward loss in humans – an event that sometimes has tragic consequences.

Some of the experiments considered in this chapter will be concerned with methodological issues, some with parameters, and some with various comparative aspects of contrast. Methodology is important, particularly in regard to successive positive contrast (SPC), which is much more difficult to demonstrate than successive negative contrast (SNC). Yet the reliability of SPC is an important issue for theory. For example, several variations on a theme of frustration have some success in describing SNC, but where do these theories stand as general explanations of contrast if SPC is a reliable and potent phenomenon? In regard to SNC, a formulation based on generalization decrement that results from a change in reward is a more conservative explanation of SNC than theories

19

based on presumed frustration. But which of these approaches incorporates more of the data?

One way of presenting this material would be to describe each theory and the data that seem to be most relevant to that theory. The approach taken here, however, will be to present the data (this chapter and Chapter 3) with relatively little theoretical comment; then, in Chapter 4, the theories will be presented with commentary on the support that each derives from the previously described data. This approach has the advantage of allowing the reader to formulate his or her own theory as the data are described.

Successive contrast in runways and mazes

In the studies by Crespi, Elliott, Spence, Tinklepaugh, and Zeaman, the animals were first trained with one reward and then shifted to a different reward. It is this procedure that is referred to as successive contrast (Spear & Hill, 1965). One definition of successive contrast specifies that performance after the shift is inversely related to the magnitude of reward before the shift (Spear & Spitzner, 1966). This was clearly the result obtained by Crespi, but this definition omits reference to an unshifted control condition. Crespi, Spence, and Zeaman all used values extrapolated from preshift levels of performance as the control condition, but this use of preshift values as a control may lead to ambiguities in interpretation, particularly in regard to positive contrast (Spence, 1956). Thus, most recent studies have included groups of unshifted animals to use as a reference point in evaluating the effects of a reward shift. Given the use of these control groups, SPC would be defined as an increment in performance in an upshifted group to a level that exceeds that of an unshifted control group receiving the same reward. Similarly, SNC would be defined as a decrement in performance to a level below that of an unshifted control group receiving the same reward.

Symmetry of successive contrast

The question of symmetry is fundamental for functional and mechanistic interpretations of contrast. For example, if both positive and negative contrast occur, then certain categories of explanation, such as inhibition and generalization decrement, are excluded as comprehensive explanations of contrast. The occurrence of symmetry in contrast suggests the operation of a perception-related process, such as deviation in either direction from a norm or adaptation level, or, alternatively, it may indicate opposing emotions, as Crespi argued. The question of symmetry has two parts: (1) Is it possible to obtain both positive and negative contrast? (2) If so, are both equivalent in magnitude, duration, and so forth? The answer to the first question seems to be yes, whereas the answer to the second question seems to be no.

Is successive contrast symmetrical? Crespi and Zeaman provided clear demonstrations of SPC, but Spence failed to obtain SPC. The outcome that reflects the true state of nature has not been easy to determine, but one thing is clear – positive contrast is a much rarer event than negative contrast (see reviews by Black, 1968; Cox, 1975; Dunham, 1968; Flaherty, 1982). The problem has been to determine whether this rarity reflects an inherent asymmetry in contrast or whether it reflects a measurement problem in runway and maze experiments.

Bower suggested that positive contrast might fail to occur because of a performance limitation (ceiling effect) – if the large-reward control group is responding at or near the upper limit characteristic of that situation (apparatus, species, etc.), then an upshifted group would not be able to demonstrate a contrast effect. Bower's experiment was not a successive contrast experiment, but his argument may well apply to such experiments. For example, it is clearly relevant to Spence's (1956) failure to obtain SPC. The irony here is that because Spence believed that Crespi's animals had not reached asymptotic running speed, he substantially increased the amount of acquisition training compared to that given by Crespi. By ensuring that his rats had reached asymptotic running speed, however, Spence may have introduced the ceiling effect problem.

If the existence of an upper limit on performance is the reason that successive positive contrast is so uncommon, how might this problem be evaded? Many approaches have been tried, and one or two may have succeeded.

Early shift

Running speed in a runway or maze typically increases in a negatively accelerated, monotonic fashion, becoming asymptotic after some number of trials. If the failure to obtain SPC is due to an upper limit in performance represented by the asymptotic level of performance, this limit should be avoidable if the reward is shifted prior to the point at which the acquisition function approaches this upper limit. This line of reasoning was followed in several studies. For example, Schrier (1967) shifted rats from 1 to 4 pellets after 17 runway trials, an acquisition period similar to that used by Crespi. However, no positive contrast occurred. Similar results were obtained in other such experiments, which included shifts from 1 to 5 pellets after 0, 2, or 4 trials (Mellgren, 1971b); shifts from 2 to 24 pellets after 0, 5, 10, or 15 trials (Campbell, Crumbaugh, Knouse & Snodgrass, 1970); shifts from 1 to 10 pellets after 0, 10, 20, or 30 trials (Ashida & Birch, 1964); and shifts from 1 to 5 pellets after 24, 54, or 108 trials (Wolach & Seres, 1971). The lack of occurrence of positive contrast in all these experiments, which varied considerably in degree of reward shift and number of acquisition trials prior to shift, suggests that shifts prior to asymptotic responding will not produce SPC in the runway.

The logic of the pre-asymptotic shift experiments seems correct. The failure to obtain SPC may suggest either that the ceiling-effect artifact is not the explanation for the rarity of positive contrast or that some combination of parameters not tapped by these experiments represents the "correct" formula for obtaining SPC.

Minimal deprivation

Another potential way to avoid a ceiling effect is to train animals under relatively nondeprived conditions. Since running speed in a runway varies directly with degree of food deprivation, testing relatively nondeprived rats would be a method of examining reward shift at performance levels clearly below the physiological limit.

However, this method has not provided a clear answer to the question of a ceiling-effect artifact. One study found evidence of both SPC and SNC in rats deprived to 85% of their free-feeding weight, but neither contrast effect was found in animals maintained at 95% of their free-feeding weight (Ehrenfreund & Badia, 1962). There were two unusual aspects of this study. First, no control groups were included – contrast determination was based on extrapolation from terminal preshift running speeds. However, since 90 preshift trials were given, there may be reason to assume that the preshift baselines represented a stable estimate. The second unusual aspect of the study was that the trials were highly massed, with all 115 trials of the preshift and postshift phases given over a 4-day period. The trials were given in blocks of 5 with a 15- to 20-second intertrial interval (ITI) and with approximately 30 minutes to 1 hour between blocks each day. Given these constraints, the conclusion from this study would be that the occurrence of both positive and negative contrast seems to be favored by more extreme conditions of food deprivation.

However, three subsequent studies failed to support this conclusion unequivocally. Ehrenfreund (1971) found no reliable positive contrast with animals deprived to either 85% or 98% of free-feeding weight, although the trend toward SPC was greater in the 85% group. Negative contrast occurred only in the 85% deprivation group. The ITI was longer (4–5 minutes) in this experiment than in the study by Ehrenfreund and Badia (15–20 seconds), but SPC occurred with even longer ITIs in the next two studies to be considered.

These two studies varied deprivation, but also varied other important procedural parameters, thus making it difficult to interpret the influence of deprivation condition directly. One study (Benefield, Oscos & Ehrenfreund, 1974) found equivalent SPC effects in rats deprived to either 90% or 98% of their free-feeding weight. However, the contrast animals in this experiment were shifted twice – first from large reward (one 190-mg pellet) to a small reward (one 45-mg pellet) and then back to a large reward (the 190-mg pellet). The control animals were maintained on the 190-mg pellet throughout. The ITI in this experiment was 2.5 hours.

In the final study to be considered, the animals were tested in a complex maze (Lashley III), which was selected "to prevent the rats from running at maximum speed" (Shanab & Ferrell, 1970). The rats in this experiment were initially trained under an 80% deprivation state, then, coincident with the reward shift (from 1 to 22 pellets), the animals were either maintained on the 80% deprivation condition or shifted to a 6-hour food deprivation state. An equivalent positive contrast effect occurred in both deprivation groups. The deprivation manipulation was clearly effective in producing differences in behavior because the 6-hour group ran reliably slower than the 80% group, but the deprivation difference did not influence SPC.

Thus, three of the four experiments considered in this section obtained SPC, with five groups showing positive contrast and three groups not showing contrast. Of the three groups that did not show positive contrast, two were under low deprivation (98% and 95%), and one was under high deprivation (85% – contrast was "reliable" in this group at the $p = .0.10$ level, but not at the 0.05 level). Of the five cases in which positive contrast occurred, the deprivation conditions were 80%, 85%, 90%, 6 hours, and 98%. Reasonable conclusions would seem to be that (1) SPC is obtainable; (2) deprivation state is not a fundamental factor; (3) greater deprivation may favor the occurrence of SPC, other parameters being optimal; and (4) using relatively nondeprived rats is not a particularly useful means of circumventing, or detecting, a ceiling-effect artifact. These experiments may also suggest that the ITI might not play a fundamental role, because the ITI values ranged from 15–20 seconds (Ehrenfreund & Badia, 1962) to 24 hours (Shanab & Ferrell, 1970) in studies that obtained SPC, and from 15–20 seconds to 4–5 minutes in studies that failed to obtain SPC.

Delay of reward

A procedure that is highly successful in revealing SPC is training the animals with a delay of reward. The rationale for such a manipulation is that delay produces lower levels of performance, including slower running speed, thereby providing the opportunity for positive contrast uncontaminated by behavioral limitations.

The first study to utilize this strategy combined an increase in amount of reward (from 1 to 22 pellets) with the introduction of a 30-second delay of reward. The delay produced a decrement in running speed, but this was partially offset by the increase in reward. Thus, the shifted group ran faster after the delay was introduced than did a group that had always received the 22-pellet reward (Shanab, Sanders & Premack, 1969). This result was termed a positive contrast effect. Though far from the typical design, this experiment did suggest that delay of reward could be used to obviate a potential ceiling-effect artifact.

Subsequent experiments have confirmed the effectiveness of reward delay. For example, Mellgren (1972) found SPC when rats were shifted either from 2 to 22 pellets or from 1 to 8 pellets, when the rats were trained with a constant 20-second delay of reward throughout the experiment. The development of positive contrast on a trial-by-trial basis is illustrated in Figure 2.1. In another study with a constant 20-second delay of reward, Mellgren (1971a) examined shifts from 1 to 6 pellets after 24, 48, or 72 acquisition trials. These data are presented in Figure 2.2. It is clear that a substantial positive contrast effect occurred after each of the shifts. Although there was not a great deal of difference in contrast as a function of the number of preshift trials, there was a statistically reliable effect –

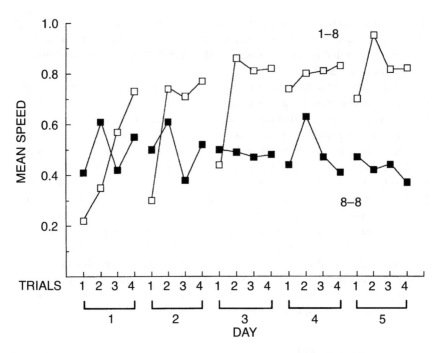

Figure 2.1 Trial-by-trial running speeds during the postshift period of rats either shifted from one-pellet to 8-pellet reward or maintained on 8 pellets. The study demonstrates successive positive contrast. (Adapted from Mellgren, 1972.)

positive contrast developed sooner the fewer the preshift trials (on the third post-shift trial after 24 preshift trials; on the fourth postshift trial after 48 preshift trials; and on the sixth postshift trial after 72 preshift trials). In this sense, the results were somewhat consistent with the rationale for the early shift studies already described. SPC was not found in any of those studies, but it was large and enduring in this study – an outcome seemingly attributable to the presence of the reward delay.

Many other experiments have demonstrated SPC when delay of reward was incorporated into the study – using either the constant delay of simultaneous shift or delay introduction procedures (Lehr, 1974; Mellgren, Seybert, Wrather & Dyck, 1973; Shanab & Biller, 1972; Shanab & Cavallaro, 1975; Shanab & Spencer, 1978; Spencer & Shanab, 1979). Although the preponderance of evidence clearly favors the occurrence of SPC when a delay is incorporated into the experiment, positive contrast is not an inevitable outcome of such experiments (Shanab & McCuistion, 1970).

Repeated shifts

Another procedure used in the investigation of positive contrast is the use of multiple reward shifts. The rats in Crespi's study that were upshifted in reward actu-

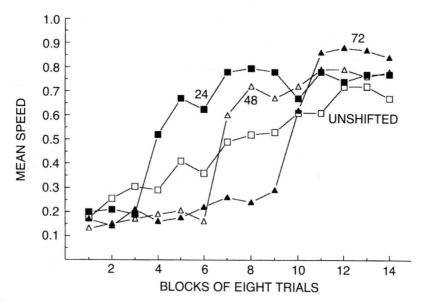

Figure 2.2 Running speed following shifts from one pellet to six pellets after 24, 48, or 72 preshift trials. All groups showed successive positive contrast. (After Mellgren, 1971b.)

ally received a double shift – first they were trained with a large reward, then they were shifted to a small reward, and then they were brought back to a large reward. There is a theoretical reason for believing that prior experience with the large reward might be an important consideration. Any change in the experimental situation from that existing during initial training is likely to produce a deterioration in performance, a process known as generalization decrement (see, for example, E. D. Capaldi, 1978). Thus, a reduction in reward would be expected to produce degraded performance because of the additive effects of two processes – the reaction to the reward reduction itself, and generalization decrement. Any enhanced performance, however, that might be expected to occur following an increase in reward would have to overcome an opposing tendency of performance decrement resulting from the occurrence of change itself. The relative contribution of generalization decrement toward offsetting SPC might then be minimized by giving animals prior experience with the large reward.

The theory is more convincing than the results. The role of previous large reward experience in enhancing the occurrence of SPC has been investigated in several experiments, but the results are inconclusive in regard to the importance of repeated shifts or prior large-reward experience as an important factor in the occurrence of SPC.

Positive contrast effects in rats with prior large-reward experience were reported in two studies (Benefield, Oscos & Ehrenfreund, 1974; Calef, 1972), but no direct comparison with rats not receiving this experience was made in either study. Studies that have made such a comparison do not present a unified set of results. Both E. J. Capaldi and Lynch (1967) and Weinstock (1971) reported no positive contrast effects following large–small–large (LSL) shifts, but Weinstock did find SPC in rats that received only the small-to-large (SL) shift.

Other studies have found positive contrast after repeated shifts, but these data do not implicate prior experience with the large reward as a particularly important variable. McCain and Cooney (1975) obtained SPC after LSL and after small–large–small–large (SLSL) shifts, but they also obtained positive contrast on the first of these SL shifts. Similarly, Shanab and Spencer (1978) also reported SPC after both SL and LSL shifts. One study that did support an important effect of prior large-reward experience used a magnitude of sucrose reward shift with water-deprived rats (Shanab, France & Young, 1976). This study demonstrated SPC in LSL rats but not in small–small–large (SSL)-shifted rats.

In a particularly interesting study, SPC was obtained following an LSL shift if the animals were shifted back to large reward while a negative contrast effect (from the initial LS shift) was still apparent in the animal's behavior, but SPC did not occur if the shift was delayed until the negative contrast effect had dissipated (Maxwell et al., 1976). These data may indicate that the probability of obtaining SPC is enhanced if the animals are shifted while experiencing a negative emotional state.

In summary, four of these studies (Capaldi & Lynch, 1967; Maxwell et al., 1976; Shanab, Domino & Ralph, 1978; Weinstock, 1971) show that prior large-reward experience is not a sufficient condition for the production of SPC. Such experience is apparently not a necessary condition either, given the many studies previously cited in which SPC occurred without a prior large-reward period.

One study combined the delay of reward with the repeated-shift procedure (Goomas, 1981). In this case, a constant 15-second delay was employed and the rats were shifted, after an initial 15 trials, from 10 pellets to 2 pellets, and then received repeated upshifts and downshifts every 6 trials (3 trials/day). An SNC effect occurred on the first two downshifts and SPC occurred on the first two upshifts. Thereafter, no contrast occurred and, in fact, changes in behavior tended to be minimal after subsequent shifts. Given the results described previously, it seems that the presence of the constant delay in this experiment, rather than the prior experience with the large reward, seems fundamental to the occurrence of SPC. The experiment is also interesting in illustrating the dampening of behavioral swings, as well as the loss of contrast, with repeated shifts – two results that do not occur when consummatory behavior is measured following shifts in sucrose concentration (see section on "Successive contrast in consummatory behavior").

Apparatus

Often overlooked is the fact that Crespi used a very long runway (20 ft) in his experiment. It could well be the case that a long runway would serve to minimize a ceiling-effect artifact, because the animals would have more space to accelerate and decelerate in such an apparatus. Some support for this idea was obtained by Seybert & Mellgren (1972), who shifted rats from 1 to 8 pellets after 28 trials way and half in a 326.75-cm U-shaped runway. Only the animals in the longer runway showed SPC.

Even given these results, runway length cannot be a sole determining variable, because many of these studies used standard 4- or 5-foot runways and Zeaman, in his early study (1949), found SPC with a runway only 3 feet long.[1]

Summary

Of the five procedures used to alleviate a potential ceiling-effect artifact, the use of delay of reward has clearly been the most effective in terms of published studies showing SPC. Shifting early in training has been the least effective. In spite of the seemingly impeccable logic behind such experiments, prior experience with the large reward does not seem to have a major effect in promoting the occurence of SPC. The effects of deprivation condition are not clear, but one could interpret the results as suggesting that deprived animals might be more likely to show SPC than nondeprived animals, if other conditions exist that favor the occurrence of such contrast. Finally, the use of a long runway, or perhaps an elevated runway or a complex maze, may favor the measurement of positive contrast, but none of these conditions is absolutely necessary.

The generally clear results obtained with delay of reward may be due to more than control of a potential ceiling-effect problem. It is conceivable that the aversiveness of delay itself enhances the effectiveness of the reward increase. Such a possibility would be consistent with the findings of Maxwell et al. (1976) that SPC is more likely to occur if the reward is increased while the shifted animals are still showing a negative contrast from a previous downshift, than if a reward increase is delayed until after the negative contrast effect has dissipated.

Overall, one would have to conclude that SPC has been obtained often enough to indicate its existence as a viable psychological phenomenon, especially when its occurrence in other paradigms is also taken into account. The data, however, also suggest that there is not complete symmetry in successive contrast. Simply in terms of a box-score count, successive negative contrast is much more likely to be obtained than successive positive contrast is (see, for example, Black, 1968; Cox, 1975; Dunham, 1968; Flaherty, 1982). Consideration of reasons why this might be the case will be deferred until after parametric data and other forms of contrast have been considered.

Variables influencing successive contrast

Reward disparity

One common factor across all the contrast designs considered in this book is that degree of contrast varies directly with degree of difference between the two rewards experienced. In SNC in runways, this has been demonstrated with shifts

---

[1] Zeaman's runway was elevated, a condition that probably contributed to slower running speeds.

rewards experienced. In SNC in runways, this has been demonstrated with shifts from 16, 8, 4, or 2 pellets to a single pellet (DiLollo & Beez, 1966) and with shifts from 32 or 8 pellets to 2 pellets (Gonzalez, Gleitman & Bitterman, 1962). Crespi himself reported that disruptions in the behavior of rats were greater with shifts from 256 units of reward to 16 units than with shifts from 64 to 16 units. An indication of greater contrast with greater reward disparity has also been demonstrated in two SPC experiments (Mellgren, Seybert, Wrather & Dyck, 1973; Shanab & Cavallaro, 1975), but Crespi (1942) did not report any substantial difference in positive contrast in animals shifted from either 1 or 4 units to 16 units of reward.

These systematic variations in degree of contrast with degree of reward difference are consistent with several theoretical explanations of contrast, including the hypothesis of an emotional effect of reward shift, as suggested by Crespi.

Deprivation condition

Within limits, degree of SNC may vary directly with degree of deprivation. Several studies have found that SNC is more likely to occur when rats are substantially deprived (Cleland, Williams & DiLollo, 1969; Ehrenfreund, 1971; Ehrenfreund & Badia, 1962; Flaherty & Kelly, 1973), with the more extreme deprivation conditions including animals deprived to 75% or 85% of their free-feeding weight and animals food-deprived for 22 hours. The less severe deprivation conditions, in which SNC was not obtained, included animals deprived to 90%, 95%, or 98% of their free-feeding weight and animals food-deprived for 6 hours.

However, no effect of deprivation on SNC was obtained in two experiments by E. D. Capaldi and Singh (1973). In these experiments, rats were deprived to either 75% or 90% of their free-feeding weight and shifted from 20 pellets to 2 pellets; in another condition, rats were deprived to 70% or 90% of their free-feeding weight and shifted from 10 pellets to 1 pellet. Equivalent degrees of SNC occurred under both sets of deprivation conditions.

These data may not be as contradictory as they appear. The conditions of the Capaldi and Singh experiment may have been more favorable to the occurrence of contrast in one or more ways than the earlier experiments. There was a greater reward discrepancy than in the Ehrenfreund studies, a shorter intertrial interval (ITI) than in the Cleland et al. study, and more trials per day and a shorter ITI than in the Flaherty & Kelly study. Thus, as Capaldi and Singh suggested, increased deprivation might be expected to enhance SNC when conditions might otherwise be less than optimal for contrast occurrence.

The effects of deprivation conditions on SPC were reviewed earlier in this chapter; the general conclusion was that more extreme conditions of deprivation may favor the occurrence of contrast, other factors being equal. However, the data favoring this generalization are not particularly strong.

Deprivation shift

Several studies have examined the effects of concurrent shifts in reward and deprivation condition. Neither positive contrast (E. D. Capaldi, 1971) nor negative contrast (E. D. Capaldi, Smith & White, 1977) were obtained when such a double shift was employed. Contrary data were reported by Shanab and Ferrell (1970), who concurrently shifted from low to high deprivation and from 1 to 22 pellets. They found an SPC in rats given the double shift as well as in rats maintained under the high deprivation condition.

It is possible that the difference in outcome obtained in these studies may be related to procedural factors, particularly those involving the instantiation of the deprivation shift. Capaldi (1971) brought her highly deprived group (11 grams per day) up to the level of the lesser-deprived group (20 grams per day) by placing them on a free-feeding schedule for 10 days and then feeding them for 4 more days at 20 grams per day. The animals were not exposed to the runway during this 2-week period, a time when aspects of the preshift reward magnitude could have been forgotten. Although there are no retention studies with exactly the same parameters of the Capaldi studies, it is clear that contrast diminishes with increasing time periods between the last experience with the preshift reward and the first experience with the postshift reward (see section on "Retention interval").

Shanab and Ferrell (1970) shifted their animals differently. The highly deprived group was trained at 80% of their free-feeding weight and then one-half of these animals were shifted to a less extreme deprivation schedule by allowing them to have access to food for 18 hours after each daily session in the postshift phase of the experiment. Thus, the deprivation shift was from 80% free-feeding weight and once-per-day feeding to a 6-hour deprivation schedule with no time gap between shift phases. Under these conditions, the concurrent deprivation and reward shift did not preclude the occurrence of SPC.

A second procedural difference between these studies was that the Capaldi experiments were conducted in runways, whereas the Shanab and Ferrell experiment was conducted in a maze, a condition that may favor the occurrence of SPC.

Capaldi's interpretation of her data was that (1) the stimulus condition correlated with deprivation state is a potent cue for reward expectancy, and (2) a shift in this cue at the same time that reward is shifted will prevent the occurrence of contrast because the preshift reward will no longer be expected. Such analysis suggests that this may not necessarily be an absolute in terms of positive contrast. The situation in regard to negative contrast awaits further parametric investigation.

Retention interval

The longer the interval between the last experience with the preshift reward and the first experience with the postshift reward, the smaller the SNC. In the runway, negative contrast is lost following a shift from 20 pellets to 2 pellets when a 68-day retention interval is inserted between shift phases, or when the same retention interval is inserted after the first experience with the postshift reward (Gleitman & Steinman, 1964). Data obtained in the runway have also shown that, following a shift from 18 to 2 pellets, negative contrast occurs with a 1-day retention interval; is smaller after 26 days; is numerically present, but not statistically reliable, after 42 days; and is not present after 68 days (Gonzalez, Fernhoff & David, 1973). There are apparently no corresponding studies that have investigated SPC.

The loss of contrast over a retention interval is not surprising because, presumably, the animals must compare the postshift reward with the memory of the preshift reward in order to show a contrast effect (Spear, 1967; Spear & Riccio, 1994).

Prior reward experience

POSTSHIFT REWARD. Initial experience with the small reward (the reward that will eventually be the postshift reward) may reduce the size of SNC. Complete elimination of SNC has been obtained in one experiment in which a 24-hour ITI was used, and reduced contrast has been obtained with shorter ITIs (E. D. Capaldi & Singh, 1973; E. J. Capaldi, 1972; Spencer & Shanab, 1979). Many studies, however, have obtained contrast in animals that have had prior experience with the small reward, including animals shifted two or more times between large and small reward (Calef, Calef, Prochaska & Geller, 1978; Maxwell et al., 1976; McCain & Cooney, 1975; Shanab et al., 1978; Shanab & Spencer, 1978).

To the extent that there is a neophobic or generalization decrement component to SNC, a reduction would be expected in the size of contrast, as a function of previous experience with the postshift reward. To the extent that contrast is not eliminated by such experience (it generally is not), neophobia and/or generalization decrement may be negated as complete accounts of SNC.

The issue of prior experience with the postshift reward in the case of SPC has already been discussed here; it was concluded that such experience seems not to be a major factor in the occurrence, or lack of occurrence, of positive contrast.

PARTIAL REWARD. Successive negative contrast may be reduced, or its appearance retarded, by prior experience with partial reinforcement. The initial demonstration of this effect showed that rats trained on a 50% reinforcement schedule with a 10-pellet reward showed no SNC when shifted to a 1-pellet reward (still on a 50% schedule – Mikulka, Lehr & Pavlik, 1967). Later studies found that prior partial reinforcement experience retarded, but did not prevent, the development of SNC (Gonzalez & Bitterman, 1969; Ison, Glass & Daly, 1969; Peters & McHose, 1974). One study found that positive contrast occurred in both partial reward and continuous reward groups shifted from a 1-pellet to an 8-pellet reward (Lehr, 1974). All subjects in this experiment were run under a constant 20-second delay of reward.

Both the Lehr (1974) SPC experiment and the Gonzalez and Bitterman (1969) SNC experiment involved shifts from partial to continuous reward concurrent with the increase in reward magnitude, whereas the Ison et al. (1969) and

Mikulka et al. (1967) experiments maintained the animals on the partial schedule after the shift. There have apparently been no direct within-experiment comparisons of these two procedures.

The specific sequence of rewarded and nonrewarded trials that rats receive in a partial reinforcement experiment may have important effects on resistance to extinction (E. J. Capaldi, 1966; Seybert, Mellgren & Jobe, 1973). The role of "sequential variables" in SNC remains unclear. One study in which effects were obtained (E. J. Capaldi & Ziff, 1969) shifted rats from a large reward where only 67% of the trials were rewarded, to a small reward in which 100% of the trials were rewarded. The variable of interest was the sequence of rewarded and nonrewarded trials during the preshift period. In the case of one group, the sequence each day was large–none–large (LNL), and for the other group the sequence was LLN. There were 15 preshift trials; the large reward was 20 pellets and the small reward was 2 pellets. A control group received the small reward throughout the experiment. After the shift, Group LLN showed an SNC but Group LNL did not.

Based on these results, Capaldi and Ziff argued that partial reward would interfere with the occurrence of SNC only when nonreward–to–reward (NR) transitions were included in the preshift experience. Such an interpretation would lead to a parallel between SNC and extinction, because the occurrence of NR transitions in a partial reinforcement schedule retards extinction (E. J. Capaldi, 1966; Seybert, Mellgren & Jobe, 1973). However, results inconsistent with this generalization were reported by Peters and McHose (1974). In this study, separate groups of rats received either a 20-pellet reward or a 3-pellet reward in one of the following sequences each day: LSL, LSS, or SSL. Following a shift to small reward (3 pellets), all groups showed an SNC, with contrast being largest in the LSL group. Since Capaldi and Ziff found no contrast in their LNL group, it is clear that SL and NL transitions are not comparable and/or the effects of sequential variables on contrast are complex and parameter sensitive.

It is difficult to make a summary statement regarding the effects of prior experience with partial reward on SNC other than to say that there apparently are conditions under which such experience will reduce or delay the onset of SNC, but these conditions may be limited. No effects of such treatment on SPC have been noted.

VARIED REWARD. Varied magnitude of reward has many effects similar to partial reward (Logan, 1960), and this similarity extends to the effects on contrast. Two studies reported that prior experience with varied magnitude of reward prevented the occurrence of SNC following a shift to a constant small reward (Calef et al., 1978; Davis & North, 1967). A systematic study by Peters and McHose (1974) found that rats given 4 and 20 pellets on a 50% schedule preshift and 1 pellet postshift showed SNC approximately equivalent to rats maintained on a constant 7 pellets and then shifted to 1 pellet. Two other studies in Peters and McHose also showed SNC following varied reward experience, and the degree of contrast was consistent with the hypothesis that the rats "averaged" the rewards received during the preshift phase and that degree of contrast was related to degree of disparity from this average value. The Peters and McHose study also unconfounded the effects of varied magnitude and prior experience with the postshift reward, by not including the specific postshift reward value in the preshift varied-reward experience.

SUMMARY – PRIOR REWARD EXPERIENCE. The impression presented by these data is that all the prior-reward experience conditions reviewed here may act to reduce SNC, but this result is far from inevitable; there is no procedural recipe yet available that one could use as a guide to produce or avoid such effects. The most attractive interpretation of the data would seem to be an incentive-averaging model like the models employed by Logan and by Peters and McHose. That is, prior experience with rewards equal to, or less than, the eventual postshift reward may retard or reduce SNC, because the degree of reward disparity is less than it would have been without this prior experience. In addition, it may be more difficult for the animals that have experienced partial or varied reward to detect the onset of the shift condition. The data regarding SPC are too few to attempt a generalization.

Successive contrast in consummatory behavior

Negative contrast is readily demonstrated in the consumption of sweet solutions. If, for example, rats are given access for 5 minutes each day to a 32% sucrose solution for 10 days and then shifted to 4% sucrose, their lick frequency for the 4% sucrose is substantially less than that of rats that receive only the 4% solution. These results are illustrated in Figure 2.3.

Positive contrast in consummatory behavior has been infrequently demonstrated. Perhaps the first attempt at such a demonstration involved shifting rats from either 4% or 16% sucrose to 32% sucrose after 20 preshift sessions (Premack & Hillix, 1962). Separate groups of rats were given access to the sucrose for either 2 minutes or 15 minutes each day. The rats in these experiments were maintained on a 3-hour food and water deprivation schedule. Preshift lick frequencies indicated an *inverse* relationship between sucrose concentration and lick frequency in the 15-minute group and no effect of concentration in the 2-minute group. The effect of the shift was consistent with this relationship – rats shifted from 4% or 16% sucrose to 32% sucrose showed a *decrement* in lick frequency, the antithesis of SPC. Evidence of positive contrast was obtained only when the first minute of access on the first postshift day was examined. In this case, an apparent positive contrast effect occurred in the group shifted from 4% to 32%, but the statistical data to support this outcome were not presented in the paper. Even this incident of SPC was transient – the data for the first minute of the last postshift day showed a decrement in licking resulting from the shift, rather than an enhancement. Thus, in this experiment, SPC was a minor and transient effect, with the bulk of the data indicating a change in direction of licking opposite to that of a positive contrast effect.

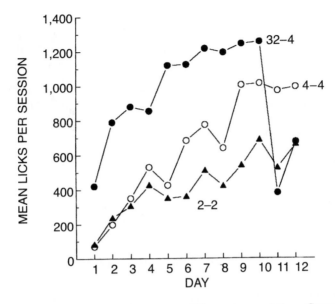

Figure 2.3 Lick frequency in groups given access to different sucrose solutions. Groups 4-4 and 2-2 received 4% or 2% sucrose on all days. Group 32-4 received 32% sucrose on days 1–10, and 4% sucrose on days 11 and 12. Lick frequency in this shifted group decreased to the level of the 2% group, thereby showing a successive negative contrast effect in comparison to Group 4-4. (After Flaherty, Becker & Pohorecky, 1985.)

Symmetry of successive contrast in consumption

Although SPC has been demonstrated much less frequently than SNC in con-summatory behavior, positive contrast, usually transient, has been obtained under special conditions.

Early shift and repeated shift

Rats exposed to 32% and 4% sucrose for a 5-minute period, on alternate days, show SPC over the first three upshifts, but not thereafter. Similarly, when rats were given double alternation shifts (32–32–4–4–32–32, etc.) positive contrast was reliable on the first two upshifts only (Flaherty, Becker & Checke, 1983). Negative contrast was reliable throughout the experiment in both cases. These data, which are illustrated in Figure 2.4, suggest that the loss of positive contrast is due to the approach of the unshifted 32% control group to an asymptotic lick frequency. Similar results were reported for the double-shift condition by Dachowski and Brazier (1991) but, in this case, SPC was reliable on only the first shift. Thus, the early-shift procedure, which was totally ineffective in leading to SPC in runway studies, seems to be a reliable method of obtaining SPC in con-summatory behavior. Furthermore, the pattern of results supports the hypothesis that an upper limit in performance may occlude the occurrence of SPC unless special precautions are taken to avoid this limitation.

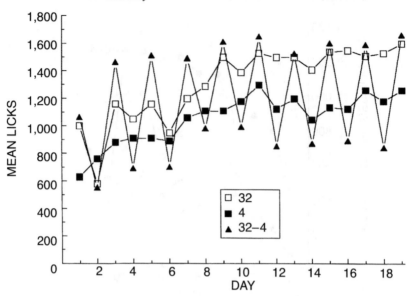

Figure 2.4a Lick frequency in three groups given access to 32% sucrose only, 4% sucrose only, or both 32% and 4% sucrose alternated daily. The alternating group showed a sustained negative contrast effect and a transient positive contrast effect. (After Flaherty, Becker & Checke, 1983.)

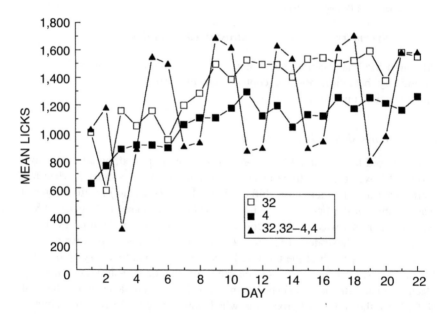

Figure 2.4b Same as 2.4a except that the sucrose solutions were alternated on a 2-day cycle. (After Flaherty, Becker & Checke, 1983.)

Minimal deprivation

An SPC effect failed to occur when nondeprived rats were shifted from 4% to 32% sucrose using either the early-shift–repeated-shift procedure or a procedure in which the rats were given a 10-day acquisition period before the shift from 4% to 32% sucrose (Brazier & Dachowski, 1991; Dachowski & Brazier, 1991). In both cases, substantial SNC occurred. These results, in comparison to those reported earlier in this chapter, indicate that increased deprivation may enhance SPC – a suggestion also derived from the runway contrast data.

Novel flavors

A procedure that was particularly effective in revealing SPC in runway behavior was the inclusion of a delay of reward. Delay is not practical in the investigation of consummatory behavior, but a technique that may have an analogous effect is the addition of a novel flavor to the sucrose solution. The experiments reported were modeled after the Shanab, Sanders and Premack paper (1969), in which delay was introduced concurrently with reward increase.

In our experiments (unpublished data), a flavor (McCormick's pure orange extract) was added to the sucrose on the shift day. In the first experiment, one group of rats received 12% sucrose preshift and flavored 12% sucrose on the shift day (Group 12-12F); a second group received 4% preshift and flavored 12% postshift (Group 4-12F); a third group received 4% preshift and unflavored 12% postshift (Group 4-12). The results, in terms of terminal preshift lick frequency and postshift lick frequency, are presented in the left panel of Figure 2.5.

The rats receiving the 12% solution licked at a higher frequency during the preshift period than did the animals receiving the 4% solution.[2] The addition of the flavor to the 12% solution produced a reliable decline in licking in Group 12-12F, but the addition of the flavor coincident with a shift from 4% to 12% sucrose resulted in no reliable change in the lick frequency of Group 4-12F. The combination of these two effects produced a reliably higher lick frequency in Group 4-12F than in Group 12-12F, an outcome indicating the occurrence of SPC analogous to that obtained in the Shanab et al. (1969) experiment.

The nonflavored group shifted from 4% to 12% sucrose showed a reliable increase in lick frequency, but their ultimate level of responding did not exceed the preshift value of Group 12-12F. Thus, positive contrast was indicated only in Group 4-12F, and only in comparison to the decremented performance in Group 12-12F.

The center panel of Figure 2.5 illustrates a replication of the flavor-shift conditions of this experiment with the same outcome: A shift from 4% to flavored

---

[2] The reliability statements are based on analysis of variance which indicated a reliable preshift x shift interaction ($F(2, 18) = 29.76, p < 0.01$) and subsequent tests using Fisher's least significant difference test ($p = 0.05$, two tail).

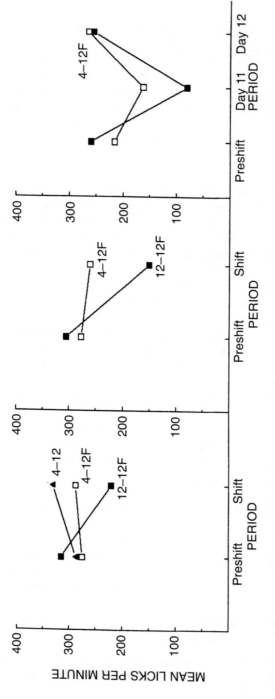

Figure 2.5 Three experiments demonstrating a type of successive positive contrast. In each experiment, one group was shifted from 12% sucrose to flavored 12% sucrose. Also in each experiment, another group was shifted from 4% sucrose to 12% sucrose with an added flavor. The first experiment (left panel) included a group shifted from 4% sucrose to 12% sucrose without an added flavor. The third experiment (right panel) included 2 postshift days. In all cases, the group shifted from 4 to 12F showed less of a decrement in licks than the group shifted from 12 to 12F.

12% sucrose offset a decrement in licking that occurred in a group shifted from 12% to flavored 12%, yielding SPC.[3]

Finally, the right panel of Figure 2.5 represents another replication with an extra postshift day included. This experiment showed the same basic result of the shift – reliable SPC, as defined in this context – and it also showed that the animals adapted rapidly to the flavor so that licking recovered on the second postshift day. After recovery, there was no positive contrast present.[4]

These experiments leave little doubt that an increase in the concentration of a sucrose solution may act to offset a decrement produced by the addition of a novel flavor to the higher concentration sucrose solutions. Although these results have been termed SPC by analogy to the Shanab et al. delay of reward experiment, whether this contrast outcome represents the same psychological process as that occurring in other demonstrations of SPC remains to be determined.

Apparatus

Although the nature of the apparatus/context would seem to have little relevance to the occurrence of contrast in consummatory behavior, such a consideration may in fact be related to the ceiling-effect problem. For example, a context with more "distractions" might lead to a low lick frequency in unshifted control rats, thereby providing the opportunity for a positive contrast to occur in shifted rats. The argument is not unlike that developed for the addition of a novel flavor to the postshift solution. As a test of this possibility, we conducted some preliminary studies of shifts from 4% to 32% sucrose in the context of an eight-arm radial maze. In one of three similar experiments a reliable SPC occurred. These experiments were too few and in too small a scale to draw any firm conclusions. However, the results are encouraging enough to pursue the use of a complex environment as a means of investigating SPC.

Saccharin shifts

Contrast following shifts in saccharin solutions is included here as a special technique because such shifts may produce positive contrast quite different from that obtained with shifts in sucrose solutions. Whereas the typical finding with sucrose shifts is a small and transient SPC, a shift in saccharin solutions may lead to large and "permanent" SPC. Such was the finding of Rabiner, Kling, and Spraguer (1988), who reported that a shift from 0.05% to 0.20% saccharin solution resulted in a large SPC (the shifted group drank over 7 ml more solution than the unshifted controls in a 30-minute session) that endured essentially unchanged for nine sessions. A smaller, but enduring, SNC was also obtained in this experiment.

---

[3] The reliability statements are based on significant group x shift interaction ($F (1, 17) = 17.30$, $p < 0.01$) followed by least significant difference tests ($p = 0.05$, two tail).

[4] Reliability statements based on a significant group x shift interaction ($F (3, 30) = 5.51, p < 0.01$) followed by least significant difference tests ($p = 0.05$, two tail).

A possibly related finding is the "saccharin elation effect," in which rats show a substantial increase in saccharin intake when a regularly available saccharin solution is removed for a period ranging from minutes to days (for further discussions of this effect, see Flaherty, 1982; Gandelman & Trowill, 1969; Pinel & Rovner, 1977; Rabiner et al., 1988).

Variables influencing consummatory contrast

There have been fewer parametric studies of contrast in consummatory behavior than of contrast in instrumental behavior but, where comparison is appropriate, similar principles seem to apply.

Reward disparity

Large SNC results from a shift in sucrose concentration from 32% to 4%, but no contrast effect follows a shift from 8% to 4% sucrose. Rats that received equal access to 2%, 4%, 8%, 16%, and 32% sucrose before being shifted to 4% showed a contrast effect intermediate between the 32% to 4% and the 8% to 4% groups (Flaherty, Becker & Osborne, 1983) – an outcome consistent with the incentive averaging effect considered in the section on "Varied reward."

Concentration disparity effects have also been obtained with shifts in saccharin solutions. Rats shifted from 0.15% saccharin to either 0.075% or 0.05% showed small but reliable negative contrast effects, but rats shifted from 0.15% to either 0.125% or 0.10% did not show contrast (Flaherty & Rowan, 1986). However, a large concentration disparity does not guarantee SNC when saccharin is shifted; for example, no contrast was obtained in one study in which the shift was from 0.1% to 0.01% saccharin (Vogel, Mikulka & Spear, 1968). It is not clear why negative contrast failed to occur in this study. It should be noted, however, that contrast, even when it did occur, was small in the Flaherty and Rowan study and that the postshift concentration in the Vogel et al. study was quite low (0.01%), perhaps creating a floor effect.

Particularly large and enduring SNC is obtained if rats are shifted from sucrose to saccharin solutions (unpublished data). Some of these effects are illustrated in Figure 2.6.

Deprivation state

Negative contrast obtained with nondeprived rats is often more durable than that obtained with deprived rats. Riley and Dunlap (1979) found that deprived rats (maintained at 80% of their free-feeding weight) shifted from 32% to 4% sucrose recovered from negative contrast within 4 days, as is typical, but free-fed rats showed no indication of recovery after 4 days. The same pattern occurred after the animals were returned to their original solutions and shifted again, and also if the animals were switched to the alternative deprivation con-

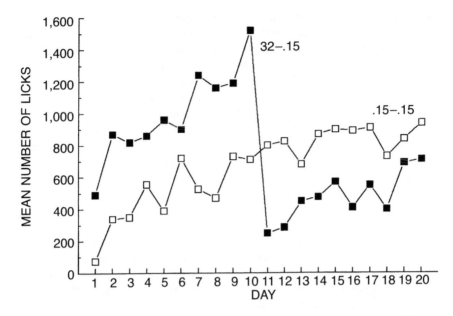

Figure 2.6. Mean licks per minute (5-minute session) in rats shifted from 32% sucrose to 0.15% saccharin compared to rats maintained on 0.15% saccharin. An enduring SNC occurred following the shift.

dition and shifted. In the latter case, contrast was influenced by current deprivation only, not by the former deprivation condition. These results were replicated and extended in two other studies in which it was shown that SNC endured for at least 11 days in free-fed rats (Dachowski & Dunlap, 1976; Dachowski, Piazza & Dunlap, 1981, reported in Dachowski & Brazier, 1991). These latter two studies also showed that SNC was enduring in animals shifted-daily between 32% and 4%, as well as in animals given a single shift. However, in some studies, free-fed rats have recovered from contrast quite rapidly. Thus, Brazier and Dachowski (1991) found recovery in free-fed rats by the fifth postshift day.

Free-fed and deprived rats differ in the microstructure of their licking behavior following a decrease in sucrose concentration. In deprived rats, SNC in lick frequency reflects contrast effects in frequency of lick bursts initiated and in burst length. However, in free-fed rats, contrast in lick frequency is correlated with contrast in (increased) interburst interval (Grigson, Spector & Norgren, 1993). Thus, downshifted free-fed rats might be characterized as less motivated to lick (long intervals), but downshifted deprived rats, although more motivated to lick, lick only for brief times when they sample the postshift solution.

The rapid recovery from SNC in consummatory behavior found almost universally with deprived animals can be compared with the resistance to recovery in nondeprived animals. This comparison, combined with the extended contrast that occurs in rats shifted from sucrose to saccharin solutions, suggests that the need for calories, in conjunction with the presence of calories in the postshift solution, is a driving force in the recovery from negative contrast. This suggestion is supported by the finding that the administration of insulin will prevent the occurrence of contrast in rats shifted from 32% to 4% sucrose (Flaherty, McCurdy, Becker & D'Alessio, 1983). That is, the need for sugar produced by the insulin administration may eliminate contrast through a mechanism similar to that which produces relatively faster recovery in deprived rats than in free-fed rats.

Prior sucrose experience

Continuous prior experience with 4% sucrose reduces the degree of SNC, when rats are shifted from 32% to 4% sucrose. The effect is graded, with 10 days prior experience having a greater effect than 3 days' prior experience (Flaherty, Grigson & Lind, 1990). These data parallel the effects observed in the runway experiments already described, and they may be amenable to the same types of explanation, such as incentive averaging.

Prior experience with 4% sucrose in the context of repeated shifts between 32% and 4% does not substantially alter contrast. Negative contrast did not diminish in degree with nine daily alternations between 32% and 4% sucrose or with five double (32–32–4–4–32–32, etc.) alternations (Flaherty, Becker & Checke, 1983). The animals in these experiments were food-deprived, but similar results have been obtained with free-fed rats (Dachowski & Brazier, 1991). Negative contrast is also maintained with multiple shifts between 32% and 4% sucrose when parameters other than single and double alternation are used (Flaherty, Becker & Checke, 1983; Flaherty, Clarke & Coppotelli, in press; Flaherty, Coppotelli & Potaki, in press), and when such shifts are made within a session every 75 seconds (Panksepp & Trowill, 1971). The durability of SNC under these conditions argues against an interpretation of negative contrast in terms of generalization decrement.

Positive contrast occurs in the initial daily shifts of a repeated-shift procedure when deprived animals are used, but contrast is lost as the control groups approach asymptote. These data were already reviewed. When shifts are made every 75 seconds within a session, then SPC tends to be maintained (Panksepp & Trowell, 1971).

Retention interval

Negative contrast is lost in an orderly fashion as the interval between the last experience with 32% sucrose and the first experience with 4% sucrose increases from 1 to 32 days, with contrast being statistically marginal at 17 days and not reliable at 30 days (Ciszewski & Flaherty, 1977; Flaherty, Capobianco &

Hamilton, 1973; Flaherty & Lombardi, 1977; Gordon, Flaherty & Riley, 1973). Some of these data are illustrated in Figure 2.7.

Retention of contrast may be enhanced, at least over a 10-day retention interval, if rats are given brief prior experience (before preshift) with both the preshift and postshift solutions in an alternating fashion (Flaherty & Lombardi, 1977). This differential prior experience had no effect after a 1-day retention interval. This effect may be interpretable in terms of Lawrence's work on transfer along a continuum. Lawrence (1949) reported that prior differential experience with two stimuli distant from one another on a stimulus continuum enhanced the later learning of a discrimination between two points close together on the same continuum. The prior experience with 32% and 4% sucrose in the Flaherty and Lombardi experiment may have served to facilitate an otherwise difficult discrimination between the sweetness value of the postshift 4% sucrose and the memory of the 32% sucrose after the 10-day retention interval.

All the animals in these experiments were food-deprived. Apparently, memory of the preshift solution is much greater when the animals are free-fed. At least, contrast will occur over much longer retention intervals in this case. Dachowski et al. (1981; reported in Dachowski & Brazier, 1991) found that contrast endured for 10 days after a shift from 32% to 4% sucrose and then remained essentially unaltered when a 78-day "vacation" was inserted before testing was continued with the postshift 4% solution. This experiment differs from the pre-

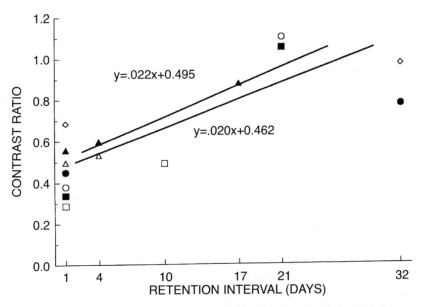

Figure 2.7 Summary of contrast retention experiments. Contrast ratio is the ratio of lick frequency in shifted/unshifted groups. Like symbols represent data points obtained within a single experiment. The top linear equation was calculated on three data points from the same experiment (1-, 4-, and 17-day retention intervals). The bottom equation is based on all of the data points. Reliable contrast is lost with about 17 days inserted between the last preshift day and the first postshift day.

vious studies not only in deprivation conditions but also in the location of the retention interval – in this case, during the postshift period itself, rather than after the last experience with the preshift solution.

Even brief exposure to 32% sucrose has long-lasting effects. One study showed that a single 5-minute access period to 32% sucrose would result in clear negative contrast when the rats were given 4% sucrose 24 hours later. Small, but statistically reliable, negative contrast was evident even some 70 hours after this single brief exposure to 32% sucrose (Flaherty, Ciszewski & Kaplan, 1979).

The potent effect of these brief exposures to 32% sucrose renders even more puzzling the failure of reinstatement treatments to enhance the memory of the preshift solution. It has been shown in a variety of experimental situations that brief exposure to the reinforcer or to the context during a retention interval can enhance memory (Rovee-Collier et al., 1980; Spear and Riccio, 1994). In the one known examination of this effect in consummatory contrast, however, brief exposures to the preshift 32% sucrose solution did not enhance contrast over 17- or 32-day retention intervals (Ciszewski & Flaherty, 1977).

Summary

Degree of contrast in consummatory behavior seems to vary directly with degree of concentration disparity (either sucrose or saccharin). Initial experience with the eventual postshift solution tends to diminish negative contrast, but not if this experience is in the context of repeated shifts between high and low concentrations. Negative contrast remains robust through repeated reward shifts under a variety of parametric conditions.

In the case of instrumental behavior, contrast tends to vary directly with degree of deprivation, but there is no such trend in consummatory behavior. Instead, initial degree of contrast is approximately equivalent in free-fed and food-deprived rats (80% to 82% of free-feeding weight) however, the deprived animals recover rapidly, whereas the nondeprived animals are very slow to recover. Several items of evidence suggest that physiological need plus the nutritional value of the postshift substance combine to drive recovery from contrast. However, the stark difference between contrast in instrumental and consummatory behaviors in the case of free-fed rats suggests some fundamental difference in the effects of food deprivation on the two behaviors.

Another difference, although not as striking, may be in the response to repeated shifts in reward. Whereas negative contrast reoccurs unabated in consummatory behavior with each shift, the outcome in instrumental behavior is much less clear, with some studies showing a rapid loss of contrast and others finding contrast with up to two or three shifts.

Like contrast in instrumental behavior, contrast in consummatory behavior can be maintained over long retention intervals, perhaps extraordinarily long in the case of nondeprived rats.

Successive contrast in comparative perspective

Species differences

There is substantial evidence that SNC and SPC do not occur in the instrumental responding of goldfish, turtles, or toads following shifts in magnitude of reward (Couvillon & Bitterman, 1985; Gonzalez, Ferry & Powers, 1974; Gonzalez, Holmes & Bitterman, 1967; Gonzalez et al., 1972; Lowes & Bitterman, 1967; Mackintosh, 1971; Papini & Ishida, 1994; Pert & Bitterman, 1970; Raymond, Aderman & Wolach, 1972; Schmajuk, Segura & Ruidiaz, 1981; Wolach & Latta, 1974; Wolach, Raymond & Hurst, 1973).

In some of these experiments with long intertrial intervals, the behavior of the subjects (fish) did not change after the reward decrease, and even when there was a change in behavior under apparently favorable conditions (that is, massed trials and a 40-to-1 reward decrease), it was gradual and did not hint at a contrast effect. In rats, consummatory behavior may be a more sensitive indicant of contrast than instrumental behavior (see the section on "Contrast in instrumental and consummatory behavior – an anomaly"). In order to test if this might be the case with goldfish, Couvillon and Bitterman (1985) examined contrast in consummatory behavior when the fish were shifted from a preferred food to the same food adulterated with quinine sulphate. Although quinine adulteration produces large contrast effects in consummatory behavior in rats (Flaherty & Rowan, 1989b), no evidence of contrast occurred in the goldfish. In fact, the initial response of the fish following the shift was to increase consumption of the adulterated food. Consumption eventually decreased, but did not fall below that of the unshifted control group.

Negative contrast in consummatory behavior has been obtained in two species of marsupials, red opossums (*Lutreolina crassicaudata*) and white-eared opossums *(Didelphis albiventris)*. Contrast occurred repeatedly in both species with repeated shifts from 32% to 4% sucrose (Papini, Mustaca & Bitterman, 1988).

These data have led to the hypothesis that a mechanism that supports contrast effects may have evolved in some common reptilian ancestry of birds and mammals (Bitterman, 1975; Papini et al., 1988).

However, a common evolutionary history may not be the only route to contrast. Couvillon and Bitterman (1984) found clear evidence of negative contrast in consummatory behavior when free-flying honeybees were shifted from 50% to 20% sucrose. Since it is unlikely that the occurrence of contrast in bees and mammals could be explained on the basis of a mechanism that evolved from a common ancestor, these data may suggest a process of convergent evolution (Bitterman, 1988). It is also possible that the mechanism that produces SNC in mammals (searching? emotional reaction?) is different from that which produces SNC in honeybees (sensory adaptation?) (Ammon, Abramson & Bitterman, 1986).

Strain differences in rats

Brush (1985) selectively bred for two strains of rats that differed in active avoidance behavior – the Syracuse Low Avoidance (SLA) and Syracuse High Avoidance (SHA) rats. When tested in the consummatory contrast paradigm, the rats from the SLA strain showed substantially larger SNC than the rats from the SHA strain (Flaherty & Rowan, 1989a). The two strains also differed in degree of plasma glucose response to a novel environment, in glycemic conditioning, and in the effects of the tranquilizer chlordiazepoxide on negative contrast.[5] The two strains, however, did not differ in another type of contrast – simultaneous contrast. Substantial independent evidence suggests that the SLA rats are more emotionally reactive than the SHA rats, but the relationship of emotional reactivity per se to contrast is not compelling (see Flaherty, Krauss, Rowan & Grigson, 1994).

For example, the Maudsley reactive (MR) and Maudsley nonreactive (MNRA) rats, originally selected on the basis of number of defecations in an open field, have been widely characterized as differing in emotional reactivity (Broadhurst, 1975; Gray, 1987). When tested in consummatory contrast, the reactive animals unexpectedly showed a reliably smaller SNC than the nonreactive animals, and the contrast effect in both groups was unaffected by chlordiazepoxide (Rowan & Flaherty, 1991). Also, both of these groups showed SNCs smaller than those obtained in an unselected population of Sprague–Dawley derived rats. Because these results were unexpected, and because the animals used in our experiments were derived from an American branch (MR/Har and MNRA/Har) of the original Maudsley strains, we tested them in a version of the original open-field apparatus used to select and classify the animals. We found that the two strains differed in the typical fashion – the MNRA defecated less and were more active than the MR animals (Rowan & Flaherty, 1991).

Taken together, the results of these two studies with rats selected on the basis of behavior in other tasks suggest that it is not a simple matter to predict the performance of rats in an SNC procedure on the basis of global conceptions of emotional reactivity.

Zucker lean and obese rats were also tested in the SNC paradigm (Flaherty, Krauss & Hill, 1994). The genetically obese rats (mean predeprivation weight = 605 grams) showed somewhat larger SNC than the lean rats (mean predeprivation weight = 402 grams). The difference, although statistically reliable, was small, and the degree of contrast shown by the obese rats was within the range seen in unselected Sprague–Dawley rats. Thus, the dietary abnormalities present in the Zucker obese strain do not have a major effect on contrast.

Successive negative contrast in consummatory behavior was also examined in three standard, commercially available, rat strains – Sprague–Dawley derived, Wistar, and Long Evans hooded rats. The sucrose solutions in this particular

---

[5] These data, and other psychopharmacological data, will be considered extensively in Chapter 3.

experiment were always given in an open-field context, and behaviors other than sucrose consumption were monitored. Although the strains differed in aspects of open-field behavior and in absolute level of sucrose consumption, they did not differ in degree of negative contrast (Flaherty, Troncoso & Deschu, 1979).[6]

Thus, standard commercially available rat strains seem not to differ in SNC in consummatory behavior, but rats selectively bred for certain other psychological differences will also differ in SNC.

Sex differences

The issues of sex differences in contrast has aroused little concern (Black, 1968; Cox, 1975; Dunham, 1968; Flaherty, 1982; Gandelman, 1983; Williams, 1983), perhaps reasonably so since the few studies available indicate little in the way of such differences (see, for example, Flaherty, Krauss, Rowan & Grigson, 1994). In a study conducted in an open field, male and female rats showed equivalent contrast effects upon the initial shift from 32% to 4% sucrose solutions (Flaherty, Powell & Hamilton, 1979). This lack of a sex difference in contrast occurred even though the female rats tended to spend twice as much time ambulating around the open field and to spend less time drinking than the male rats. The experiment in question was primarily concerned with the effects of septal lesions on contrast, and sex did interact with lesion status in terms of recovery from contrast. Female rats with lesions of the septum were the slowest to recover from contrast.

Another study of consummatory contrast also found no sex difference in degree of contrast in rats shifted from 32% to 4% sucrose (Flaherty & Rowan, 1989b). A sex difference was obtained, however, when the shift was from a sucrose solution to a quinine-adulterated sucrose solution. In this case, the female rats showed a larger overall contrast effect across five postshift days, an effect which was due to a slower recovery process in the females rather than to initial differences in degree of contrast. There were no sex differences in recovery in rats whose shift involved unadulterated sucrose solutions.

Thus, sex differences may not normally exist in SNC in consummatory behavior, but sex differences in recovery from consummatory contrast may be revealed under special circumstances that include, at least, lesions of the septum and a shift to a quinine–sucrose solution.

Developmental differences

Very young rats do not show SNC in runway behavior. Roberts (1966) obtained an SNC in 180-day-old rats, but not in 25-day-old rats (actually, 46-day-old rats

---

[6] We also examined SNC in consummatory behavior in Sprague–Dawley derived rats purchased from three American breeders: Camm, Charles River, and Blue Spruce (subsequently acquired by the Harlan Sprague–Dawley company). No differences in degree of contrast were obtained in this study (Flaherty and Rowan, unpublished data).

related phenomena (Amsel, 1992; Amsel & Stanton, 1980; Chen, Gross & Amsel, 1981; Daly, 1991; Stanton & Amsel, 1980; Stanton, Lobaugh & Amsel, 1984). One study found that 11-, 14-, and 16-day-old rats showed a decrease in performance when reward (access to milk) was downshifted, but they did not show a contrast effect. Another study found SNC in 61–68-day-old rats and in 34–35-day-old rats, a marginal contrast effect in 25–26-day-old rats, and no contrast in 17–24-day-old rats. These latter data were collected with food pellets as the reward. With a milk reward, an SNC was obtained in 25–26-day-old rats, some evidence of contrast in 20–21-day-old rats, but none in 16–17-day-old rats. However, Stanton, Lobaugh and Amsel (1984) did find contrast in 17-day-old rats, but not in 14-day-old rats. These same investigators found that simultaneous contrast may develop earlier than successive contrast, an interesting result because simultaneous contrast is readily demonstrable in fish, whereas successive contrast is not.

It may also be of some interest that successive contrast first appears just before, or at about the time of, weaning, around 17–21 days of age. In Chapter 4 we will consider a possible functional role for successive contrast in foraging, and the appearance of contrast at about the time the young rat is "on its own" may be relevant for this discussion.

Individual differences and selective breeding

Although, as a group phenomenon, SNC in consummatory behavior is robust, there is a range of individual differences in degree of decrement in lick frequency that occurs when rats are shifted from 32% to 4% sucrose. An example of different degrees of decrement, based on the shift ratio (postshift/preshift lick frequency) of 397 rats, is presented in Figure 2.8. On the basis of these data, a breeding program was initiated with five male and five females selected from each tail of the distribution. Contrast data for the F_7 generation (the only generation in which unshifted controls were used) are presented in Figure 2.9. Differences between the large and small contrast lines developed in degree of shift by the third filial generation and were present, along with differences in contrast compared to unshifted control groups, in the contrast test conducted in the seventh generation (Flaherty, Krauss, Rowan & Grigson, 1994).

Regression functions of offspring on the parental generations are presented for the sixth and seventh filial generations in Figure 2.10. The estimate of heritability (h^2) of degree of shift obtained was 0.40 in the sixth generation and 0.64 in the seventh generation.

Animals from the two lines differed in activity, but this did not correlate with contrast. They did not differ in responsivity to the absolute rewarding values of 32% and 4% sucrose, nor in the response to the rewarding value of cocaine, nor in anticipatory contrast. Thus, the breeding data suggest that responsivity to sucrose concentration reduction may involve a relatively delimited psychological process that is amenable to selection. This genetic factor may account for indi-

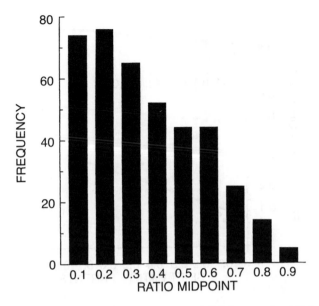

Figure 2.8 Frequency distribution of shift ratios (postshift lick frequency/preshift lick frequency) obtained from a sample of 397 rats. Low ratios (e.g., 0.1) represent large contrast effects. (Adapted from Flaherty, Krauss, Rowan & Grigson, 1994).

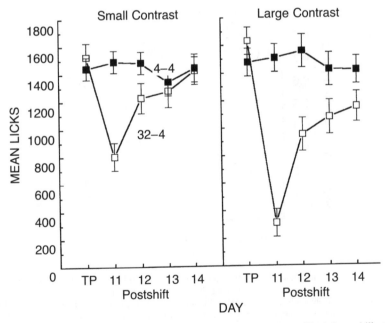

Figure 2.9 Mean lick frequency in shifted (32-4) and unshifted (4-4) rats. The left panel illustrates data from rats selectively bred to show small contrast (SC), and the right panel shows rats selectively bred to show large contrast (LC). (Adapted from Flaherty, Krauss, Rowan & Grigson, 1994.)

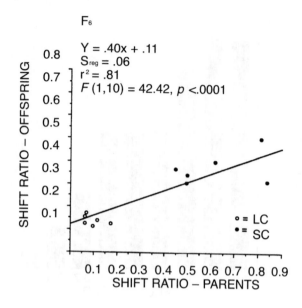

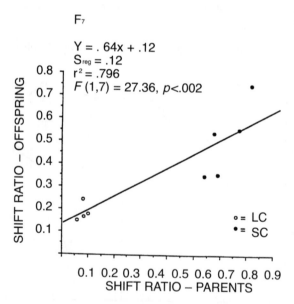

Figure 2.10 Regression functions of offspring on their parents in terms of shift ratio (postshift lick frequency/preshift lick frequency). Top panel illustrates the sixth filial generation and the bottom panel illustrates the seventh filial generation. SC indicates rats bred to show small contrast and LC indicates rats bred to show large contrast. (Adapted from Flaherty, Krauss, Rowan & Grigson, 1994.)

sucrose concentration reduction may involve a relatively delimited psychological process that is amenable to selection. This genetic factor may account for individual differences in response to reward loss in rats; the possibility that a similar factor exists in humans merits investigation.

Successive contrast in complex feeding situations

Laboratory studies of SNC have almost always involved animals that are exposed to the experimental conditions for brief periods each day and are shifted in food pellets or sucrose solutions that constitute just a small part of their daily diet. Two experiments have demonstrated the occurrence of SNC in situations in which rats received, or earned, all their food and in which the shift was made in complex aspects of their diet. In one study, Rogers (1985) maintained separate groups of rats on either lab chow or a cafeteria diet. One-half of each group was allowed to free feed and the other half had their weight controlled by restricted periods of access. Over the period of "preshift," the rats allowed to select freely on a cafeteria diet became obese, but the free-fed lab chow rats did not. In the postshift period, all rats were shifted to free feeding on the lab chow diet. Both cafeteria-fed groups became hypophagic following the shift to the lab chow diet, an apparent SNC. The hypophagia was due to a reduction both in average meal size and in meal frequency, and it was initially larger and longer lasting in the overweight rats than in the normal weight rats. This latter result parallels effects obtained with free-fed rats in consummatory negative contrast effects, already described.

In another study (Johnson, Ackroff, Peters and Collier, 1986), rats that earned all their food by completing a chain Fixed Ratio 80, Fixed Ratio 10 schedule[7] were shifted from high-caloric-density diets to low-caloric-density diets, or vice versa. The initial response of the downshifted rats was to eat less per meal and consume fewer kilocalories per day compared to preshift levels – an SNC effect. These animals recovered by approximately 3 days. The upshifted animals initially ate more per meal and consumed more kilocalories per day compared with preshift levels – an SPC effect. These animals also recovered in about 3 days.

The data from these two experiments considerably extend the potential generality of contrast effects by indicating that they may be a normal part of feeding when diet is shifted. A contrast effect from a shift in sucrose concentration that carried over to influence daily food intake was demonstrated by Valle (1990). In this study, rats were given access to sucrose for 2 hours per day – one group receiving 4% sucrose each day and the other alternating between 15% and 4% sucrose each day. All animals were given their daily food ration (Purina chow) for 2 hours following the sucrose period. Valle found that the group alternating between 16% and 4% sucrose consumed 4% less than the 4% control group did, demonstrating SNC.

---

[7] The rats had to complete 80 responses on one lever and then go to a second lever and complete 10 responses in order to get access to a meal.

More interesting, this group also consumed less Purina chow on days in which they had the 4% sucrose compared to when they had the 16% sucrose. The total loss in calories in the contrast group, including their reduced intake of sucrose and their reduced meal, was 17% – a potent negative contrast effect.

Contrast with aversive stimuli

There is little to report in the category of contrast with aversive stimuli. Neither positive nor negative contrast effects were obtained in one study of escape[8] learning (Bower, Fowler & Trapold, 1959), but both were found in a similar study (Nation, Wrather & Mellgren, 1974). There are some principal differences between the studies. Nation, Wrather and Mellgren shifted the level of electric current, and the animals were shocked only in the start and run sections of the runway, not in the goal section; however, Bower, Fowler, and Trapold shifted voltage level and the animals received shock in all sections of the runway. Perhaps the effective "reward" disparity was greater in the Nation et al. experiment. The importance of reward disparity in escape learning was suggested by a series of experiments in which the similarity of shock and escape chambers was varied (McAllister et al., 1972). An SNC effect was obtained only in the third of three studies, the one in which there was the greatest difference between the two chambers (thereby, perhaps, allowing for the greatest "relief" [Denny, 1991]). There was no evidence of SPC in any of the three experiments. A final study utilizing an escape paradigm with differential water temperature as the reinforcer also reported SNC but no SPC (Woods, 1967).

Contrast has also been reported using punishment procedures. Nation, Mellgren, and Wrather (1975) found SNC but no SPC when a shift of current levels was used as a punishment in a runway task. An SPC was reported when a shift from a 1-pellet to 12-pellet reward was combined with the removal of a shock punishment (Shanab & White, 1972).

A series of studies using a one-way shuttle avoidance procedure has reported a consistent pattern of results. These studies showed that reducing the time spent in the nonshock compartment from 30 seconds to 1 second produced a substantial decrement in avoidance performance, compared to rats who always were allowed 1 second in the "safe" compartment. This SNC effect was obtained with a variety of parametric conditions (Candido et al., 1992). The SNC in avoidance responding was blocked by diazepam (Morales et al., 1992; Torres et al., 1994 – see Chapter 3), thereby supporting the possibility that the reward for avoidance learning is "relief" (Denny, 1991) and that contrast in this paradigm is similar to that obtained with positive reinforcers.

---

[8] In the escape learning studies, the animals were placed in the start box of a runway and had to run to the goal box to escape an electric shock – complete escape from shock in the case of the Nation et al. experiment, or reduced shock in the case of the Bower experiment.

In summary, the data that are available show that SNC does occur with shifts in aversive stimuli, that these contrast effects may be functionally similar to SNC obtained with positive reinforcers, and that SPC is a rarer event than SNC.

Consummatory versus instrumental contrast – an anomaly

It is clear by now that successive negative contrast is readily demonstrable in both consummatory and instrumental behavior under a wide variety of experimental conditions. However, there is one condition in which it has been virtually impossible to demonstrate SNC – the measurement of runway behavior following a decrease in the concentration of a sugar solution.

This failure to obtain SNC has occurred in many experiments with a variety of parametric variations (Barnes & Tombaugh, 1973; Burns, 1984; Burns & Burns, 1978; Burns, Dupree & Lorig, 1978; Burns, Lorig & McCrary, 1986; Collier, Knarr, & Marx, 1961; Flaherty & Caprio, 1976; Flaherty, Riley & Spear, 1973; Goodrich & Zaretsky, 1962; Homzie & Ross, 1962; Rosen, 1966; Rosen & Ison, 1965; Shanab, France & Young, 1975; Spear, 1965).

In examining the parameters used in these experiments, it seems unlikely that variations in factors such as concentration disparity, trials per day, intertrial interval, or differential massing or spacing of trials in the preshift and postshift periods is responsible for the failure to obtain SNC in instrumental behaviors following a shift in sucrose concentration. Given the number of published studies that have failed to obtain SNC, and the difficulty in publishing papers with negative results, it would not be surprising if there were many more failures to find contrast in runway behavior following a shift in sucrose concentration. In our laboratory, we have tried using an eight-arm radial maze as a runway, with rats starting from the extreme end of one arm and running to the extreme end of another arm (64 inches). The rationale for this experiment was that the availability of the alternative six arms would provide an opportunity for responses that would compete with goal approach and thereby enhance the likelihood of obtaining negative contrast. However, in two experiments involving shifts from 32% to 4% sucrose, negative contrast in approach behavior failed to occur, although contrast in consummatory behavior was reliable in both experiments (Flaherty & Kops, unpublished data). Unpublished data from our laboratory also indicate that using a very long runway (32 feet) does not alter the failure to obtain contrast in runway behavior when the concentration of a sucrose solution is decreased.

The failure of contrast to occur in runway behavior is particularly striking because substantial contrast in consummatory behavior occurs when the rats reach the end of the runway (Flaherty & Caprio, 1976). The dissociation between the two measures of behavior was further analyzed by examining correlations between lick frequency and the various measures of runway behavior at three points during the preshift period and three points during the postshift period.

None of the 36 correlations obtained during the preshift period between lick frequency and instrumental behavior were reliable. In comparison, 7 of 12 correlations between run speed and goal speed were reliable; 3 of 12 between start speed and goal speed; and 2 of 12 between start speed and run speed. In the case of the postshift data, 2 of 60 correlations between lick frequency and instrumental behavior were reliable, compared to 18 of 60 between different measures of instrumental behavior (Flaherty & Caprio, 1976).

Other instances of a dissociation between instrumental behavior and consummatory behavior may be found in the literature. For example, Knarr and Collier (1962), after a systematic investigation of different aspects of consummatory behavior in the runway, concluded that "variations in consummatory activity are neither necessary nor even sufficient conditions for producing variations in acquisition and performance" (Knarr & Collier, 1962, p. 587). In a lever-press study, either prefeeding with saccharin or pairing saccharin with a toxin was found to decrease consumption of saccharin, but not bar pressing for saccharin (Holman, 1975). In the same experiment, it was found that both consummatory and instrumental behaviors were suppressed if the animals were prefed with dextrose. These data indicated to Holman that instrumental behavior was influenced by the need for food but not by the appetite for food.

Holman's interpretation cannot directly be applied to contrast for three reasons. First, the dissociation in the case of contrast applies only in the case of sucrose concentration reductions, not in the case of food pellet reductions, or reductions in volume of sucrose (Shanab et al., 1975; Shanab, France & Young, 1976), or, probably, reductions in the number of sucrose pellets (Burns et al., 1978). Second, another type of contrast, "simultaneous contrast," does occur in runway behavior when sucrose concentration is varied (Flaherty, Riley & Spear, 1973). Third, Holman's experiments involved lever pressing and the relationship of lever pressing to runway behavior in regard to the occurrence of contrast is not yet clear. As Bindra's analysis of instrumental learning (Bindra, 1974) made clear, the lever-pressing task is quite different from the runway task because the route to the goal (reward) is usually indirect with lever pressing – the animals typically must deviate from a direct approach to the food magazine in order to press the lever – but the approach is direct in the runway. Thus, a great deal of runway behavior may well represent a Pavlovian goal-tracking response rather than instrumental learning per se (Hearst & Jenkins, 1974). Whether this difference has functional meaning for contrast is not clear; very few successive negative contrast studies have been conducted with a lever-press task, and those that have been done using sucrose as a reward have produced ambiguous results.

One early study (Collier & Marx, 1959) seemed to provide evidence of durable positive and negative contrast effects following shifts in the concentration of sucrose solutions. However, this result has been shown to be due to a confounding of body weight differences with the shift conditions. When body weight was equated, no contrast occurred (Dunham & Kilps, 1969). Two other small-scale studies with rats have provided some evidence of SNC in lever pressing with sucrose concentration decreases (Weinstein, 1970a, 1970b). In addition, two studies required monkeys to lever press on a variable-interval (VI) schedule for sequence of increasing or decreasing sucrose solutions. Limited evidence of contrast was provided in one experiment, and no evidence was provided in the other experiment (Schrier, 1965, 1969). Thus, the lever-press experiments have not systematically addressed the parallel between runway and lever-press measures of contrast following downshifts in sucrose concentration, nor have they addressed the more general question of the dissociation between instrumental and consummatory responding.

Another example of the dissociation between instrumental and consummatory measures of contrast will be presented in Chapter 3, where data will be presented showing that lesions of the hippocampus or entorhinal cortex affect contrast in instrumental behavior but not contrast in consummatory behavior.

Summary

"Ubiquitous" may be too strong a term, but successive contrast is a frequent consequence of abrupt shifts in reward. Negative contrast is much more common than positive contrast, but positive contrast may be obtained with special manipulations, such as using delay of reward or a long runway in the shift situation.

Contrast in consummatory behavior may be both more sensitive and more enduring than contrast in approach (instrumental) behavior. There may be adaptive reasons for this, in that the "best" solution to reward variability may be to continue to approach and sample previously bountiful sources of nutrition and then reject them if they still fall below the level of expectation produced by continued interaction with the environment. A potential adaptive role for contrast in mammalian behavior is indicated by its widespread occurrence across the mammalian spectrum; a potential genetic role is indicated by differences in selectively bred species, both those bred for non-contrast behaviors and those selectively bred for contrast.

The occurrence of contrast in complex feeding situations and in aversive as well as appetitive tasks indicates that relativity mechanisms may play an important role in a variety of situations in an animal's interactions with its hedonic environment.

3   Successive contrast: psychopharmacology and neurobiology

Brains compute value.
      – Joseph LeDoux, 1990

One of the established findings of animal learning research is that different amounts of reward produce different levels of behavior. There are many parameters that affect the final level of performance, but the simple message is that the brains of lower animals have mechanisms that permit the scaling of reward value in a host of different forms and that produce behavior based on differences in value. These brains, at least the brains of mammals and birds, also have mechanisms that permit the comparison of rewards and that activate behavior based on the *relative* value as well as the absolute value of rewards. Insight into this mechanism has been provided by studies of the effects of drugs and lesions on SNC.

Because the majority of these studies have involved the acute effects of drugs in consummatory contrast experiments, these data will be considered first.

Acute drug administration

Consummatory contrast

A summary of the effective and ineffective drugs administered on either the first or second postshift day is presented in Table 3.1.

The benzodiazepines

The benzodiazepine tranquilizers facilitate recovery from contrast. For example, chlordiazepoxide (CDP), flurazepam, and midazolam reduce contrast in a dose-related manner when the drug is administered on the second postshift day (Becker, 1986; Becker & Flaherty, 1983; Flaherty, Becker, Checke, Rowan & Grigson, 1992; Flaherty, Grigson & Lind, 1990; Flaherty, Lombardi, Wrightson & Deptula, 1980; Flaherty, Grigson, Demetrikopoulos, Weaver, Krauss & Rowan, 1990; Vogel & Principi, 1971). Cross-experiment comparison suggests that midazolam is the most potent of these drugs and flurazepam the least potent. The effects of CDP and midazolam are illustrated in Figure 3.1.

Given the frequent suggestion that SNC involves a negative emotional

Table 3.1. *Listing of drugs that have been investigated in the consummatory negative contrast procedure. All drugs, except imipramine, were administered acutely. All measurements are in mg/kg, unless otherwise noted. (*) = significant effect.*

Effective Drugs	Ineffective Drugs
Chlordiazepoxide (2, 4, 6* ,8*, 10*)	Imipramine (8, 16)
Midazolam (0.25, 0.5, 1.0*, 1.25*, 2.0*)	Chlorpromazine (1, 3, 5)
Flurazepam (5, 10, 20*)	Haloperidol (0.1, 0.5, 1.0)
Sodium Amobarbital (15, 17.5*, 20)	Amphetamine (0.125, 0.25)
Ethanol (250, 500, 750*, 1,000*, 1,500, 2,000)	Naloxone (0.25, 0.5, 1.0)
Morphine (0.5, 1, 2, 4*, 8*, 16)	Methysergide (3, 6, 12)
Cyproheptadine (3*, 6, 12)	Buspirone (0.125, 0.25, 0.5, 1, 2, 15)
Cinanserin (5, 10*, 15*, 20)	Gepirone (2.5, 5, 10)
Muscimol (0.025 μg, 0.05* μg)	Propanolol (5, 10)
	Clonidine (0.00312, 0.00625, 0.0125, 0.025, 0.05)
	Scopolamine (0.25, 0.5, 1.0)
	Pyrilamine (3, 6)
	PCPA (150, 300)
	Ketanserin (2, 8)
	Ritanserin (0.63, 2.5)
	Mianserin (2.5, 10)

response, a reasonable hypothesis is that the benzodiazepines facilitate recovery from contrast by moderating this emotional reaction. However, the benzodiazepine tranquilizers have a number of effects in addition to anxiety reduction. The benzodiazepines are muscle relaxants, anticonvulsants, sedatives, and, most importantly for the current issue, they are appetite stimulants (see, for example, Cooper & Estall, 1985). Could the enhanced recovery from contrast be a reflection of the appetite-stimulating effects of benzodiazepines?

There are several controls for this possibility. One is the unshifted 4% animals that are injected with the drug. If the effect of the tranquilizers was simply to increase sucrose consumption, then this group should be affected as much as the shifted group and, thus, there would be no contrast reduction. This is not the case; the rats shifted from 32% to 4% sucrose show a much greater increase in lick frequency than the rats that have been maintained on 4% sucrose. Thus, there is something special about the shift that determines the effectiveness of CDP.

There are also cases in which CDP is ineffective in reducing contrast; in some of these cases, however, it does have an appetite-stimulating effect – suggesting that the two effects are not necessarily related. The first case involves drug effects on the first postshift day. Although CDP does not reduce contrast, it often does have appetite-stimulating effects. These are illustrated in Figure 3.2. In this experiment, shifted and unshifted rats were injected with 8 mg/kg of CDP on the first postshift day – which occurred either 24 or 48 hours after the last preshift day. In both cases, rats given CDP showed increased lick frequencies,

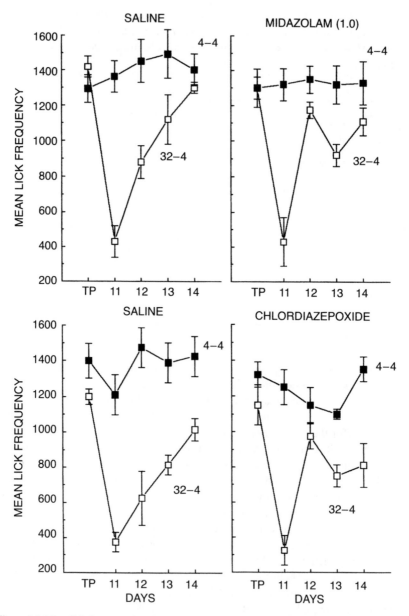

Figure 3.1 Mean lick frequency in shifted (32-4) and unshifted (4-4) rats injected with saline, chlordiazepoxide (CDP), or midazolam on the second postshift day (day 12). Both drugs reliably reduce contrast. (Top panel: Flaherty, Grigson, Demetrikopoulos, Weaver, Krauss & Rowan, 1990; bottom panel: Flaherty & Rowan, 1989.)

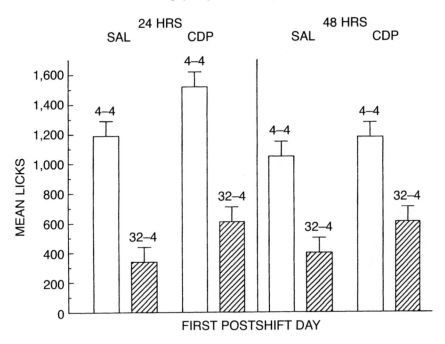

Figure 3.2 Chlordiazepoxide (CDP), administered on the first postshift day, failed to reduce successive negative contrast both when the first postshift day was 24 hours after the last preshift day and when the first postshift day was 48 hours after the last preshift day. The drug did have an appetite-stimulating effect. (After Flaherty, Grigson & Rowan, 1986.)

but the increase occurred equivalently in shifted and unshifted groups. Thus, CDP had an appetite-stimulating effect without reducing contrast (Flaherty, Grigson & Rowan, 1986).

The second control involves the effects of CDP in free-fed rats. Preliminary data suggest that CDP does not reduce contrast when administered on the second postshift day under these conditions, but it does have an appetite-stimulating effect (Flaherty, 1991b). CDP is also ineffective in reducing two other types of contrast in consummatory behavior – simultaneous contrast and anticipatory contrast – even though it has appetite-stimulating effects in both cases (Flaherty & Rowan, 1988; Flaherty, Lombardi, Kapust & D'Amato, 1977).

Given the effectiveness of CDP in reducing SNC when administered on the second postshift day, it was surprising to find that the drug was without effect when administered on the first postshift day (Flaherty et al., 1980). Several potential reasons for this difference in the effectiveness of CDP across the first two postshift days have been investigated. One possibility is that there is a different dose/response function on the first postshift day than on the second postshift day. However, doses of 3, 5, 10, and 15 mg/kg of CDP were ineffective on the first postshift day, even though doses of 3, 5, 6, and 8 mg/kg were effective on the second postshift day in reducing contrast (Flaherty et al., 1990). Thus, it does not appear that different dose/response function is the answer.

Another possibility is that the effectiveness of CDP on the second postshift day, but not on the first postshift day, is due to differential retention intervals between the last preshift day and the first and second postshift days. In order for the animals to show a contrast effect, they must be able to compare the postshift solution with the *memory* of the preshift solution (Spear, 1967). On the second postshift day there has been a 48-hour retention interval from the last experience with the preshift solution, whereas there has been only a 24-hour interval on the first postshift day. Perhaps CDP is effective on the second postshift day because the contrast is weaker, due to a less effective comparison with the memory of the preshift solution.

In order to test this hypothesis, we conducted an experiment in which the *first* postshift day was given either 24 or 48 hours after the last preshift day. Chlordiazepoxide did not reduce contrast under either condition, although it did have an appetite-stimulating effect (see Figure 3.2) (Flaherty et al.,1986). Thus, retention interval is not responsible for the differential effectiveness of CDP.

Still another hypothesis on the timing of CDP's effectiveness is that the animals must have some experience with the postshift solution before the CDP becomes effective. The designation of first and second postshift day is some-what arbitrary because it is based on the procedure of giving the animals access to the sucrose solutions for only 5 minutes per day. In order to investigate the role of this time factor, rats were given access to the postshift solution for 20 minutes on the first postshift day. Thus, all four postshift "days" were incorporated into the first experience with the postshift solution. Lick frequency was then recorded on a minute-to-minute basis in animals injected with either saline or CDP (8 mg/kg). The results of this experiment showed that CDP was without effect during the first 5 minutes of exposure but it reliably reduced contrast in the second 5-minute period. Similar results were obtained in a replication of this experiment (Flaherty et al., 1986).

These data indicate that experience with the postshift 4% solution may be necessary for CDP to be effective in reducing contrast. However, is it necessary that this experience be during the postshift period? Would any prior experience with the 4% solution render CDP effective under conditions in which it is not normally effective? In order to test this, experiments were conducted in which the animals were given an initial period (prior to preshift training) of experience with the 4% sucrose solution. Some animals were given a period of either 4 or 10 days with the 4% sucrose, then experienced the usual 10-day preshift period, and then were shifted to 4% again. Other animals were given prior experience with the 4% sucrose in the context of a simultaneous contrast procedure (alternating 32% and 4%) for 3 days prior to preshift training. On the first postshift day, one-half of each group was injected with CDP (10 mg/kg) and one-half with saline. In no case did CDP lead to a reliable reduction of contrast, even though the prior training experience (in the case of the 10-day pre-exposure condition) did lead to a smaller contrast effect on the first postshift day (Flaherty et al., 1990). Thus, experience with the 4% solution prior to experience with the preshift 32% solution does not enhance the effectiveness of CDP on the first postshift day.

The collective results of the experiments designed to investigate this issue, particularly those from the 20-minute postshift studies, suggest that some period of experience with the *postshift* solution is necessary before CDP becomes effective. Later we will argue that this is because SNC may involve an initial period of searching behavior, rather than a type of emotional response that is susceptible to the tranquilizing effects of the benzodiazepines.

Recent investigations of the effects of CDP in the context of repeated shifts in sucrose concentration have produced several findings. The procedure used in these experiments was 32% sucrose for 3 days (5 minutes per day) and then 4% sucrose for 2 days in the shifted groups, and 4% sucrose for 5 days in the unshifted groups. A total of eight shifts were examined (40 days) with a 2-day break between successive 5-day cycles (Flaherty, Clarke & Coppotelli, in press). The basic findings were as follows: Contrast was still reliable after eight shifts in one study, and after seven shifts in another; CDP administered on the second postshift day continued to reduce contrast; CDP administered on the first postshift day was ineffective over the first three shift cycles (which is the usual finding with CDP), but on the fourth cycle CDP had a contrast-reducing effect, and on the fifth shift cycle (and subsequently), it eliminated contrast.

Thus, the repeated administration of CDP, and/or repeated experience with reward reductions, rendered CDP effective where it had been previously ineffective. Preliminary data suggest that the combination of both drug and shift experience is necessary for sensitization to the contrast-reducing effect of CDP to occur.

The lack of tolerance to the anti-contrast actions of CDP on the second postshift day is particularly interesting, given that these same experiments showed that tolerance did develop to the sedative effects of CDP as measured in open-field behavior. Because the open-field tests were given in a completely different context from the contrast studies, it seems unlikely that the tolerance to the sedative effects of the drug was based on conditioning. These data further suggest that the anti-contrast action of CDP is mediated by a different mechanism than the mechanism that controls the sedative effects of the drug.

Ethanol

The administration of ethanol reliably reduces SNC in a dose-dependent manner (Becker & Flaherty, 1982, 1983). No dose of ethanol we investigated was effective enough to eliminate contrast completely – the higher doses produced motor incoordination in both shifted and unshifted rats. Like the benzodiazepines, ethanol seems to be ineffective when administered on the first postshift day (Becker & Flaherty, 1982). Ethanol and CDP also influenced contrast in an additive fashion. That is, marginally effective doses of CDP (4 mg/kg) and ethanol (0.50 g/kg) given together on the second postshift day substantially reduced contrast (Becker & Flaherty, 1983).

This interaction of CDP and ethanol is consistent with other evidence that suggests ethanol promotes recovery from contrast through actions at the gamma-amino butyric acid (GABA)/benzodiazepine receptor complex. This evidence includes the finding that the indirect GABA agonist valproate enhances the effectiveness of a marginal (0.50 g/kg) dose of ethanol. Also, picrotoxin, a chloride channel blocker and GABA antagonist, antagonized the contrast-alleviating effects of ethanol (Becker & Anton, 1990). The effects of ethanol on contrast were also countered by Ro 15-4513, a partial inverse agonist at the benzodiazepine receptor (Becker & Hale, 1991).

Barbiturates

The only barbiturate investigated in the consummatory contrast paradigm, sodium amobarbital, reduced SNC in a dose-dependent manner when given acutely during the postshift stage (Flaherty, Becker & Driscoll, 1982; Flaherty & Driscoll, 1980). Unlike CDP, amobarbital was equally effective when administered for the first time on either the first or second postshift day, but the degree of contrast reduction was considerably less than that produced by CDP. Amobarbital was not effective when given during both the preshift and postshift periods.

Like the benzodiazepines and ethanol, the actions of sodium amobarbital are probably mediated through the GABA/benzodiazepine/chloride channel receptor complex (Morrow, Suzdak & Paul, 1988). However, unlike ethanol and the benzodiazepines, barbiturates may also directly stimulate the chloride channel without the necessity of GABA mediation (Morrow et al., 1988). This latter property may account for the fact that sodium amobarbital is effective on the first postshift day, whereas CDP and ethanol are not.

Dopaminergic agents

The neuroleptic chlorpromazine does not affect contrast when administered on either the first or second postshift day (Flaherty, Becker, Checke, Rowan & Grigson, 1992). The more specific dopamine antagonist, haloperidol, was also without effect on contrast when administered on the second postshift day, but this drug did produce a dose-related decrease in consumption of the postshift sucrose solution. This decrease was proportional in shifted and unshifted rats, suggesting that the drug may affect the absolute rewarding value of sucrose (and/or have sedating or motor-impairing effects), but it apparently does not affect the relative reward value of sucrose (Flaherty et al., 1992). Amphetamine (0.125, and 0.25 mg/kg), an indirect dopamine agonist, also had no effect on contrast (Flaherty, unpublished data).

The failure of dopaminergic agents to influence contrast was somewhat unexpected. The literature suggests that dopaminergic transmission mediates aspects of reward (Wise, 1982) and that dopamine receptor blockers may blunt the effects of reward and enhance the effects of nonreward (Ettenberg & Camp, 1986a, 1986b; Feldon, Katz & Weiner, 1988), although they do not exactly mimic the effects of nonreward (see, for example, Gramling, Fowler & Collins, 1984; Tombaugh, Szostak, Voorneveld & Tombaugh, 1982). These data may suggest that dopaminergic agents, whatever their involvement in the absolute effects of reward, are not involved in the relative effects of reward. However, until further research is conducted with specific dopaminergic blockers (and with the apparently functionally different dopaminergic systems that exist in the central nervous system), it would be premature to completely exclude dopaminergic involvement in contrast at this point. In fact, some studies using different contrast procedures have produced evidence that blockade, and release from blockade, of dopaminergic systems may produce contrast (Kentridge & Aggleton, 1993; Phillips & LePiane, 1986; Royall & Klemm, 1981).

Noradrenergic agents

Little work has been done with this category of drugs. Clonidine, one of the alpha-2 agonists (compounds that generally lead to antagonistic effects on norepinephrine release), has had anxiolytic effects in some animal models of anxiety and in some clinical situations; however, the drug had no effect on contrast on the second postshift day (Flaherty, Grigson & Demetrikopoulos, 1987). Low doses (3.12, 6.25 µg/kg) did not influence contrast, and high doses (12.5, 25.0, 50.0 µg/kg) reduced sucrose intake in both shifted and unshifted rats.

Unpublished data have shown that clonidine is also ineffective on the first postshift day; the ß-adrenergic blocker propranolol is ineffective on both the first and second postshift day, although it may have a slight appetite-stimulating effect on the second postshift day. Unpublished data have suggested that imipramine, which blocks the re-uptake of norepinephrine, has no effect on SNC when administered acutely or subchronically (7 days).

Serotonergic agents

The neuropharmacology of serotonin is complex, given the variety of receptor subtypes and receptor-specific agents (see, for example, Green, 1985; Whitaker-Azmitia & Peroutka, 1990). The effect of serotonergic agents on contrast is also complex and not well understood. For example, methysergide, cinanserin, and cyproheptadine are generally regarded as nonspecific serotonin antagonists, yet they have different effects on contrast – cyproheptadine and cinanserin reduce contrast, whereas methysergide has no effect (Becker,1986; Coppotelli & Flaherty, 1993; Grigson, 1990; Grigson & Flaherty, 1991). The effects of cyproheptadine are particularly intriguing because the drug reduces SNC when it is administered acutely on the first postshift day, and it promotes recovery from contrast when administered acutely on the second postshift day. Other than insulin, cyproheptadine is the most effective agent in blunting the initial occurrence of SNC that we have encountered (Flaherty, McCurdy, Becker & D'Allesio, 1983).

It is unlikely that the effects of cyproheptadine are mediated by serotonin, because other serotonergic agents are generally ineffective. For example, buspirone, a selective 5-HT$_{1A}$ agonist, has no effect on contrast over a wide dose range when administered acutely on either the first or second postshift day or when administered chronically (Flaherty, Grigson, Demetrikopoulos, Weaver, Krauss & Rowan, 1990). Similarly, the 5-HT$_{1A}$ agonist gepirone, the 5-HT2 antagonist ketanserin, and the 5-HT2 antagonist ritanserin all failed to influence contrast (Flaherty et al., 1990).

Antidepressants such as imipramine have substantial serotonergic activity. For example, imipramine inhibits serotonin binding at re-uptake sites (Briley, 1985). Chronic treatment with antidepressants, including imipramine, leads to a decrease in the number of serotonin receptors (Ogren & Fuxe, 1985). The previously mentioned failure to find an effect of acute or subchronic imipramine administration on contrast again raises questions about the role of 5-HT mechanisms (Becker & Flaherty, unpublished data). In the subchronic study, the drug was administered for only 7 days, and current evidence suggests that a period of 2–3 weeks of imipramine administration is necessary before a decrease in 5-HT receptors is obtained (Ogren & Fuxe, 1985). However, chronic treatment (30 days) with the specific serotonin re-uptake blocker fluoxetine (10 mg/kg) failed to alter the degree of shift following a reduction from 32% to 1% sucrose (Flaherty, Portugal & Coppotelli, 1995).

In a further attempt to explore serotonergic involvement in SNC, Grigson depleted brain serotonin with the synthesis inhibitor para-chlorophenylalanine (PCPA) and subjected the rats to a shift from 32% to 4% sucrose. Substantial depletion of serotonin had no effect on the rats' response to the shift (Grigson, 1990; Grigson & Flaherty, 1991). Furthermore, there was no effect of the shift on serotonin levels, measured in the striatum, in rats not treated with PCPA. All this evidence suggests that serotonin does not play a functional role in successive negative contrast.

What then of the anti-contrast actions of cyproheptadine? Because cyproheptadine also has antihistaminergic actions, Grigson investigated the effects of the antihistamine pyrilamine. This drug had no effect on contrast when administered on the first postshift day (Grigson, 1990; Grigson & Flaherty, 1991) and was equally ineffective when administered on the second postshift day (Becker, 1986).

Cyproheptadine also has anticholinergic effects, but it seems unlikely that these mediate the effects of cyproheptadine on contrast, because the anticholinergic scopolamine does not affect contrast (Becker, 1986; Flaherty & Meinrath, 1979).

Given that cyproheptadine affects at least three neurotransmitter systems (serotonin, histamine, and acetylcholine), it may be that a combined antagonism of all of these, or some subset, mediates the effects of cyproheptadine in blocking SNC. However, experiments in which combinations of methysergide (a general serotonin antagonist that does not affect contrast) and pyrilamine (antihistamine) or methysergide plus scopolamine (anticholinergic) found no anti-contrast activity of the compounds (Flaherty & Coppotelli, unpublished data).

Thus, the situation at the present is that cyproheptadine reduces contrast, but its mode of action – as well as that of cinanserin, which is effective on the second postshift day but not on the first postshift day (Becker, 1986; Coppotelli & Flaherty, 1993) – is entirely unknown. One unexplored possibility is that the effects of cyproheptadine are not due to a psychoactive property of the drug at all, but instead to an influence on the blood glucose regulatory system. It has been reported that low doses of cyproheptadine promote the release of insulin from the pancreas with resultant hypoglycemia (Bryce & Jacoby, 1979). It has previously been shown that administration of exogenous insulin on the first postshift day will prevent the occurrence of contrast (Flaherty, McCurdy, Becker & D'Allesio, 1983). However, the hypoglycemic effect of cyproheptadine, in comparable doses to those used in the contrast studies, was much less than that of insulin (Bryce & Jacoby, 1979; Flaherty et al., 1983), suggesting that this may not be the mechanism of cyproheptadine's effect on contrast.

Opiates

The opiate agonist morphine has small, but reliable, contrast-reducing effects (Rowan & Flaherty, 1987). The opiate antagonist naloxone blocks the effects of morphine but appears to have no intrinsic effect on contrast. Unlike CDP and ethanol, but like sodium amobarbital, morphine appears to be equally effective on the first and second postshift days. The actions of drugs specific for different opiate receptor subtypes remain to be investigated.

The fact that morphine has effects similar to those of sodium amobarbital is of potential interest, because morphine is not known to act at the benzodiazepine/GABA/chloride ionophore complex. These data may indicate a parallel effect at some subsequent stage on a contrast system.

Acetylcholine

The only specific cholinergic drug investigated thus far is the antagonist scopolamine. As previously discussed, it has no influence on contrast (Becker, 1986; Coppotelli & Flaherty, 1993; Flaherty & Meinrath, 1979).

Histamine

Similarly, only one histaminergic drug has been studied – the antagonist pyrilamine, which has no effect on contrast (Becker, 1986; Coppotelli & Flaherty, 1993; Grigson & Flaherty, 1991).

Quantitative effects

An appreciation of the relative magnitude of the influence produced by some of the effective and ineffective drugs may be gained from an examination of Figure 3.3, in which drug effectiveness ratios[1] are presented for the most effective dose of each drug investigated. The larger the ratio, the greater the effect on contrast.

Summary – acute drug effects

The pattern of effective drugs clearly indicates a role for the GABA/benzodi-azepine/chloride ionophore complex in mediating recovery from contrast. The benzodiazepines, ethanol, and sodium amobarbital, all of which have actions at this complex, are effective in alleviating contrast. No drug that has agonist properties at this complex has been found ineffective and, with three exceptions, no drug that does not act at this complex has been found effective. The three exceptions are morphine (which has a statistically reliable, but numerically small, contrast-reducing effect), cyproheptadine, and cinanserin. The mode of operation of these drugs, as they affect contrast, has not been determined.

This pattern of activity suggests that a GABA-related mechanism may be involved in recovery from contrast, but that some other process, which is not serotonergic (and probably not dopaminergic, histaminergic, or cholinergic), is involved in the initial occurrence of contrast. This issue will be discussed in Chapter 4, when theories of successive contrast are considered.

Contrast in instrumental behavior

I am unaware of any studies in which the acute effect of drugs on successive contrast have been investigated in discrete-trial instrumental tasks with appetitive reinforcers.

There are two interesting studies in avoidance learning. It was initially shown that reducing the time spent in the nonshock compartment of a one-way shuttle avoidance task (for example, shifting from 30 seconds to 15 seconds) produces SNC in avoidance performance (Candido, Maldonado, Megias & Catena, 1992). Subsequently, it was shown that this SNC is alleviated by diazepam in a dose-dependent manner (Morales, Torres, Megias, Candido & Maldonado, 1992)

---

[1]The drug effectiveness ratio (DER) discounts preshift differences in lick frequency by examining postshift data in terms of proportions (P) of terminal preshift values; for example: (terminal preshift lick frequency)/(first postshift day lick frequency plus terminal preshift lick frequency). The effectiveness of the drug is then examined by obtaining a ratio of the difference between vehicle-injected shifted and unshifted animals and drug-injected shifted and unshifted animals:

$$DER = \frac{[P(\text{unshifted vehicle})] - [P(\text{shifted vehicle})]}{[P(\text{unshifted drug})] - [P(\text{shifted drug})]}$$

The greater the effect of the drug in reducing contrast, the larger the DER.

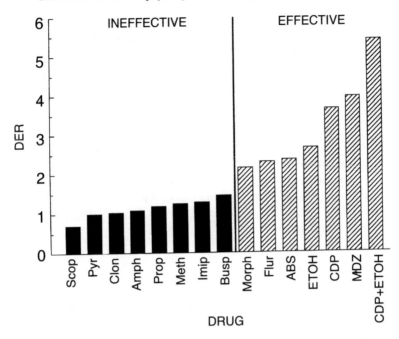

Figure 3.3 Drug effectiveness ratio (DER) is a measure of the relative effectiveness (or lack thereof) of drugs in reducing contrast (see footnote 1 in Chapter 3). The greater the ratio, the greater the contrast-reducing effect of the drug. The data presented here are for the most effective doses of selected drugs on the second postshift day. (From Flaherty, 1991b.)

and that the effect of diazepam is blocked by the benzodiazepine antagonist flumazenil (Torres, Morales, Megias, Candido & Maldonado, 1994). The latter study also showed that flumazenil itself had no effect on SNC, suggesting that an endogenous ligand for the benzodiazepine receptor is not involved in SNC in avoidance learning.

The benzodiazepine effects obtained in these avoidance studies are similar to those obtained in studies using appetitive reinforcers; this supports the contention that the reward for avoidance learning may be "relief" – an appetitive event (Denny, 1991).

Chronic drug administration

Consummatory contrast

The effects of chronic benzodiazepine administration on contrast when rats are shifted from 32% to 4% sucrose is quite different from the acute effects: Chronic or subchronic administration of CDP (8 mg/kg) did not reduce SNC when rats were shifted from 32% to 4% sucrose (Flaherty, Lombardi, Wrightson &

Deptula, 1980, experiments 1 and 3). Acute administration of the same dose on the second postshift day, but not on the first postshift day, eliminated contrast in this same study (experiments 2 and 4). The effect of repeated acute doses of CDP on either the first or second postshift day, across repeated shifts (Flaherty, Clarke & Coppotelli, in press), was considered in this chapter under the section on "Acute drug administration."

Subchronic administration of sodium amobarbital (15, 17.5, and 20 mg/kg) did not reduce SNC and, in fact, the highest dose prevents recovery from contrast. Acute administration (17.5 mg/kg) on the first and second postshift days reduced contrast in the same study (Flaherty, Becker & Driscoll, 1982).

As mentioned in the section on "Serotonergic agents" in this chapter, unpublished data have indicated that subchronic, as well as acute, administration of the antidepressant imipramine has no effect on SNC, and neither does chronic administration of fluoxetine.

Instrumental contrast

Chronic administration of anxiolytics prevents the occurrence of SNC in runway behavior. This outcome was obtained with CDP (5 and 10 mg/kg, but not 2.5 mg/kg; Rosen & Tessell, 1970) and with sodium amobarbital (15 mg/kg; Rosen, Glass & Ison, 1967).

Negative contrast in runway behavior is unaffected by chronic chlorpromazine (1, 3, 5, and 10 mg/kg; Roberts & Pixley, 1965; Rosen & Tessell, 1970).

There is one report that sodium amobarbital (20 mg/kg) prevented the occurrence of SPC and interfered with the increase in running speed normally demonstrated in a group upshifted in reward (Rabin, 1975). Another experiment, however, using a somewhat different runway procedure, failed to find SPC in drug or vehicle groups and reported no indication that sodium amobarbital (20 mg/kg) interfered with an increase in running speed following an increase in reward (Ison & Northman, 1968). Similar disagreement regarding the effects of sodium amobarbital on positive contrast will be seen again when behavioral contrast is considered in Chapter 6.

Summary – pharmacological studies

With the exception of the consummatory negative contrast procedure, the pharmacological analysis of contrast is far from complete. However, there are some generalizations and many questions that emerge from the data.

1. The benzodiazepines, ethanol, amobarbital, and morphine all promote recovery from SNC, but to different degrees, with the benzodiazepines' being the most effective.
2. The conditions in which these agents are effective vary somewhat in the different procedures. Perhaps the most intriguing problem is the disparity in the effectiveness of acute administration of CDP and ethanol on

the first and second postshift day, combined with the effectiveness of amobarbital on both of these days in the consummatory contrast procedure. The conjunction of these results suggests a pivotal role for the benzodiazepine/GABA/chloride ionophore receptor complex in mediating these effects.

Also puzzling is the finding that chronic CDP and amobarbital are each ineffective in consummatory contrast but effective in runway contrast as preventors of the occurrence of contrast. Meaningful speculation is difficult at this juncture, given the absence of runway studies with acute drug administration and the still unresolved differences between consummatory and instrumental measures of contrast when sucrose solutions are used as the reward (see Chapter 2).

3. The failure of a wide variety of other agents suggests that contrast is particularly sensitive to GABAergic-related agents and insensitive to compounds that affect other neurotransmitter systems. The negative evidence is strongest regarding serotonergic agents, but it is also a serotonin antagonist, cyproheptadine, that presents a major puzzle. To date, there is no clue as to what mediates the effectiveness of cyproheptadine both in moderating the initial occurrence of contrast and in promoting recovery from contrast.

Lesion studies

Consummatory contrast

The septal area

Lesions of the septum produce apparent deficiencies in inhibition (see for example, Dickinson, 1972; Donovick, 1968; McCleary, 1961), an outcome that would suggest that contrast should be reduced by such lesions (Lombardi & Flaherty, 1978). However, septal lesions also enhance intake of preferred solutions (sucrose and saccharin) and exacerbate the rejection of quinine-adulterated solutions (Beatty & Schwartzbaum, 1967, 1968); these reactions suggest that septal lesions might exaggerate consummatory contrast. Neither is the case – SNC in consummatory behavior was unaffected by septal lesions (Flaherty, Capobianco & Hamilton, 1973; Flaherty, Powell & Hamilton, 1979). The lesions were not entirely without effect – contrast was lost over a shorter retention interval in the lesioned rats than in the control rats (Flaherty et al., 1973). Also, the increase in activity that normally accompanies contrast was enhanced in lesioned rats (Flaherty et al., 1979). But the initial degree of contrast in lick frequency was uninfluenced by the lesion.

The hippocampus

The effect of lesions of the hippocampus on consummatory contrast are not quite as clear. As in the case of septal lesions, there is reason to believe that damage to the hippocampus should reduce contrast because of widespread deficits in inhibition following such lesions (Gray, 1982). In fact, Gray's theory of behavioral inhibition suggests an important role for the hippocampus in contrast (Gray, 1982, 1987).

The data on this issue are inconsistent. One electrolytic lesioning study found that hippocampal lesions had no effect on the negative contrast that occurs when rats are shifted from 32% to 4% sucrose (Kramarcy, Mikulka & Freeman, 1973), but another study using a nearly identical procedure reported that such lesions prevented the occurrence of negative contrast (Murphy & Brown, 1970). There were differences in the size of the lesions reported in these studies – small lesions restricted to the dorsal hippocampus in the Kramarcy et al. (1973) experiment, and larger lesions in the Murphy and Brown experiment – but there was still some sparing of the ventral tips of the hippocampus in the latter study.

We examined the effects on contrast of damage to the hippocampal granule cells produced by the neurotoxin colchicine. Colchicine substantially reduced the granule cell population, an effect that should have interrupted Gray's postulated hippocampal circuit involved in anxiety. However, there was no effect at all on contrast. In these same rats, spatial learning in an eight-arm radial maze was substantially impaired (Flaherty, Rowan, Emerich & Walsh, 1989), indicating a functional effect of the lesion.

How can the discrepancies among these three studies of consummatory contrast be resolved? Other than lesion size, the parameters in the Kramarcy et al. and Murphy and Brown experiments were nearly identical. The colchicine experiment differed from both in having a 10-day preshift period instead of the 18 days used in the earlier studies. However, it seems unlikely that this is a relevant factor, because the results obtained in the colchicine study were similar to those obtained by Kramarcy et al., and since the 10-day preshift period was used in the studies of septal lesions already described, (and in a study of amygdala lesions, which eliminated contrast – see discussion later in this chapter).

There is, however, a potentially important procedural difference between the two studies that found no effect of the lesion (Kramarcy et al. and the colchicine study) and the Murphy and Brown experiment, which found that the lesion eliminated contrast. In the Murphy and Brown experiment, the animals were given several other tests before they were used in the contrast procedure. That is, the rats were first given a sucrose preference test (8% versus water), a procedure that occupied approximately 17 days. The animals were then exposed to two sodium depletion tests, each requiring 5 days, before the start of the reward-shift study. In addition, there was a 10-day break between phases, when the animals were returned to a free-feeding schedule and then food was deprived again before the next test. Thus, the animals were exposed to appetitive and aversive tests and to repetitive deprivation cycles before the contrast experiment began. It is possible that this experience in some way acted to moderate the behavioral effects of the reward shift in the lesioned animals. It is interesting to note that the lesioned animals in the Murphy and Brown experiment did show a decrement in licking to a point slightly below the unshifted 4% control group subsequent to the shift, but this decrement did not approach reliability.

In addition to these procedural differences, is it possible that characteristics of the lesion contribute to the differences among the studies? Murphy and Brown reported large aspiration lesions of the hippocampus, with substantial incidental damage to overlying neocortical tissue with some sparing of the ventral tips of the hippocampus. Kramarcy et al. reported small radio-frequency lesions restricted to the dorsal hippocampus with minimal cortical involvement. The colchicine lesions produced in our own study were discrete and produced destruction of the granule cells throughout the hippocampus without incurring damage to other hippocampal neuronal populations, surrounding structures, or neocortex. Thus, the procedure by Murphy and Brown appears to have produced the most widespread damage. However, it seems unlikely that this alone accounts for the difference in results because, in a recently completed study, we found that large hippocampal lesions produced by the neurotoxin ibotenic acid had no effect on SNC in consummatory behavior, whereas the same lesions (the same rats) interfered with contrast in runway behavior (Flaherty, Otto, Hsu & Coppotelli, 1994).

The implications of these data for Gray's theory will be considered in more detail in the next chapter. For now, though, it should be noted that Gray specifically restricted his theory of septo-hippocampal function to conditions in which "secondary aversive stimuli warn the animal" of impending aversive events (Gray, 1982, p. 142). The importance of such secondary or signalling stimuli would presumably be minimized in consummatory response tasks, compared to instrumental procedures – where Gray's theory might be more applicable.

The amygdala

If the evidence indicates minimal involvement of the septo-hippocampal system in consummatory contrast, it also suggests a major role for the amygdala. There is a convergence of data that suggests a potential role for the amygdala in contrast. For example, the central nucleus of the amygdala has a high density of benzodiazepine and opiate receptors (Mohler & Okada, 1977), and the benzodiazepines and opiates reduce contrast (as discussed earlier in this chapter). The central nucleus of the amygdala also receives taste fibers from the pontine taste area and from the cortical taste area (Norgren, 1984), a fact that may be particularly important for consummatory behavior. Also, a role for the amygdala in anxiolytic action is strongly suggested by studies showing anticonflict effects of intra-amygdala benzodiazepine administration in consummatory punishment and in operant conflict tasks (Hodges, Green & Glenn, 1987; Scheel-Kreuger & Petersen, 1982). Furthermore, application of the benzodiazepine antagonist flumazenil or the inverse agonist FG-7142 to the amygdala blocks the anticonflict effects of CDP given peripherally (Hodges et al., 1987).

Although lesions of the amygdala affect contrast, they do not replicate

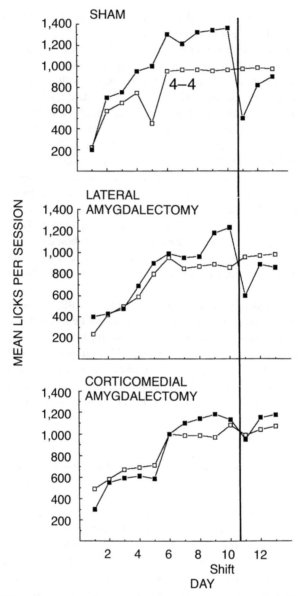

Figure 3.4 Effect of amygdala lesions on successive negative contrast. Lesions of the basolateral area produced a small reduction in degree of contrast; lesions of the corticomedial area eliminated contrast. (After Becker, Jarvis, Wagner & Flaherty, 1984.)

exactly the effects of benzodiazepines or other anxiolytics. Thus, lesions of the basolateral aspects of the amygdala reduce contrast, whereas lesions of the corticomedial aspects of the amygdala, including the central nucleus, prevent the occurrence of contrast (Becker, Jarvis, Wagner & Flaherty, 1984). These results are illustrated in Figure 3.4.

Damage to the amygdala may affect contrast through a variety of mechanisms. The taste system is one possibility. However, although the amygdala receives input from taste afferents and sends efferent fibers to various waystations in the ascending taste circuit, it is not likely that the effects of the amygdala lesions on contrast are due to abnormal taste reactivity per se. This is because taste reactivity to a variety of sapid solutions, including sucrose, is essentially normal in rats with large amygdala lesions (Kiefer & Grijalva, 1980). The preshift data from the Becker et al. study show that the lesioned rats responded to the 32% and 4% sucrose solutions in a manner quite similar to the sham-operated rats (see Figure 3.4). There were some differences. Both the sham-operated and lesioned rats tended to lick at a higher frequency for the 32% than for the 4% sucrose solution during the preshift period, but these differences were reliable only in the case of the sham-operated groups. These preshift differences are probably not related to the effects of the lesion on contrast, because the sham-operated group and the group with corticomedial lesions did not differ in lick frequency for the 32% sucrose, yet they differed substantially in response to the shift. Also, during the preshift phase there were no reliable differences among the three lesion groups in response to the 4% sucrose solution. Thus, the effects of the lesion were much more pronounced in the postshift phase than in the preshift phase. These postshift effects of the lesion, plotted in terms of proportion of preshift lick frequency, are illustrated in Figure 3.5.

Five psychological deficits – diminished neophobic response, response perseveration, diminished emotional reactivity, diminished memory of reward, and inability to compare rewards – seem relevant as potential explanations for the effects of the lesion on postshift behavior. First, there may be a deficit in the recognition of, or the response to, novel stimuli. Amygdala lesions, at least in monkeys, have been reported to eliminate the autonomic component of orienting to novel stimuli (see, for example, Bagshaw & Benzies, 1968; Bagshaw, Mackworth & Pribram, 1972). Diminished neophobic responses to taste stimuli have also been found in rats following amygdala lesions (see Kemble & Schwartzbaum, 1969; Nachman & Ashe, 1974). An explanation in these terms, applied to contrast, would suggest that the corticomedial lesion group failed to show contrast because they did not distinguish the postshift 4% solution as being different from the preshift 32% sucrose solution. But such an explanation does not seem tenable for two reasons: (1) There were no differences among the three lesion conditions in lick frequency on the first *pre*shift day, when all solutions were novel, and (2) the shift from 32% to 4% sucrose did lead to a reliable decrement in responding in all shifted groups. The decrement was simply greater in

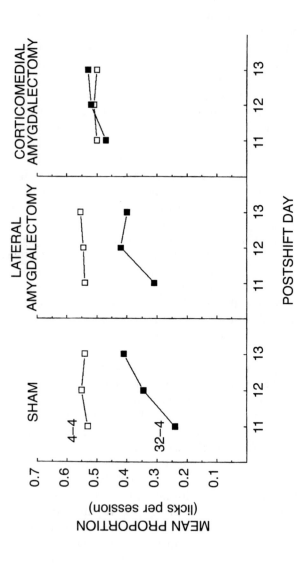

Figure 3.5 Same data as in Figure 3.4, but only postshift data are presented. These postshift data are presented in terms of proportion of preshift lick frequency, where proportion = (postshift day lick frequency)/((terminal preshift + postshift day lick frequency). (After Becker, Jarvis, Wagner & Flaherty, 1984.)

the sham-lesioned and lateral-lesioned group than in the corticomedial-lesioned group. The occurrence of a decrement clearly indicates that the lesioned animals responded in some degree to the change in solutions.

This same point, the occurrence of a reliable decrement, also argues against response perseveration as a sufficient account of the lesion effect.

A third possibility, reduced emotional reaction to reward loss, is suggested by evidence of reduced emotionality in a variety of situations following amygdala lesions (see Blanchard & Blanchard, 1972; Davis, 1992; Everitt & Robbins, 1992; LeDoux, 1992; Rolls, 1992). A problem with this explanation is that current evidence is not clear regarding the point at which emotion-related behaviors might be causally involved in contrast. Thus, the evidence previously reviewed showed that CDP and ethanol are not effective in reducing contrast until the second postshift day. Also, elevations in corticosterone, an indicator of stress, are not obtained until the second postshift day in this paradigm (Flaherty, Becker & Pohorecky, 1985). Furthermore, as reviewed in Chapter 2 under the heading "Strain differences in rats," "emotionality" has proven to be a concept of little value for understanding SNC. In addition to the evidence from the selective breeding experiments, experiments with the Denenberg–Levine early-handling procedure have failed to indicate a role for general emotional reactivity in contrast. The Denenberg–Levine early-handling treatment, which reduces emotionality as defined by open-field measures (Ader, 1970; Levine, 1956; Levine, Haltmeyer, Karas & Denenberg, 1967), does not influence SNC in consummatory behavior (Meinrath & Flaherty, 1987) or instrumental behavior (Daly & Rosenberg, 1973). Thus, to assume that the lesion reduced contrast because it reduced the emotional reaction to reduced reward would not be saying much at the present time.

Another possible reason for the effect of the lesion on contrast is that the lesion rendered the animals unable to remember characteristics of the reward previously experienced. The involvement of the amygdala in reward detection and memory has long been suspected (Gaffan, 1992; Kesner, 1981; Kesner & Andrus, 1982; McGaugh et al., 1992); such an interpretation would be compatible with the postshift behavior of the rats with the medial lesions, because their postshift behavior appeared to reflect the value of the current 4% postshift solution uncompared with the preshift 32% solution. However, an absolute deficit in reward memory is incompatible with the fact that the animals showed an acquisition function during the preshift period – an outcome that suggests the animals remember aspects of the reward experienced on the preceding day.

The final possible explanation is that the lesioned animals do not compare the postshift reward with the preshift reward. Rather, they respond to each reward on the basis of its absolute value. This possibility is consistent with the data and is not excluded by any of the preceding arguments. It is also consistent with the results of the selective breeding experiment, which indicated that response to a sucrose shift was independent of other aspects of reward substances (Flaherty, Krauss, Rowan & Grigson, 1994). This explanation also corresponds to the effects of haloperidol on contrast, which suggest that absolute and relative

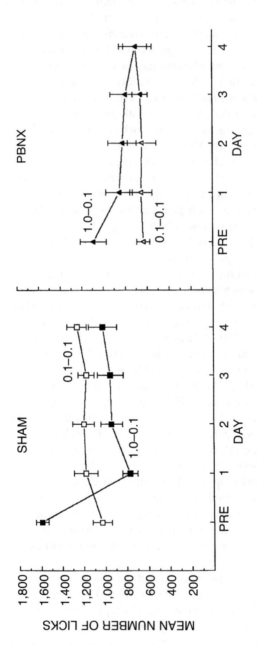

Figure 3.6. Effect of lesions of the parabrachial nucleus of the pons (PBNX) on successive negative contrast. The shift was from a 1.0 molar to a 0.1 molar sucrose solution concentrations that approximate the 32% to 4% shift used in other studies. The lesions eliminated the contrast effect, producing results similar to those obtained with lesions of the corticomedial amygdala (Figure 3.5). (After Grigson & Norgren, 1994.)

reward may be mediated by different mechanisms (Flaherty et al., 1990). However, there is no independent evidence for this interpretation of corticomedial amygdala function. It should be noted that Gray (1982) posited just such a comparator function for the hippocampus – a function that may apply for instrumental behavior but perhaps not for consummatory behavior.

The parabrachial nucleus

The parabrachial nucleus (PBN) of the pons is the second major relay station for taste input. After synapsing in the nucleus of the solitary tract, afferent taste fibers course to the PBN, then to the thalamus, and from there to the taste cortex (Norgren, 1984). Most, if not all, of these areas also send fibers to the central nucleus of the amygdala and receive reciprocal fibers from the amygdala. Thus, the amygdala is in a position to integrate taste information from various levels of input and, in turn, perhaps to influence the nature of the input signals. If the amygdala is involved in a comparative function, as already speculated here, it may alter sensory responsivity at one of the lower levels of input as a result of this comparison process. Although electrophysiological data would be the best method of examining this possibility, there are none available. There is, however, a recent study of lesions of the PBN. As illustrated in Figure 3.6, lesions of the PBN prevented the occurrence of SNC – the shifted rats showed a gradual decline to the level of the unshifted controls, rather than the abrupt decline typical of unlesioned rats (Grigson & Norgren, 1994).

Three aspects of these data should be noted. First, because the experiment was terminated after 4 postshift days, it is not clear whether the lesioned animals would have shown a delayed contrast effect with greater postshift experience. Second, the lesioned animals licked at a lower frequency than the nonlesioned animals during the preshift period. This may have been due to a motoric effect of the lesion, or an alteration in the absolute value of the sucrose solutions. Third, even with the lower lick frequencies, a sucrose concentration function was maintained – the lesioned animals licked more for the 32% than for the 4% solution during the preshift phase.

In comparison to lesions of the corticomedial amygdala (see Figure 3.4), the PBN lesions seemed to have less effect in eliminating the preshift concentration function; the PBN lesions may perhaps have produced a more prolonged and gradual reduction in lick frequency following the shift than was the case following amygdala lesions. The latter effect, though, is difficult to analyze because recovery from contrast appeared more rapid in the unlesioned animals in the amygdala study than in the unlesioned animals in the PBN study.

The effect of PBN lesions suggests that relativity mechanisms operate very early in the ascending taste system, but it cannot be determined from this study whether the failure of contrast to occur in the lesioned animals was a direct effect of PBN damage itself, or if it was related to the loss of signals transmitted from (or through) the PBN to other structures.

Instrumental contrast

Septal area

Although there apparently have been no studies of runway contrast per se, a study of reward-shift behavior showed that shifted lesioned rats and shifted sham rats did not differ reliably in the reaction to a reward shift from 15 pellets to 1 pellet. There were no unshifted control animals in this study; thus, the issue of contrast per se cannot be addressed. Numerically, the rats with septal lesions had a greater reaction to the shift, but the reaction was in terms of increased running speed, not a "depression" effect (Hammond & Thomas, 1971). The gap in our knowledge of the effects of septal lesions on contrast needs to be closed before any serious brain model of this topic can be constructed.

Hippocampus

Hippocampal lesions completely prevented the occurrence of SNC in one study (Franchina & Brown, 1971) and reduced the degree of SNC in another study (Strong, data described in Isaacson, 1982). In the Franchina and Brown study, lesions prevented any change in behavior on the part of the shifted animals – postshift running speeds were controlled entirely by preshift reward values. The failure of the lesioned animals to show any change in behavior was striking, because large SNC occurred in unoperated controls and in controls that had the cortex overlying the hippocampus ablated (see Figure 3.7).

Franchina and Brown also tested for SPC and, not unusually, they found no SPC in either of their control groups. It may be worth noting, however, that the upshifted animals with hippocampal lesions, like the downshifted animals described earlier, showed no change at all in running behavior whereas both control groups did show change (see Figure 3.7).

A more recent study used the neurotoxin ibotenic acid to produce large lesions of the hippocampus. These lesions had no effect on consummatory contrast, but they did affect contrast in the runway following a shift from 12 pellets to 1 pellet. However, only the start-speed measure was influenced by the lesion. The lesioned animals showed reliable contrast effects in both run and goal measures (Flaherty, Otto, Hsu & Coppotelli, 1994). These data suggest that the hippocampal lesion interfered with a hesitation to initiate behavior that occurs in shifted-unlesioned rats, but once the approach behavior was underway, the lesioned animals behaved normally (that is, shifted rats ran proportionally slower than unshifted rats). The Franchina and Brown study reported only total alley speed, not behavior in different segments of the runway.

Entorhinal cortex

The entorhinal cortex serves one of the major sensory input pathways to the hippocampus, but lesions of this structure do not have the same effect as hippocampal lesions. Aspiration lesions of the entorhinal cortex eliminated contrast,

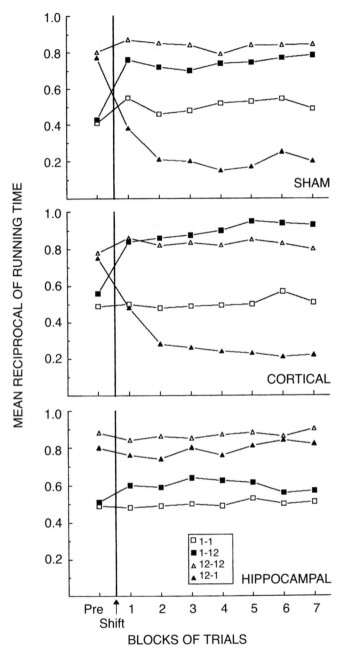

Figure 3.7 Effect of lesions of the hippocampus on successive negative contrast in the runway. The rats were either shifted from a 12-pellet to a 1-pellet reward or remained on a 1-pellet reward throughout the experiment. The rats with hippocampal lesions showed no change in behavior when the reward was reduced. Both nonlesioned rats and rats with control lesions to the cortex showed normal negative contrast effects. No successive positive contrast was obtained in rats shifted up from 1 pellet to 12 pellets. (From Franchina & Brown, 1971.)

but only in the goal section of the runway. These same lesions had no effect on contrast in consummatory behavior (Flaherty, Otto, Hsu & Coppotelli, 1994). It is often the case that SNC contrast is largest in the goal region, thus the entorhinal lesions seem to have had an effect just at the point where hesitation (inhibition?) may be at its greatest in normal rats. The differences in results obtained with hippocampal and entorhinal lesions suggest that the entorhinal cortex serves as more than just a simple input to the hippocampus.

Cingulate cortex

Lesions of the cingulate cortex were found to reduce the magnitude of SNC that followed a shift from 15 pellets to 1 pellet, but the contrast was still reliable in the lesioned animals (Gurowitz, Rosen & Tessel, 1970). The lesioned animals also ran faster than the controls did in the start section of the runway but slower in the goal area during the preshift period. This pattern of results often occurs in animals that receive intermittent reinforcement in the runway, compared to animals that receive continuous reinforcement (see Amsel, 1992). It is impossible to say whether these effects of the cingulate lesion are related, but it should be recalled that prior experience with intermittent reinforcement may reduce, or retard, the development of SNC (see Chapter 2).

Amygdala

One study examined the effects of inactivation of the amygdala by injections of lidocaine into the area of the central nucleus of the amygdala immediately *following* the first postshift trials. On the next day, the vehicle animals shifted in reward showed a large SNC in running speeds, but the animals that had been injected with lidocaine were much less affected by the shift – particularly in trials 2–6 of this second postshift day. The authors' interpretation of these results was that the amygdala is important for the storage of memory for the shifted reward (Salinas, Packard & McGaugh, 1993).

Olfactory bulbs

One study in which the olfactory bulbs were removed by aspiration reported SNC in both lesioned and control animals, but there was some evidence that contrast developed more slowly in the anosmic rats (Davis, Harper & Seago, 1975).

Overview – drug and lesion studies

There are too few lesion experiments to allow for any definitive conclusions. The available data do suggest that there is a difference in the control of consummatory and instrumental contrast, with the septal–entorhinal–hippocampal complex possibly uninvolved in consummatory contrast. The data available on entorhinal, hippocampal, and cingulate lesions do indicate an involvement of all three structures in SNC in instrumental behavior. These data suggest that the effect of lesions in all these structures is consistent with Gray's theory, which places major emphasis on this system as the control mechanism for behavioral inhibition (Gray, 1982, 1987). However, since the data available indicate that lesions in the entotrhinal cortex (an input channel to the hippocampus), the hippocampus, and the cingulate cortex (an output channel from the hippocampus) have somewhat different effects, each may contribute differently to the control of instrumental approach behavior.

The finding that the lesions of the hippocampus, septum, and entorhinal cortex do not affect contrast in consummatory behavior suggests that the actual comparator mechanism (or system) lies elsewhere. Perhaps a system including aspects of the amygdala may be involved in the re-evaluation of shifted rewards and may circulate the results of this new evaluation to other structures involved in instrumental approach behavior (entorhinal–hippocampal–cingulate–striatal system?) and consummatory behavior (parabrachial nucleus, nucleus of the solitary tract, and the hypothalamus?).

The drug data suggest that anxiolytics may hasten the recovery from SNC via a GABAergic mechanism, but they have provided little evidence regarding which other systems are influenced by this GABA activity. Because GABA is inhibitory and because recovery from contrast represents an increase in consummatory or instrumental behavior, GABA activity must have a disinhibitory effect on some other system.

Lesions that affect contrast, such as those to the corticomedial area of the amygdala or the parabrachial nucleus of the pons, do not produce effects like those seen with the benzodiazepines, ethanol, or the barbiturates, although they may be similar to the effects of cyproheptadine on consummatory contrast.

Chronic benzodiazepine administration may have effects somewhat like hippocampal lesions on instrumental behavior, but chronic benzodiazepine treatment has little effect on consummatory behavior. There are many loose ends to be investigated and there are no clear data regarding causal mechanisms in the initial occurrence of contrast, other than the fact that corticomedial amygdala lesions, parabrachial lesions, and cyproheptadine may prevent the occurrence in consummatory behavior, and hippocampal lesions, entorhinal lesions, and chronic CDP prevent or modify SNC in instrumental behavior.

Overall, the drug/lesion data offer support for a role of emotional behavior in SNC, but they also suggest that a complex neurochemical and neurophysiological network underlies judgments of incentive relativity and the translation of these judgments into behavior.

4   Successive contrast: theories

It is on the discovery of general principles in experimental
work on lower animals that our chief hopes of progress in the
understanding of man's nature must rest.

– J. A. Gray, 1987

This chapter will review the applicability of traditional theories of contrast in
view of the data considered in the previous chapters. It will also present and
evaluate a multistage theory as an alternative to the traditional theories.
Finally, this chapter will provide a comparison of successive negative contrast
with four selected animal models of anxiety in regard to comparability of drug
effects.

Generalization decrement

It may be a universal property of perception and behavior that animals respond
to stimuli other than those previously rewarded, but this generalized responding
tends to decline, perhaps in an invariant fashion, as the psychological distance
between the stimuli increases (Shephard, 1987). A generalization decrement
interpretation of contrast is simply that the change in reward is also a change in
the stimuli that existed during initial training (E. J. Capaldi & Lynch, 1967;
Mackintosh, 1974; Spear & Spitzner, 1966). The reward change, therefore,
leads to a decrease in responding just as would any other change in context,
such as a change in the brightness of a runway from the level used in original
training (E. D. Capaldi, 1978).

The most thorough treatment of SNC as generalization decrement has been
by E. J. Capaldi (Capaldi, 1972; Capaldi & Lynch, 1967). Capaldi assumed that
the memory, or "aftereffects," of reward entered into an association with the
instrumental response and that this association was specific for each reward
experienced. Therefore, rats shifted from large to small reward in a runway will
have less associative control over their responding than animals that had received
only the small reward, because there will be no association between the memory
of small reward and the performance of the instrumental response, except for
what generalizes from the large-reward association. It is because of this defi-
ciency in associative strength that SNC occurs following a decrease in reward.
The theory predicts recovery from negative contrast because, over the course of

the postshift trials, an association develops between the memory of the small reward and instrumental responding.

Capaldi's theory also predicts that initial experience with the eventual post-shift reward should diminish contrast, because this initial experience would function to establish an association between the small reward and the instrumental response, thus reducing the degree of generalization decrement. Data on the effects of prior reward experience on SNC (see Chapter 2) tend to be consistent with this contention. Support for this theory was also provided by Capaldi and Lynch (1967), who found that SNC occurred in runway behavior following a downshift from 24 to 2 pellets if the rats had no prior experience with the 2-pellet reward. However, no negative contrast occurred if the animals had such prior experience (either 2–24–2, or 24–2–24–2). Spear and Spitzner (1966) had previously reported that the SNC that occurred in runway and T-maze responding following a shift from 12 pellets to 1 pellet was greatly reduced if the animals had prior experience with the small reward (1 pellet) by having been rewarded with 12 pellets or 1 pellet in a differential conditioning task. Spear and Spitzner further noted that contrast following the same 12-pellet to 1-pellet shift was not reduced if the prior training was with a 12-pellet versus 0-pellet reward discrimination – suggesting remarkably specific effects of prior reward experience (or associations between memory of reward and responding, in Capaldi's terms).

It was found subsequently that prior experience with the postshift reward was much more effective in reducing SNC when trials were spaced (24-hour ITI) than when they were massed (3–5-minute ITI). Capaldi (1972) suggested, in considerably more detail than will be presented here, that the reason for this ITI effect was that the stimulus characteristics of small reward differed in comparison with those of large reward when there was a short ITI – thus, there would be greater generalization decrement, and greater SNC, under short ITI conditions.

Generalization decrement is an appealing interpretation of SNC because it is parsimonious and it has face validity; also, generalization decrement is readily demonstrable when contextual or discriminative stimuli are changed. There is also some evidence that generalization decrement may occur when rewards themselves are changed. This was demonstrated by selecting two conditions, five 45-mg Noyes pellets and 35 seconds access to water, that apparently possessed equal rewarding potency (rats ran at equivalent speeds for them in a runway) (Huang, 1969). After stabilized running was achieved, one group was shifted from water to the five Noyes pellets. By the fifth block of three trials, the group showed a gradual decrement in running speed that became reliably slower than the speed of a five-pellet control group. A group shifted from five pellets to a single pellet did not show SNC. The decrement shown following the food-to-water shift was interpreted as SNC caused by generalization decrement rather than by a reduction in reward. A similar result was reported by Spear (1968) when he switched rats from one 45-mg Noyes pellet to three drops of a 4% sucrose solution (which produced approximately equivalent running speeds); there was a transient decrement in running speed in the shifted group.

Evaluation

It seems probable that generalization decrement, or a related process such as neophobia or caution, occurs when rewards are shifted and that such a process con-
tributes to SNC (and antagonizes SPC). However, the evidence is not compelling
that generalization decrement is a major contributor to SNC. The contrast effect
that developed in the Huang study was very slow in coming, requiring some 15
postshift trials (at 1 trial per day), nothing like the immediate drop demonstrated
in the classic runway studies of Crespi and Zeaman or the rapid drop demonstrated in more recent studies (for example, 8 trials to maximum contrast in E. J.
Capaldi, 1972; 6 trials in E. J. Capaldi & Lynch, 1967; within 3 trials in E. D.
Capaldi & Singh, 1973; within 8 trials in Flaherty & Kelly, 1973; 4 trials in
Gleitman & Steinman, 1964).

It is usually assumed that the effects of generalization decrement would be
rapid. For example, Mackintosh, in his description of the generalization decrement interpretation of SNC, stated that generalization decrement would account
for "an abrupt, transient decrement" in behavior (Mackintosh, 1974, p. 399). The
slow change in the Huang study could indicate that reward magnitude reduction
per se is responsible for the rapid decrease frequently encountered in contrast
studies, whereas generalization decrement is responsible for a slower decline in
behavior. However, this does not seem intuitively plausible; if it is correct, it
would leave only a minor role for generalization decrement, because SNC most
often occurs abruptly.

Whatever the meaning of the Huang results, there are other data that dis-
credit generalization decrement as a comprehensive account of SNC. Although
Capaldi and Lynch (1967) found contrast following *only* the initial shift to small
reward, other studies have obtained repeated contrast in runway behavior with
repeated shifts between large and small rewards (Calef, Calef, Prochaska &
Geller, 1978; Maxwell, Calef, Murray, Shephard & Norville, 1976; McCain &
Cooney, 1975; Shanab, Domino & Ralph, 1978; Shanab & Spencer, 1978). A
particularly striking example of maintained contrast with repeated shifts
occurred in a study of contrast in consummatory behavior in which SNC showed
no sign of diminution after nine single-alternation shifts (32% sucrose to 4%
sucrose to 32% sucrose, etc.) or five double-alternation shifts (32–32–4–4, etc.)
(Flaherty, Becker & Checke, 1983). These data were illustrated in Figure 2.4.
Repeated SNC in consummatory behavior has also been obtained when rats were
exposed to eight cycles of 3 days of 32% sucrose and 2 days of 4% sucrose.
Although contrast showed a slight diminution, it remained reliable over all eight
shifts (Flaherty, Clarke & Coppotelli, 1993).

There are other problems for generalization decrement theory, particularly
from consummatory contrast experiments. Black (1968) suggested that SNC
may involve an active inhibitory process, rather than passive generalization
decrement. As one test of this hypothesis, Lombardi and Flaherty (1978) introduced a novel stimulus (loud tone) 30 seconds after a downshift from 32% to 4%

sucrose. The novel tone had no effect on licking on the first postshift day, but the shifted animals exposed to the tone showed a higher lick frequency (smaller contrast) on subsequent postshift days. Thus, the added tone did not enhance contrast on the first postshift day, as might be expected from a generalization decrement interpretation, but it did reduce contrast on subsequent days, suggesting a disinhibitory effect. Additional control experiments showed that the enhanced licking produced by the tone could not be due to an energizing effect or a rate-dependent energizing effect[1] of the novel stimulus. Thus, the effect of the novel stimulus was to reduce contrast (as would be expected from a disinhibition account), rather than to enhance contrast (as would be expected from a generalization decrement account).

The effect of drugs on contrast argues against generalization decrement in two ways. Like the added tone in the Lombardi and Flaherty experiment, administration of drugs during the postshift period should effectively enhance the degree of stimulus change correlated with reward reduction. However, anxiolytic drugs reduce contrast (Chapter 3); they do not enhance it, as a generalization decrement theory would predict. A second aspect of the drug data – that stress-relevant drugs seem to be particularly effective in reducing contrast – supports an account of contrast that reflects the occurrence of a stress/emotion-related process rather than a passive associative process. Similarly, the elevation of corticosterone levels by reward reduction suggests an active stress response.

Further evidence against a passive generalization decrement process is provided by studies showing a substantial increase in activity subsequent to a reward reduction. The activity increase may take the form of increased ambulation and rearing in an open field (Flaherty, Blitzer & Collier, 1978; Flaherty, Powell & Hamilton, 1979; Flaherty, Troncoso & Deschu; 1979) or increased arm entries in an eight-arm radial maze (Flaherty, 1991b), but reward shift does not lead to increased wheel running when the running wheel is attached to one arm of a radial maze (Flaherty, Krauss & Noctor, unpublished data). Increases in activity following shifts to nonreward have previously been noted by other investigators (for example, Amsel, Work & Penick, 1962; Devenport, 1984; Gallup & Altomari, 1969; Klinger, Barta & Kemble, 1974; Wookey & Strongman, 1974). These activity increases are consistent with the searching or exploratory behavior originally suggested by Elliott (1928) and also observed by Tinklepaugh (1928), but they seem inconsistent with a passive loss of associative strength.

A quite different type of experiment also questions a role for generalization decrement in contrast, at least in consummatory contrast. The experiments in question shifted the context in which the animals experienced the sucrose reward. The context shift, of varying degrees in different experiments, was made coincident with the shift from 32% to 4% sucrose. These experiments showed

---

[1]It is conceivable that the tone could have energized licking only when lick frequency was at a low level, as in the shifted animals. However, inclusion of a group of rats given access to 2% sucrose, which produced lick frequencies the same as in rats shifted from 32% to 4% sucrose, showed that the tone did not affect this group.

that the context change produced disruptions of licking, but the disruptions were approximately equivalent in shifted and unshifted animals – leaving degree of contrast unaffected by the context change (Flaherty, Hrabinski & Grigson, 1990). The failure of radical context changes to disrupt contrast, even though licking itself was disrupted, suggests that rats are able to compare rewards independently of the context in which they are received; thus, reward shifts are different than context shifts.

Overall, the data indicate that, in some circumstances, prior experience with the small reward does reduce SNC (see Chapter 2, as well as the preceding discussion), but this is not enough evidence to argue that generalization decrement is the sole, or even an important, contributor to SNC. Prior experience and repeated reward shifts may have a greater effect on reducing contrast in runway experiments than in consummatory contrast studies; this may suggest a greater role for generalization decrement in instrumental behavior. However, direct comparisons of the two behaviors have not been examined within a single experiment.

Adaptation level and incentive averaging

Psychophysical judgments concerning a point along a stimulus continuum – such as weight of lifted objects, temperature, brightness, or hue – are not determined solely by the value of the given point, but are also influenced by concurrent or prior experience with other stimuli lying along the same continuum. Some success in understanding the relativity of these judgments has been achieved by assuming that individuals form an average of the stimuli they experience and then judge each new stimulus in reference to this average or "adaptation level" (Helson, 1964).

The application of this approach to reward contrast effects was explored by Bevan (for example, Bevan, 1968). The theory and application will not be presented in detail here because its applicability to the typical successive contrast experiment seems limited. A few comments, however, would be appropriate. Taken at face value, adaptation level theory predicts symmetrical positive and negative contrast effects. The paucity of clear demonstrations of positive contrast led Black (1968) to dismiss adaptation level as a useful account of contrast. Even though there is now more evidence for positive contrast, it is clearly more difficult to obtain and subject to apparent constraints not considered by the advocates of adaptation level theory.

Furthermore, many of the byproducts of reward shift, and many of the parameters of contrast, seem to be beyond the initial and boundary conditions of adaptation level theory. For example, reward reduction is accompanied by increases in activity (see previous discussion), by increases in variability, and by a sharply skewed distribution of latencies in runway speed (Spear, 1968). All these effects would seem to be uncalled for by an alteration in perception or judgment. Furthermore, the powerful and specific effect of anxiolytic drugs on negative contrast would seem to lie outside the realm of a perceptual theory. Also, adaptation level theory would seem to predict that contrast should diminish in animals given repeated shifts as they form an average somewhere between the two extremes of reward experienced. However, the data for consummatory contrast, at least, clearly show no diminution of contrast (Figure 2.4).

Even though a perceptually based adaptation level theory does not directly apply to reward contrast, the notion of averaging does have an appeal – an appeal that has been captured in incentive-averaging approaches to reward contrast. Thus, McHose (McHose, 1970; McHose & Moore, 1976; McHose & Peters, 1975) assumes that the degree of SNC is proportional to the degree of difference between the postshift reward and the *average* value of the preshift reward. This average for the preshift reward is a function of the magnitude and frequency of the different rewards received during the preshift period. For example, rats rewarded with either 20 pellets or 4 pellets on a 50% schedule preshift and with 1 pellet postshift showed SNC roughly equivalent to that of animals receiving a constant 7-pellet reward preshift (Peters & McHose, 1974). Two other studies in the same paper were consistent with the hypothesis that rats averaged rewards received during the preshift period and that the degree of SNC was related to the reward disparity from this average value. A shift from a continuous reward to a varied reward, the average of which is lower than the preshift reward, also leads to a SNC (Calef, Hopkins, McHewitt & Maxwell, 1973). A discussion of reinforcement level, another variant of averaging, may be found in Capaldi (1974) and Flaherty (1982).

In consummatory contrast, rats exposed to 2%, 4%, 8%, 16%, and 32% sucrose (in that order) during preshift, and shifted to 4% sucrose postshift show SNC that is smaller than that shown by rats exposed to only 32% sucrose – but show larger SNC than that shown by rats exposed to 8% sucrose (the geometric average of the varied sucrose group). These data suggest averaging, perhaps influenced by a recency effect and/or an average related more closely to the arithmetic mean (12.4%) than to the geometric mean (Flaherty, Becker, & Osborne, 1983).

Thus, one aspect of adaptation level theory – that rats average rewards – is supported by the available evidence. However, other aspects of adaptation level as a perceptual theory of reward contrast do not fit well with the data.

Exploration

Elliott (1928) reported a substantial increase in both blind-alley entries and time to traverse the maze when a group of rats with a history of receiving a wet mash was shifted to sunflower seeds (see Chapter 1). The change in performance occurred after a single trial with the substitute reward and showed no sign of diminishing after 6 days of testing. Elliott argued that the increase in blind-alley entrances errors reflected a search process on the part of the rats. Tinklepaugh

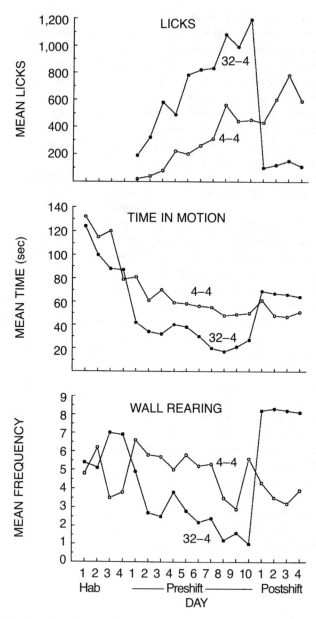

Figure 4.1 Three measures of successive negative contrast in an open field. Correlated with a reduction in lick frequency following the shift from 32% to 4% sucrose was an increase in wall-rearing and time in motion. No sucrose solutions were presented during the initial 4-day habituation period. (After Flaherty, Blitzer & Collier, 1978, exp. 2.)

(1928) also reported that his monkeys looked under and around the area where the banana was usually found when they encountered lettuce that had been substituted for banana.

In an effort to obtain evidence relevant to the search hypothesis, a series of consummatory contrast studies was conducted in a large open-field apparatus. These studies showed that, concurrent with a shift from 32% to 4% sucrose, there was a large increase in ambulation and rearing (see Figure 4.1). Although mutually exclusive, these two activities tended to be highly correlated, suggesting that both of them represented a common underlying dimension of activity (Flaherty, Blitzer & Collier, 1978; Flaherty, Powell & Hamilton, 1979; Flaherty, Troncoso & Deschu, 1979). Although elevated activity levels are consistent with an increase in exploration, they are also consistent with increased arousal (see, for example, Royce, Poley & Yeudall, 1973). Examination of other aspects of the open-field data did not yield convincing evidence of exploration subsequent to the reward reduction. For example, in one study a single source of sucrose (32% or 4%) was mounted on one wall of the open field during the preshift stage, but four sources (all containing 4% sucrose) were available during the postshift period, one mounted on each wall (Flaherty et al., 1978). During the postshift phase, both shifted and unshifted animals sampled from all four sources and a negative contrast effect was present at all locations. An examination of the number of times the rats switched to a different tube once they had stopped, and then reinitiated, drinking showed that the unshifted animals switched to a different tube more than the shifted animals. Similarly, the unshifted animals initiated drinking more often than the shifted animals. Both of these results would seemingly argue against the exploration hypothesis of contrast. However, it could be that a brief exposure to the 4% sucrose in the novel tubes was enough to signal the shifted rats that there was no better source of sucrose than that present in the original tube.

In another open-field study, the shifted group made a greater proportion of its licks at the novel tubes than did the unshifted groups, with the greatest proportion of licks being made at the tube spatially furthest from the original tube (Flaherty et al., 1979). These data might reflect exploration and/or they might reflect an aversion to the former 32% location.

In more recent experiments, we have examined contrast in an eight-arm radial maze. Sucrose was located in one of the eight arms. Following the shift from 32% to 4% sucrose, there was a substantial increase in arm entries (see Figure 4.2). Subsequent experiments investigated the possibility that this increase represented simply an increase in activity engendered by the shift, an increase in random exploration, or a specific search. This was done by presenting the preshift solutions in either of two arms on a regularly alternating basis. In the postshift period, the 4% sucrose was located in both arms for both the shifted and unshifted animals. Thus far (two experiments), we have found that the shifted animals, after discovering the 4% in the first arm they entered, tended to go immediately to the alternative arm that had contained 32% during the preshift period (4/4 rats in one

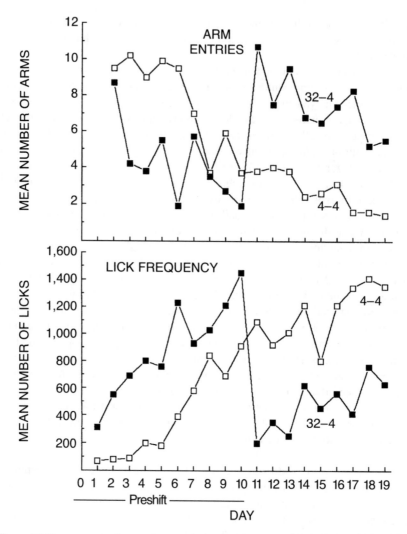

Figure 4.2 Two measures of successive negative contrast in an eight-arm radial maze. Correlated with the negative contrast in lick frequency following the shift from 32% sucrose to 4% sucrose on day 11 was an increase (and contrast effect) in arm entries. (After Flaherty, 1991b.)

experiment, 4/6 in another). Animals from nonshifted groups or animals that had experienced the preshift solutions in only one location did not show this tendency. The activity aspect of the hypothesis was investigated by including a running wheel as an option at the end of one of the alleys. The shifted rats did not show any tendency to increase running immediately after the shift.

Thus, these data are consistent with Elliott's hypothesis that part of the reaction to reward reduction is a search for the "missing" substance.

Emotional/motivational theories

... the enormous disappointment
With a smiling sigh softly flings her
Indolent apron over our lives
And sits down on our day.

> – W. H. Auden
> *The Age of Anxiety*

Most persistent of all interpretations of successive contrast have been those relying on emotional and motivational constructs. As reviewed in Chapter 1, Tinklepaugh, and another observer present during the experiments, used the terms "apparent anger," "frustrated," and "disappointment" in their descriptions of the behavior of the monkeys and young children in negative contrast experiments. Crespi (1942, 1944) argued that both reward increases and decreases led to "heightened emotional drive"; in the case of reward increases, this drive ("elation or joy") facilitated behavior, but in the case of reward decreases, the emotion ("anger") led to "frustration" symptoms such as jerky and hesitant running, delayed consumption (or lack of consumption) of the postshift reward, retracing in the runway, attempts to escape the food box, and "general excited peering." The description of contrast in terms of emotional processes was adopted in many of the earlier studies, as described in Chapter 1.

The general concept of "emotionality" has not been helpful in the understanding of contrast effects. As reviewed in Chapter 2, studies with selected strains – the Syracuse High and Low Avoidance lines, the Maudsley Reactive and Nonreactive lines, and our own selectively bred Large and Small contrast lines – did not lead to a simple pattern of contrast responses. The SLA rats, reported to be highly emotional on the basis of other measures, showed larger contrast effects than the SHA rats – a result consistent with a role for "emotionality" in contrast. However, the opposite pattern was obtained in the case of the Maudsley rats – the high-emotional MR strain showed smaller contrast effects than the low- emotional MNRA strain. The data obtained with the Rutgers large-contrast and small-contrast rats showed no consistent relationship between emotionality and degree of SNC.

Data derived from preweaning "handling" studies also question the applicability of a generalized emotionality concept to contrast. Rats separated from their litters for brief periods over several days during the preweaning period are less emotionally reactive as adults. Compared to nonhandled rats, the handled rats ambulate more and defecate less in an open field, show less elevation of corticosteroids in response to novel stimuli, investigate novel environments more, and show smaller conditioned taste aversions than nonhandled rats do (Ader, 1970; Denenberg & Grota, 1964; Haltmeyer, Denenberg & Zarrow, 1967; Hess, Denenberg, Zarrow & Pfeiffer, 1969; Levine, 1956; Levine, Haltmeyer, Karas & Denenberg, 1967; Weinberg, Smotherman & Levine, 1978). However, the early-handling treatment had no effect on consummatory negative contrast, even though such handling did reproduce the typical open-field effects in the same rats (Meinrath & Flaherty, 1987). Furthermore, correlational analyses undertaken in this study showed no relationship between measures of open-field behavior and degree of contrast in consummatory behavior. A lack of effect of early handling on SNC in runway behavior following a decrease in food quantity has also been obtained (Daly & Rosenberg, 1973).

Collectively, these studies question the utility of predictions based on a general emotionality concept for the understanding of contrast. The concept of emotionality itself has often been criticized (see, for example, Archer, 1973, 1975; Satinder, 1981; Suarez & Gallup, 1981). However, the lack of usefulness of emotionality as a general concept does not exclude the possibility that a *particular* emotion might be involved in contrast. The Daly and Rosenberg early-handling study did find that the handling procedure reduced the suppressive effects of punishment on the handled rats. These authors suggested that the effects of handling might be specific to fear-related behaviors – leaving frustration-related behaviors uninfluenced. A role for frustration in contrast was suggested by Crespi, Spence, and Tinklepaugh, and this implied role has been elaborated in the context of a theory of frustration suggested by Amsel.

Amsel's frustration theory

Amsel's theory was originally developed as an explanation of the partial reinforcement extinction effect and, later, as an explanation for aspects of discrimination learning (Amsel, 1958, 1962, 1971, 1992). Simplified, the hypothesis is that, through conditioning, animals come to anticipate reward in the presence of stimuli previously paired with reward (for example, the goal box of a runway). This anticipation generalizes to similar stimulus situations (for example, the start box of a runway) and enters into an associative relationship with the instrumental response, thereby facilitating goal approach. When the animal encounters a reduced reward in the goal box, there is a Primary Frustration reaction elicited by the discrepancy between the anticipated and obtained rewards. The frustration reaction, which is aversive and tends to produce unconditioned withdrawal, becomes conditioned to the goal-box cues and generalizes to the start-box cues. The subsequent anticipation of an aversive event (from this conditioning), and/or the conflict between anticipation of reward and the anticipation of frustration, produces behaviors that compete with the approach response – the kinds of behaviors observed by Crespi – and thus produce the slower running that is the measured SNC.

A great deal of evidence is consistent with this hypothesis in at least a general way. First, the aversiveness of reward reduction is indicated by the following: (a) Rats will learn a response to escape from a cue paired with reward reduction (Daly, 1974); (b) the stress hormone corticosterone is elevated following reward reduction (Flaherty, Becker & Pohorecky; 1985; Goldman, Coover & Levine, 1973); (c) rats may tend to withdraw from the locus of a reduced reward (Flaherty, Powell & Hamilton, 1979); (d) drugs classified as anxiolytics in humans tend to reduce the effects of reward reduction or reward elimination (Flaherty, 1991a; Gray, 1977, 1982, 1987); and, finally, (e) in a human infant analogue of contrast, a substantial reduction in the number of elements in a mobile hanging over the crib induced crying and gaze redirected away from the mobile (Fagen & Prigot, 1993; Fagen & Rovee, 1976; Mast, Fagen, Rovee-Collier & Sullivan, 1980).

Second, the effects of many of the variables reviewed in Chapter 2 may be interpreted in terms of Amsel's frustration theory: (a) The direct relationship between preshift magnitude of reward and degree of SNC is consistent with the hypothesis that large reward disparity leads to greater frustration (DiLollo & Beez, 1966); (b) the apparent tendency for SNC to vary directly with degree of deprivation in runway studies is consistent with the hypothesis that greater deprivation leads to greater frustration when reward is reduced (Cleland, Williams & DiLollo, 1969); (c) the fact that prior exposure to the postshift reward reduces SNC could be interpreted as incentive averaging, which would effectively reduce the preshift reward magnitude and, thus, the reward disparity, leading to less frustration; (d) the finding that varied magnitude of reward and partial reward experience may reduce contrast could be interpreted in the same way as in point (c)[2]; (e) the effect of the variables in points (c) and (d) could also be interpreted in terms of Amsel's explanation of the partial reinforcement extinction effect – prior experience with intermittent reinforcement trains the animals, through counterconditioning, to persist under frustrating conditions; (f) the finding that anxiolytic drugs generally antagonize contrast is also consistent with a causal role for a frustration-related response.

Thus, a great deal of the contrast data are at least consistent with Amsel's frustration theory. The theory, however, does not specifically address searching behavior, nor is it specific enough to explain the findings that the benzodiazepines and ethanol are ineffective on the first postshift day, whereas sodium amobarbital does reduce contrast at this point. The theory also does not address the mechanism of action of these drugs, nor does it address neurobiological mechanisms of contrast and potentially related phenomena. An ambitious theory that has attempted the latter is Gray's theory of anxiety and inhibition.

Gray's behavioral inhibition theory

A comprehensive model of the effects of reward variables on behavior has been developed by Gray (for example, 1982, 1987, 1990). The principle focus of this model is anxiety, but it is consonant with, and in many ways incorporates, Amsel's frustration theory and its explanation of the partial reinforcement extinction effect. Gray envisions three distinct emotional systems: a "go" system controlling approach to *conditioned* stimuli that signal reward or the absence of punishment; a "stop" system that controls the inhibition of responding to *condi-*

---

[2]There is disagreement in the literature here. One study indicates that contrast is reduced by prior partial reward, but another indicates only that the onset of contrast is delayed (see Chapter 2). The latter finding is not consistent with frustration theory.

tioned stimuli signalling punishment or nonreward; and a "fight/flight" system controlling reaction to unconditioned stimuli. Gray's theory is an elaborate and detailed attempt to integrate behavioral, psychopharmacological, and neurophysiological data. Only aspects of the theory that seem directly related to contrast will be considered here.

Two features of the theory are especially relevant. First, Gray argues that anxiolytic drugs do not affect the fight/flight system – the unconditioned reaction to aversive events. Thus, the initial reaction to nonreward or reduced reward (Amsel's primary frustration reaction) would not be expected to be influenced by tranquilizers. Gray martials evidence from a number of studies supporting this conclusion. One example is the Frustration Effect (FE), first demonstrated by Amsel and Roussel (1952). Briefly stated, rats given random 50% reinforcement in the first of two sequential goal boxes in a runway, and 100% reinforcement in the second goal box, run faster when leaving the first goal box after nonrewarded trials than after rewarded trials. Although many interpretations of this effect are possible, the evidence favors Amsel's suggestion that the faster running reflects an energizing effect of frustrative nonreward (see, for example, Dunlap & Frates, 1970; Gray, 1977; Hughes & Dachowski, 1973; Scull, 1973; Wagner, 1959).

The finding that the FE is not affected by anxiolytic drugs (Gray, 1977) is one of the bases of Gray's assumption that unconditioned emotional reactions in general are not affected by such drugs (see Gray, 1977, 1982, 1987, for other evidence). This assertion by Gray connects with the contrast literature reviewed in Chapter 3, because chlordiazepoxide and ethanol do not modify SNC in consummatory behavior on the first postshift day. Interpreted in terms of Gray's theory, contrast on the first postshift day may represent a primary emotional reaction to the reward shift. Subsequent postshift days, when CDP and ethanol are effective, may then involve conditioned cues predicting both the preshift and postshift reward – evoking conflict much as in Amsel's theory of partial reinforcement. It is exactly under these conditions that Gray would expect anxiolytics to be effective in reducing contrast.

The application of Gray's theory to the contrast data is plausible, but there are three problems. First, the anxiolytic sodium amobarbital, unlike CDP and ethanol, has a small, but reliable, contrast-reducing effect on the first postshift day. However, sodium amobarbital does not modify the FE (Gray, 1977). This suggests that the emotional state induced immediately following reward reduction is not directly analogous to the FE. Furthermore, the finding that Maudsley Reactive rats show a larger FE than Maudsley Nonreactive rats (Savage & Eysenck, 1964), but a smaller SNC in consummatory behavior (Rowan & Flaherty, 1991), indicates that the two behaviors are not measuring the same psychological phenomenon (or, once again, that there is a dissociation between instrumental and consummatory behavior). Thus, Gray's suggestion that primary frustration is not affected by anxiolytics, and the use of FE data in partial support of this conclusion, cannot be used as an explanation of the profile of anxiolytic effects seen on the initial occurrence of contrast.

Secondly, the septum and the hippocampus play a fundamental role in Gray's behavioral inhibition system. In brief, one of the many functions of the hippocampus is presumed to be that of a comparator – comparing actual environmental events with expected events. When a rewarding event is less than expected, circuits in the hippocampus are hypothesized to inhibit the behavior that led to that event. The medial septal area influences the hippocampus by providing a timing mechanism (the "theta" wave) that coordinates the flow of information in the hippocampal circuit. Aspects of this theta mechanism (firing at the rate of 7.7 Hz) are specifically sensitive to anxiolytics and are thought to be involved in the response to aversive events (Gray, 1987).[3]

However, as reviewed in Chapter 3, lesions of the septal area, the hippocampus, or the entorhinal cortex do not influence contrast in consummatory behavior. There is evidence, however, that this system (at least the hippocampus and entorhinal cortex) is involved in contrast in instrumental behavior. It may be reasonable to interpret Gray's model specifically in terms of instrumental behavior (the model refers to "action patterns"; see Gray, 1987, p. 295) and as not applicable to consummatory behavior. Also, Gray states that his theory is related to the signalling properties of stimuli correlated with reward or punishment. Such signalling stimuli would be much more of a factor in instrumental behavior than in consummatory behavior. As reviewed in Chapter 2, there are substantial differences in the occurrence of SNC in instrumental responding, compared to consummatory responding, when sucrose solutions are used. The relationship of consummatory behavior to instrumental behavior is relatively unexplored, even though it has always had an important role in conditioning model theories of behavior (see, for example, Amsel, 1991, 1992; Spence, 1956). Some of the evidence previously considered here has suggested functional differences between instrumental and consummatory behavior, including the occurrence of contrast with shifts in sucrose concentration (Chapter 2) and the effects of anxiolytic drugs on contrast and extinction (Chapter 3 and Flaherty, 1991a). Other evidence has suggested a difference between consummatory and instrumental behavior in measuring the effects of shifts in deprivation conditions (Balleine, 1992).

The third problem with applying Gray's model to contrast occurs with regard to his neuropharmacological and neurochemical hypotheses. Gray argues that ascending serotonergic fibers, from the raphe nuclei, and ascending noradrenergic fibers, from the locus coeruleus, are functionally involved in behavioral inhibition, possibly through actions in the hippocampus at the dentate gate/CA3 area. The contrast data do not speak directly to these hypotheses, but these data do suggest that, if these hypotheses are correct, the system does not influence contrast in consummatory behavior. We say this because, as reviewed

[3]This is a grossly simplified presentation of Gray's theory, which has functioned to integrate a remarkable amount of behavioral and neurophysiological data. The issue here is the applicability of the theory to negative contrast, particularly negative contrast in consummatory behavior, and not other aspects of the theory.

in Chapter 3, there is virtually no evidence that manipulations of the serotonergic system influence consummatory contrast. That is, the serotonin$_{1A}$ agonists buspirone and gepirone, over a wide range of doses, did not affect contrast, nor did the general antagonist methysergide or the specific serotonin$_2$ antagonists ritanserin and ketanserin. Also, the substantial depletion of serotonin by administration of PCPA did not affect contrast. Finally, serotonin levels, as measured in the striatum, were not altered by the shift from 32% to 4% sucrose. Although these data strongly suggest the noninvolvement of serotonin in consummatory contrast, the puzzle remains as to why cyproheptadine and cinanserin, two general serotonin antagonists, are effective in reducing contrast (see Chapter 3). Our current hypothesis is that these drugs are influencing contrast through a nonserotonergic mechanism, but, as yet, no supportive evidence for that conjecture has been obtained (Coppotelli & Flaherty, 1993; Grigson, 1990; Grigson & Flaherty, 1991).

Less work has been done with noradrenergic agents, but a study using the α_2 agonist clonidine, over a wide dose range, found no indication that the drug reduced contrast on the second postshift day (Flaherty, Grigson & Demetrikopoulos, 1987), and unpublished data indicated no effect of clonidine on the first postshift day, nor of propranolol on either the first or second postshift day (see Chapter 3). Clonidine inhibits locus coeruleus activity, and it would be expected to reduce contrast if Gray's behavioral inhibition circuit were involved (see, for example, Gray, 1987, pp. 301–302).

Overall, the data question the applicability of Gray's model to contrast in consummatory behavior. The fit of the model to contrast in instrumental behavior is much better, suggesting a fundamental difference in brain control mechanisms involved in approach to a potential reward location and the actual consumption of the reward once it is reached.

A multistage model of negative contrast

Evidence reviewed here and in Chapter 3 suggests that anxiolytics alleviate SNC, a finding consistent with an interpretation of contrast in terms of an emotional process. However, an unexpected outcome of these experiments was that the anxiolytics were much more potent in promoting recovery from contrast than in preventing its occurrence. Evidence reviewed here also suggests some role of exploration/search in contrast. A puzzle that we have addressed is how to reconcile these two interpretations (emotion and search) and how to explain the lack of effect of CDP and ethanol on the initial occurrence of contrast (the first postshift day).

Why is CDP ineffective in preventing the occurrence of contrast? As reviewed in Chapter 3, the answer does not seem to lie in different dose/response functions, because there is no evidence that high doses of CDP are any more effective than low doses on the first postshift day, whereas there is a dose/response function on the second postshift day. Another possibility relates to memory. In order to show a contrast effect, the animals must remember the preshift reward and compare the postshift reward to this memory. A specific experiment designed to examine memory as a possible modulator of the effectiveness of CDP showed that CDP's greater effectiveness on the second postshift day is not due to a weaker memory trace, because there is a 48-hour interval since the last experience with the preshift sucrose solution (see Chapter 3 for details).

Degree of experience with the postshift solution and/or time since the initial experience with the postshift solution does influence the point of effectiveness of CDP – the drug becomes effective during the second 5 minutes of a 20-minute access period following the shift, a point that corresponded to the normal second postshift day. Because the memory study described here showed that the passage of time between preshift and postshift was not a factor in the effectiveness of CDP, it would seem that passage of time *since the beginning of the postshift period* and/or degree of experience with the postshift substance is the critical factor. Another study demonstrated that experience with the 4% solution must be during the postshift period itself – giving exposure to the 4% solution prior to the start of the preshift phase and then shifting to 4% (that is 4%–32%–4%) does not alter the effectiveness of CDP, although it does alter contrast itself.

These and other data suggested a multistage hypothesis of contrast occurrence and recovery. Our hypothesis is that the differential effectiveness of CDP reflects the operation of different psychological/neurochemical processes in contrast occurrence (day 1) and recovery (subsequent postshift days). The initial response to reward reduction (day 1) may involve detection, rejection, and search processes. Evidence bearing on this includes the Tinklepaugh and Elliott studies cited here and more recent evidence from our laboratory. Informal observations indicate that shifted rats lick the postshift solution for 10 to 20 seconds as if it were the 32% sucrose solution. At this point, they stop licking and begin rearing and sniffing around the apparatus, alternating this behavior with brief returns to licking. These observations were supported by a microstructure analysis of contrast that showed that shifted rats had more lick bursts, but fewer licks per burst, than unshifted rats (Grigson, Spector & Norgren, 1993). When contrast studies are conducted in an open-field or radial maze, rats downshifted in reward show activity increases and search behavior.

Thus, these data are consistent with the hypothesis that an early reaction to reward reduction might be considered to be cognitive – a search for the "missing" substance. An initial "search" stage may have ecological validity: Foraging animals may form an expectancy of the average level of reward density available to them, and they may leave a particular location if the reward availability there falls below the expectation (Waddington & Heinrich, 1981). Such a search stage is also consistent with the data on human separation and loss, in which case a search, or other attempts to retrieve the lost object, is often the first response to loss (Bowlby, 1973; Klinger, 1975).

A second stage of contrast, recovery, may be triggered by the occurrence of contrast itself, as an opponent process mechanism (Solomon & Corbit, 1974), or by the failure of the search stage to locate a source of nutrition better than the postshift solution. This stage may involve stress. In the standard small apparatus that has been used in most of our experiments, recovery almost invariably begins on the second day and is typically complete within 4 days. However, contrast endures for a much longer period of time in the open-field and radial maze (see Figure 4.2) – at least 8 days in some experiments. This process may reflect an expanded search stage (a delayed emotional reaction?) occasioned by a complex environment.

The recovery stage may involve conflict between approaching the postshift 4% sucrose solution (because of its absolute reward value) and withdrawing from it and searching (because the relative value of the postshift reward is less than that of the remembered preshift 32% solution). Rats downshifted in reward eventually recover and this recovery may be driven by deprivation state (the rats are deprived to 82% of free-feeding weight in our experiments – ad lib rats show greatly prolonged contrast; see Chapter 3).

It may be during this conflict stage that corticosterone is elevated (day 2) and that CDP is effective in reducing contrast (day 2 or the second 5 minutes of access).

A neurochemical hypothesis to parallel the behavioral recovery processes is as follows. Benzodiazepines (such as CDP) potentiate the effectiveness of the inhibitory neurotransmitter GABA. The benzodiazepines do this by attaching to a specific benzodiazepine binding site that is a component of the GABA receptor complex on many neurons. When GABA is released by the presynaptic neuron, it binds to its receptor and opens Cl⁻ ionophores, thereby hyperpolarizing the postsynaptic neuron. If a benzodiazepine is bound to its location, it potentiates the effects of GABA on the Cl⁻ ionophore, thereby enhancing the inhibitory effects of GABA (Biggio & Costa, 1986; Costa, 1983).

The relevance of this is that the benzodiazepines are neuromodulators, not neurotransmitters. That is, in the absence of GABA, the benzodiazepines do not, in and of themselves, affect the Cl⁻ ionophore. Thus, the benzodiazepines would not be expected to have an effect in the absence of GABA. It is possible, then, that the occurrence of a contrast effect, or the failure to find a better reward, triggers an endogenous recovery process that involves GABA and, until this recovery process is underway, the benzodiazepines have no effect. Two recent papers provided evidence that a GABAergic system is involved in recovery from contrast. These studies showed that the contrast-reducing actions of ethanol on the second postshift day were blocked by the benzodiazepine partial inverse agonist Ro 15-4513, and by the chloride channel blocker picrotoxin (Becker & Anton, 1990; Becker & Hale, 1991). On the other hand, the indirect GABA agonist valproate potentiated the effects of ethanol on the second postshift day (Becker & Anton, 1990).

Preliminary experiments from our laboratory have examined an implication of the hypothesis that CDP is ineffective on the first postshift day because a relevant GABA circuit is not operative. In this experiment, the direct GABA agonist muscimol was administered into the lateral ventricles on the first postshift day. The results of the first experiment showed that a dose of 0.05 μg of muscimol prevented the occurrence of contrast, whereas a dose of 0.025 μg was ineffective

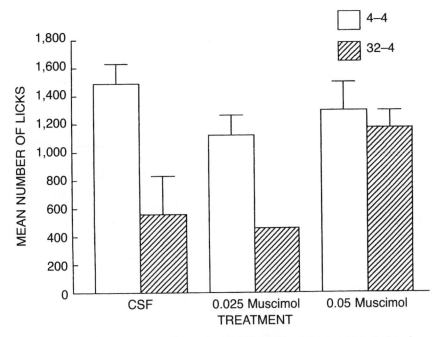

Figure 4.3 Effect of the GABA agonist muscimol (0.025 or 0.05 μg/μl) injected into the lateral ventricle on the first postshift day. Artificial cerebrospinal fluid (CSF) was used as the vehicle. The successive negative contrast effect in lick frequency following a shift from 32% to 4% sucrose was eliminated by the higher dose. (Flaherty and Lazar, unpublished data.)

(see Figure 4.3). Ongoing experiments are concerned with the interactive effects of CDP and muscimol. The hypothesis is that sub-effective doses of muscimol, administered on the first postshift day, will permit CDP (administered on the first postshift day) to be effective in reducing contrast. This follows from the role of CDP as a neuromodulator – it is only effective in modulating ongoing activity in a GABA circuit.

Although these data support the hypothesis that a GABAergic circuit may be involved in recovery from contrast and that activation of a GABA circuit may impede contrast occurrence, they shed no light on how this hypothetical system might be activated under natural conditions. Recent research in other laboratories suggested one possibility for the normal course of events that would activate a GABAergic system following reward reduction, thereby promoting recovery and enabling anxiolytics to be effective in accelerating recovery.

This research showed that exposure to a physical stressor (brief swim test at ambient temperature) led to a rapid (5 minutes or less) increase in two steroids, allopregnanolone (3α–hydroxy-5α-pregnan-20-one), a metabolite of progesterone, and allotetrahydrodeoxycorticosterone (3α,21-dihydroxy-5α–pregnan-

20-one) (THDOC), a metabolite of deoxycorticosterone (Purdy, Morrow, Moore & Paul, 1991). Elevations of these steroids were measured in the cortex, in the hypothalamus, and in plasma.

These data are important because several synthetic and naturally occurring steroids have been shown to modulate $GABA_A$ receptor function. For example, THDOC and other steroids enhance muscimol binding to GABA receptor sites, enhance flunitrazepam binding to benzodiazepine receptor sites, and inhibited TBPS binding to picrotoxin-sensitive sites (Gee, Chang, Brinton & McEwen, 1987; Turner, Ransom, Yang & Olson, 1989); THDOC and other steroids potentiate muscimol-stimulated Cl- ion flux (Morrow, Suzdak & Paul, 1988); and THDOC and progesterone metabolites enhance GABA-stimulated membrane currents (Peters, Kirkness, Callachan, Lambert & Turner, 1988). Progesterone and corticosterone metabolites function like barbiturates in many respects (Majewska, Harrison, Schwartz, Barker & Paul, 1986) but are more potent (Morrow et al., 1988) and act at a different site (Turner et al, 1989). Furthermore, THDOC has been shown to possess anxiolytic properties in rats and mice (Crawley, Glowa, Majewska & Paul, 1986).

These steroid data, in conjunction with the background and preliminary data described here, suggest the following hypothesis regarding negative contrast.

1. Rats develop a representation of the preshift sucrose solution. This representation is established via a conditioning process (Colwill & Rescorla, 1986; Holland, 1989; Rescorla, 1992) and is reflected by shorter latencies to initiate licking for the 32% solution than for the 4% solution (see, for example Grigson, Spector & Norgren, 1993). These latency differences are often maintained through the postshift period, even though the animals show a contrast effect in consummatory behavior. However, the representation of the sucrose concentration is not elicited only by the training context, because changing the context radically before the shift in reward does not eliminate the contrast effect (Flaherty, Hrabinski & Grigson, 1990). Thus, the initial taste of sucrose may function to retrieve the representation of the preshift solution independently of the context.

2. The shift to a lower concentration of sucrose initiates a sequence of psychological processes involving detection of the change, evaluation of the new solution, and reaction to the change.

3. In SNC, the reaction involves a search for the "missing" substance and subsequent activation of a stress response that includes the elevation of analgesic/anxiolytic steroids in plasma and brain.

4. These, and perhaps other mechanisms, activate a GABA circuit that promotes recovery from negative contrast.

5. The activation of this circuit requires time, perhaps a minimum of 5 minutes after the encounter with the reduced reward under the conditions of the typical consummatory contrast. Until this circuit is activated, GABA-

dependent anxiolytics, including the benzodiazepines and ethanol, will be ineffective in alleviating contrast.

6. GABA-independent anxiolytics, such as anesthetic barbiturates, will function to alleviate contrast earlier in this process than GABA-dependent anxiolytics. (Sodium amobarbital, a barbiturate, is effective on the first postshift day, whereas CDP and ethanol are not; see Chapter 3.)

7. The duration of the search process and the point of activation of the stress response may vary depending on the complexity of the context in which the reward is reduced.

8. Contrast dissipates during the postshift period through the concurrent action of a GABA circuit, which reduces the stress-related aspects of the reward shift, and the replacement of the preshift sucrose representation with a representation appropriate for the postshift solution.

This multistage hypothesis thus incorporates the search and emotion aspects of early interpretations of contrast. Substantial evidence is already available in support of points 3, 5, 6, and 7. Other points are testable. For example, the role of GABAergic mechanisms may be further investigated by using the GABA antagonist bicuculline, which, according to the hypothesis, will block the effects of muscimol, block the effects of CDP, and, if GABA is involved in the natural recovery from contrast, block this recovery. The effects of CDP, but not muscimol, should be blocked by the benzodiazepine antagonist flumazenil. Furthermore, if a GABAergic mechanism enables CDP to become effective, then low doses of muscimol on the first postshift day should allow CDP to become effective in reducing contrast. The chloride channel blocker picrotoxin should block not only the effects of CDP, but also those of sodium amobarbital, which is effective on the first postshift day, when CDP is ineffective. Bicuculline should not block the effects of sodium amobarbital on the first postshift day.

One uncertain question is the nature of the event that activates the recovery process (possibly mediated by the anesthetic steroids). At first glance, the reward downshift itself would seem to be the logical candidate, particularly given the time course of the effectiveness of CDP and the measurable steroid response in the brain following the swim stress. However, preliminary data obtained in the radial-arm maze present a problem for this interpretation. A recently completed experiment has shown that CDP (8 mg/kg) failed to reliably reduce contrast on either the second or fourth postshift day.[4] Because this dose of CDP readily eliminates contrast in a small cage, there may be something about the radial-arm maze that alters the effectiveness of CDP. The magnitude of the initial contrast

---

[4]These data are unpublished. An analysis of variance across the first four postshift days revealed an overall contrast effect [$F(1, 20) = 101.49, p < 0.001$], but no contrast-reducing effect of the drug. On the second postshift day, there was a reliable appetite-stimulating effect of CDP [$F(2, 20) = 4.85, p < 0.02$] but no interaction of the drug with shift condition ($F < 1.00$). On the fourth postshift day, there was still a reliable contrast effect [$F(1, 20) = 35.82, p < 0.001$], but no effect of the drug ($F < 1.00$); nor was there a drug x shift interaction ($F < 1.00$).

effect is not appreciably different in the two circumstances. The critical difference between the two situations may be the opportunity to search that is provided by the complex environment of the maze. It may be the failure of the search – that is, the failure to find the missing 32% sucrose or an acceptable alternative – that triggers the stress response rather than the shift per se.

One way of examining this question may be to measure corticosterone levels during a radial-maze experiment. Previous experiments in the small-cage apparatus have shown that corticosterone is elevated after the second postshift day, not on the first (Flaherty, Becker & Pohorecky, 1985). This correlates with the point of effectiveness of CDP and ethanol, and it may be reflective of the release of the central nervous system stress steroids. Thus, the prediction that would be made in the case of the radial-maze data is that corticosterone would not be elevated on the second or fourth postshift day and, in fact, its point of elevation would correspond to the point of effectiveness of CDP. Another prediction that would be made about the radial maze is that sodium amobarbital would be effective in reducing contrast at an earlier point than CDP.

In any case, the activated GABA circuit apparently inhibits a system that functions to reduce licking – a "stop" circuit as envisioned by Gray, but probably one not mediated via the septal-hippocampal complex. Thus far, the pharmacological studies have not yielded much information on what this circuit might be (but many clues on what it probably is not). The circuit is apparently sensitive to cyproheptadine; it is also sensitive to need for carbohydrates, because insulin administration will prevent the occurrence of contrast (Flaherty, McCurdy, Becker & D'Allesio, 1983). The interaction between the GABA circuit and the "stop" circuit must also be sensitive to environmental complexity, because contrast endures much longer in an open or complex environment and CDP does not become effective until later in the postshift phase in a complex environment.

In terms of neuroanatomy, the best guess at the present time is that the amygdala is an important nodal point for this circuit, because damage to this area (particularly the corticomedial area) prevents the occurrence of contrast. However, the parabrachial lesion data suggest that there may be multiple points within the taste circuit that control contrast in consummatory behavior (see Chapter 3).

Summary – emotion-related theories

The concept of a general emotionality has not been helpful in understanding negative contrast because of inconsistency in results derived from predictions based on this concept. However, much of the negative contrast data are compatible with some implications of Amsel's frustration theory and Gray's theory of anxiety and behavioral inhibition. The latter theory may be more applicable to the instrumental ramifications of SNC.

The multistage hypothesis is closely tied to recent data and narrowly applied to SNC. It has the advantage of incorporating the activity (search) aspects of contrast and the emotion-related aspects of contrast into a feasible sequence. Many neuropharmacological and behavioral implications remain to be tested, but initial results are promising. One of the potentially interesting aspects of the model is the suggestion that SNC may operate in nature to produce "behavioral dispersion" (Devenport, 1984) – to bias the decision function toward leaving a depleting food patch, rather than staying – and that the stress–emotion aspect of contrast becomes important when there is no better alternative and the animal must stay in, or return to, the unfavorable reward condition.

Successive positive contrast effects are not incorporated into any of these models simply because there are not enough parametric or analytical data to make any sense of the effect. It is possible that positive contrast has been more difficult to detect because of the operation of at least three factors that oppose its occurrence: (1) In some experimental tasks there are probably performance ceilings that prevent the measurement of SPC (Chapter 2); (2) processes related to neophobia or generalization decrement may minimize positive contrast; (3) SPC simply may not be an important feature of animal behavior. Some of the data from the selective breeding experiment described in Chapter 2 are relevant to this possibility. This experiment suggested that it is easier to breed for large SNC than for small SNC – perhaps indicating that large contrast effects have had adaptive value for rodents, possibly because of a dispersal and environment-sampling consequence of the behavior. Because of this value, the mechanisms underlying SNC are more plentifully represented in the species gene pool. An extension of this hypothesis could be that positive contrast, which would promote a tendency to stay in the same place, is not as adaptive for rodents and is less prevalent in their behavior.

Selected animal models of fear and anxiety

The analysis given here suggests that SNC is psychologically complex. Aspects of the data reviewed – particularly strain comparisons, effects of early handling, and some of the pharmacological data – also suggest that the emotional component of SNC may be different from the emotional components of other behaviors. This is not too surprising; the early investigators of contrast described shifted rats as appearing frustrated, angry, or disappointed, but not as being afraid. The possibility that lower animals are capable of responding with different emotional states has frequently been a tacit or explicit assumption in the study of animal learning. For example, among proponents of conditioning model theories it has been common to consider the degree of uniqueness or commonality of proposed emotions such as hope and relief, or fear and frustration (see, for example, Gray, 1987; Mowrer, 1960; Wagner, 1969).

One approach to isolating the degree of emotional commonality between contrast and other tasks is to compare psychopharmacological profiles obtained in the various tasks. Differences in such profiles could be used to generate hypotheses for further neurobiological and behavioral research. What follows is a comparison of the drug effects obtained in consummatory SNC with those obtained in four animal models of anxiety: potentiated startle, punished drinking, operant conflict, and elevated plus maze.

Generally speaking, an animal model of anxiety is a situation in which behavior that has been suppressed by some experimenter-contrived conflict situation (such as concurrent punishment and reward) is released from that suppression by a drug that reduces anxiety in humans (see Davis, 1991; File, 1987, 1991; Gray, 1987; Gray, Davis, Feldon, Rawlins & Owens, 1981; Green & Hodges, 1991; Iversen, 1983; Lal & Emmett-Oglesby, 1983; Sepinwall, 1985; and Treit, 1985, for further discussions of the concept of an animal model of anxiety). Well over 20 such situations have been used at one time or another, but the 4 selected for comparison with contrast here include a model involving consummatory conflict (punished drinking), a model based on a Pavlovian procedure (potentiated startle), an instrumental conflict model (Geller–Seifter operant conflict), and one involving a nonshock situation (elevated plus maze).

This will not be an exhaustive review of the behavioral pharmacology of these procedures, but rather an examination of the effects of those drugs that have been used thus far in the contrast procedure.

The models

Punished drinking

In the punished drinking test, rats are given some minimal experience with a water deprivation schedule, then, after a 23-hour period of water deprivation, they are given access to water from a drinking tube. After a given number of licks or a brief access time, subsequent licks are shocked. The number of licks made during the shock period by drugged and undrugged rats is used to determine the anxiolytic efficacy of a drug (Vogel, Beer & Clody, 1971).

A number of variations of this procedure are used, often incorporating signalled and unsignalled shock periods to allow for a better assessment of the effect of a drug on drinking per se and not just drinking when a shock is present (see, for example, Commissaris & Retch, 1982; Kilts, Commissaris & Retch, 1981; Pich & Samanin, 1986; Soderpalm & Engel, 1988). The punished drinking procedure is simple, fast, and widely used as an anxiolytic screen in the pharmaceutical industry. The theory behind this test is that the animals are placed in a conflict situation – a conflict between the availability of needed water and the response-contingent shock associated with that water.

Potentiated startle

The potentiated startle test is quite different from the other paradigms in that it probably does not involve a conflict component (and, perhaps, therefore no suppression of behavior). Instead, this procedure, which has been extensively investigated by Davis (see Davis, 1991, 1992; Davis, Hitchcock & Rosen, 1988), involves a Pavlovian fear-conditioning paradigm. The behavior of interest is the animal's startle response to a brief, loud sound. In Davis's procedure, animals are first conditioned by pairing a light with a shock for a number of trials. The effect of this conditioning is then measured by preceding some noise presentations by the light. The basic result is that the startle amplitude is enhanced when the light precedes the noise. Controls for conditioning include the use of paired and unpaired light–shock groups.

Operant conflict

The operant conflict test developed by Geller and Seifter (for example, 1960) is also widely used as an anxiolytic screen. The procedure involves a multiple schedule that typically consists of a period of a variable interval 2-minute (VI-2) schedule of reinforcement that alternates with a period of continuous reinforcement (CRF) plus shock punishment. Variations on this basic procedure include modifications of the schedules, usually in the direction of using a low fixed ratio (FR) punishment contingency and/or the inclusion of a time-out period (no reinforcement or punishment) in addition to the two reinforcement periods. Also, the shock intensity is often adjusted for each animal to ensure a baseline level of responding from which measurable deviations produced by a drug treatment may be obtained (see Howard & Pollard, 1977).

The theory is that the animals are placed in a conflict – they "must balance the positive features of reward payoff against the negative features of accepting pain shocks" (Geller & Seifter, 1960, p. 483). A "good" anxiolytic should increase responding during the shock component without affecting responding during the nonpunished component or the TO (time out) component.

Elevated plus maze

This test differs from the other three in that there is no shock and no traditional reinforcer involved. The maze consists of two elevated open arms and two elevated closed arms. Rats tend to spend more time in the closed arms than the open arms; confinement to the open arms produces a corticosterone elevation, compared to home-cage controls and confinement to a closed arm, but less of an elevation than that produced by the Vogel punished drinking test (Lister, 1991; Pellow, Chopin, File & Briley, 1985). Anxiolytic agents tend to increase the relative amount of time that rats spend in the open arms (Lister, 1991). Although a seemingly simple apparatus, factor analysis of 13 behaviors exhibited by rats in this apparatus led to four independent factors, the first of which seemed related to anxiety (number of entries into open arms, time spent in open arms, proportion of open to total arm entries, percentage of time in open arms, scanning over the edge of an open arm, and open arm end-exploring) (Cruz, Frei & Graeff, 1994).

Table 4.1. *Paradigm comparisons. (+) indicates anti-anxiety effect; (−) indicates anxiogenic effect; (0) indicates no effect; (?) indicates unknown; (+/−) indicates contradictory; (∗) indicates postinjection delay of recovery.*

	Negative contrast day 1	Negative contrast day 2	Punished drinking	Operant conflict	Potentiated startle	Plus maze
Benzodiazepines	0	+	+	+	+	+
Barbiturates	+	+	+	+	+	+
Ethanol	0	+	0	+/0	+	+
Morphine	+	+	+/?	0/?	+	
Muscimol	+?					
Methysergide	0	0	+/0	+/0	+/?	
Cyproheptadine	+	+	+/0	+/0	0	0/−
Cinanserin	0	+	+/0	+/0	0	
Mianserin	0	0?				
Buspirone	0	0	+/0	+/0	+	+/0/−
Gepirone		0	+?	+?	+	
Ritanserin	0	0		0		−
Ketanserin		0			0	
Imipramine		0	0	0	0	0
Chlorpromazine	0	0	0	0		
Haloperidol		0	+/?			0
Clonidine	0	0	+/0/−	+	+	+/0
Propranolol	0	0?	0	0	+/0	0
Scopolamine	0	0	0			
Caffeine	0/∗	0/∗				−
Inverse agonists		−			−	−
Pyrilamine	0	0				
Methy plus scopolamine		0				
Methy plus pyrilamine		0				
MK801		0				+
Zolpidem		0?	+			

Comparative drug effects

Table 4.1 provides a listing of the drugs that have been investigated in consummatory negative contrast, as well as a comparison of the effectiveness of these drugs in contrast and in the four animal models of anxiety described here.

The data from the four comparison models on which this table is based are described in the Appendix. The mechanism of action of the drugs presented was reviewed when these agents were considered in Chapter 3. The grouping of the drugs in the table reflects a more or less commonality of action.

The first impression gained from Table 4.1 is the similarity of the models in terms of drug effectiveness in spite of radically different paradigms.

Certainly, the benzodiazepines and barbiturates are almost universally effective in the models presented. The exception is the failure of the benzodiazepines to influence SNC on the first postshift day. The generality of these effects suggests the involvement of a GABAergic mechanism in anxiolytic action in all models. The exception suggests that a relevant GABAergic circuit has not been activated during the initial occurrence of contrast. The effectiveness of the barbiturates at this point may be explained by the fact that sodium amobarbital may function both as a GABA-mimetic, acting in the absence of GABA, and also as a GABA potentiator.

In general, all the models seem unaffected by serotonin$_2$ antagonists, with the possible exception of the plus maze, where ritanserin was reported to have an anxiogenic effect. Imipramine is also broadly ineffective, and there is scant evidence of neuroleptic effects in any model.

Beyond this simple generalization, the most striking aspect of the data is the uncertain or contradictory nature of the effects of many drugs. However, given this, certain other conclusions are at least suggested by the available data.

Contrast may be distinguishable from the other models in several ways: (1) in the effectiveness of cyproheptadine; (2) in the total failure of buspirone and gepirone, compared to mixed results in other models and clear effectiveness in potentiated startle; (3) in the failure of clonidine, given the suggested positive results in most other models; (4) in the possible reversal of the pattern of effectiveness of methysergide, cinanserin, and cyproheptadine compared to potentiated startle; and (5) in the unique pattern, in these models, of the clear effectiveness of ethanol and chlordiazepoxide on recovery from contrast without any effect on the initial occurrence of contrast.

Some other questions may be given tentative and partial answers from the available data. Does contrast (disappointment/frustration?) differ from shock-induced fear? The comparison of contrast and potentiated startle suggests a commonality in the effects of anxiolytics, particularly on the second postshift day, but a difference in the effects of serotonin$_{1A}$ agonists (buspirone and gepirone) and in drugs that affect the noradrenergic system (clonidine and propranolol), as well as in the pattern of effectiveness of general serotonin antagonists already mentioned.

Does contrast differ from fear engendered by open spaces (elevated plus maze)? Again, the anxiolytics have a common effect, at least on the second postshift day of contrast, but a stark difference seems to exist in the effects of cyproheptadine, and possibly in the effects of clonidine and ritanserin.

There are three major problems in making such judgments based on Table 4.1. The judgments are qualitative, not taking into account the degree of effectiveness, or relative degree of effectiveness, of the various agents. They are based largely on across-laboratory and across-experiment comparisons. They are made in the presence of still scanty data and thus may be altered as the blanks in the table are completed and as the results of experiments using more transmitter-selective drugs are reported.

For now, however, the data do support the notion that contrast does involve an emotional response, one that shares a common property with other presumed emotion-engendering situations, but one that also differs in probable neurotransmitter and psychological properties from those other situations.

Summary and conclusions

It has been over 60 years since the initial observations of Elliott and Tinklepaugh, and 50 years since Crespi's experiment. The keen behavioral observations made in these experiments have been amply supported, at least in terms of SNC, and the two theoretical interpretations developed in these studies remain current. There is little doubt that the constellation of behaviors that arise following reward reduction – the hesitant approach to the location of the original reward and increased ancillary activity – is reasonably characterized as reflecting a negative emotional state and probable incipient search behavior.

Alternative interpretations, such as generalization decrement and adaptation level, may reflect processes involved in some contrast under some conditions, but they are not adequate as general accounts of contrast.

Progress has been slow in getting beyond descriptions to the mechanisms of contrast. It is likely, however, that a GABAergic process mediates the modulating effects of anxiolytics on contrast. It also seems likely, but not proven, that a GABAergic process is normally involved in contrast recovery and that this process is initiated by the occurrence of contrast itself or, more probably, by the failure to find a better alternative than the postshift reward.

Contrast recovery cannot be due entirely to a "corrective" GABAergic mechanism. It is probable that an associative representation of the preshift reward is replaced by a representation of the postshift reward through the postshift period and, thus, deviation from expectation is minimized.

The amygdala seems to be the most likely location for these events, to the extent that they are localized. Amygdala-related processes probably also account for the commonality of tranquilizer effects in the various animal models described here and in the Appendix, because there are substantial data showing the necessity of amygdala function for fear- and anxiety-related tasks. However, it is also likely that a network involving other structures plays a role in input–output functions, representational and other associative aspects of contrast, and corrective feedback functions. The hippocampus seems likely to play a functional role in the case of contrast in instrumental behavior.

Negative contrast may be important in nature, and thus it has probably been selected for as an aid in dispersing animals geographically when food supply falls below expectation.

Little may be said about SPC other than that it is almost certainly a legitimate phenomenon. However, the difficulty of demonstrating SPC may reflect a true asymmetry in magnitude of positive and negative contrast, perhaps related to differential adaptive value. Alternatively, SPC may simply be a phenomenon waiting for the correct experimental procedure to demonstrate its robustness.

5   Anticipatory and simultaneous contrast

I was seated one day at a very important banquet, and saw across
from me an exquisite girl whose face was completely sensual.
I leaned toward my neighbor, and murmured to him that it was
impossible that this young lady be anything but a *gourmande,
given such physical characteristics.*
*... "Ridiculous!" he answered me. "She is at most fifteen, and
that is hardly the age for gourmandism. What is more, just let us
watch her ... "*
The beginnings were not at all favorable for me, and I began
to fear that I had made a foolish wager, for during the first two
courses the girl ate so lightly that I was astonished ...But finally
the dessert arrived, a dessert as impressive as it was generous,
and I felt more hopeful. I was not deceived: not only did she
eat everything that was offered to her, but she even asked
for portions from those plates which were farthest from her.
Finally, she had tasted every one and my neighbor confessed
his astonishment that this little belly could hold so many things.
Thus, my diagnosis was confirmed; thus science once more
triumphed.

> – Brillat-Savarin, 1825
> *The Physiology of Taste*

This chapter will address two forms of contrast in consummatory behavior that
occur when rats are given repeated experience with a pair of sweet solutions.
The first, *anticipatory contrast*, occurs when brief access to two solutions is
given sequentially (such as saccharin followed by sucrose) in once-per-day
pairings. The data of interest concern changes in the intake of the initial solution in each pair as the animal receives repeated experience with the sequence.
The effect of this pairing on intake of the initial solution is evaluated by comparison to a control group that receives the same solution (for example saccharin – saccharin) twice each day, or by comparison to a control group that
receives only the first solution. This paradigm may model aspects of feeding
behavior, reflecting the factors that influence a foraging animal's decision to
accept a currently available meal or wait for a future meal; the model may also

shed some light on meal choice in humans. More generally, the anticipatory contrast paradigm may provide a model of situations in which a currently available event of a given value may be compared to a differently valued event that will occur in the future.

The second procedure, termed *simultaneous contrast*, may be considered an extension of anticipatory contrast, because the solution pairs are presented repeatedly within a day. This procedure allows for taste interaction (such as sensory adaptation) between both solutions. The simultaneous contrast procedure may model aspects of psychophysical judgments used in human research, such as use of the magnitude estimation procedure for determining relative sweetness functions; it may also model taste interactions that occur during meal consumption by humans.

The anticipatory contrast procedure, in comparison, provides only for the second solution to be influenced by the first within a day. Thus, the contrast of interest in the anticipatory procedure, intake of the initial solution, occurs in the absence of immediate sensory interaction.

Negative anticipatory contrast

Rats presented a sequence of two palatable solutions each day may suppress intake of the first solution if the second solution is preferred. The initial demonstrations of this in our laboratory occurred in experiments in which some rats were given a 3-minute access period to a 0.15% saccharin solution and, following a 15-second intersolution interval, a 5-minute access period to 32% sucrose. A control group received only the saccharin access period. This control group showed an acquisition function, increasing their intake of saccharin across days – an effect that had been previously demonstrated (Domjan, 1976). The acquisition function was substantially depressed in the group that received the saccharin–sucrose sequence (see Figure 5.1).

A relationship of this suppression to contrast was suggested by the failure of suppression to occur when the second substance was 2% sucrose, a solution that is less rewarding than 0.15% saccharin (Flaherty and Checke, 1982; Flaherty, Grigson, Checke & Hnat, 1991). If the suppression was a form of contrast, the questioned remained whether it was a form of successive contrast (that is, comparison of the current 0.15% saccharin solution with the 32% sucrose received as the second solution on the previous day), or something different.

The basic between subjects (between-S) anticipatory contrast experiment contained two groups – a control group that received two brief access periods to 0.15% saccharin, separated by a brief intersolution interval (called Group .15-.15), and a contrast group that received the 0.15% saccharin solution followed, after the intersolution interval, by 32% sucrose (called Group .15-32). In this procedure, the suppressed licking of the saccharin that occurs in Group .15-32 could

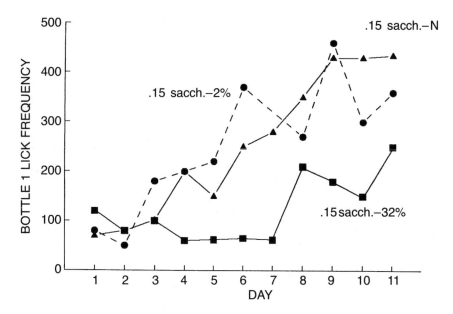

Figure 5.1 Mean lick frequency for the initial solution (0.15% saccharin) in three groups; one group that received no second solution (N); one group received 2% sucrose as the second solution; one group received 32% sucrose as the second solution. Group .15-32 demonstrated anticipatory negative contrast. (After Flaherty & Checke, 1982.)

reflect residual effects from the 32% sucrose received on the previous day. That is, because this group receives 0.15% followed by 32% each day, the suppressed intake that occurs on day $n+1$ could be due to the 32% sucrose received last on day n, rather than to the anticipation of the 32% sucrose to be received next on day $n+1$. If this were the case, then anticipatory contrast would simply be a form of successive negative contrast.

In order to test this, a within-subjects (within-S) study was conducted. In this study, both the contrast condition (.15-32) and control condition (.15-.15) were presented to the same subject, in a regularly alternating fashion across days; each condition was correlated with specific contextual cues (Flaherty & Rowan, 1985). The logic of the within-S study was as follows. If the suppressed intake of the 0.15% saccharin solution seen in the between-S experiment was due to a retrograde process (suppressed saccharin intake in the .15-32 group because 32% sucrose had been received on the previous day), then intake of the initial saccharin solution should be suppressed on days when the rats receive the .15-.15 sequence, because those are the only days in which 32% sucrose precedes access to the saccharin. On the other hand, if this contrast represents an anticipatory process, then intake of the initial saccharin solution should be suppressed on .15-32 days, when the sucrose follows the saccharin on the same day. As is indicated in Figure 5.2, the latter effect

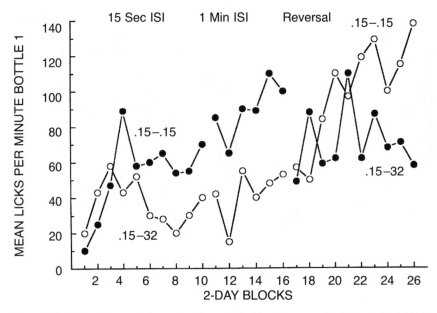

Figure 5.2 Within-subjects anticipatory negative contrast. The same group of animals received 0.15 % saccharin in both first and second bottles when one cue was present; on different days, the group received 0.15% saccharin followed by 32% sucrose when another cue was present. The rats showed negative contrast at both the 15-second and 1-minute intersolution interval times and reversed their licking behavior when the cue–solution pairings were reversed. The data presented are for first bottle (0.15% saccharin) intake in both conditions. (After Flaherty & Rowan, 1986.)

occurred. Thus, contrast in this paradigm is an anterograde process.[1]

Two recent within-S studies in which the contextual cues were omitted support this conclusion (Flaherty, Coppotelli, Grigson, Mitchell & Flaherty, 1995). The only cue as to which consequent the initial saccharin solution signalled was provided by the daily alternation of contrast and control condition (i.e., day 1, .15-32; day 2, .15-.15, day 3, .15-32; etc.). In both of these studies, the rats licked less for the initial saccharin on the days in which it *preceded* the 32% sucrose. The outcome of one of these studies is illustrated in Figure 5.3. Thus, the negative anticipatory contrast paradigm is a situation in which the learning of a daily sequence of a lesser reward followed by a greater reward results in a reduction in consumption of the initial substance – a reduction apparently related to the *relative* value of the two rewards.

The mechanism by which this anticipatory contrast effect is produced will be considered after a review of the conditions that influence the magnitude of the contrast effect.

---

[1] An extensive analysis of operant behavioral contrast by Ben Williams has also suggested the contrast on multiple schedules is largely controlled by the nature of the impending reinforcement schedule rather than by the previous reinforcement schedule. These data will be considered in the next chapter.

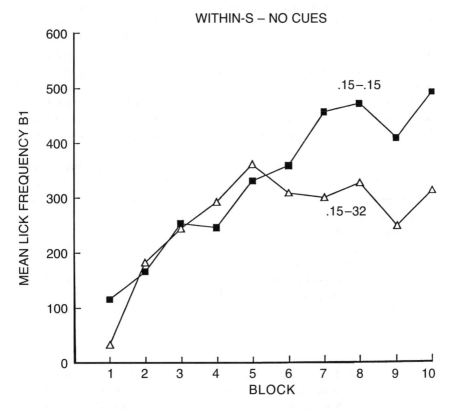

Figure 5.3. Within-subjects anticipatory negative contrast. The same subjects received 0.15% saccharin followed by more 0.15% on some days, and the saccharin followed by 32% on other days. The two conditions alternated across days. Thus, the contrast that occurred was apparently based on the rats' memory of the temporal alternation pattern (i.e., which condition had occurred on the previous day). B1 = Bottle 1. (From Flaherty, Coppotelli, Grigson, Mitchell & Flaherty, 1995).

Parametric studies

Relative reward value

Degree of anticipatory contrast varies as a function of the reward values of the first and second substances. There is a sparsity of parametric studies, but there are enough data to suggest that variations in either the first or second substance available will influence degree of contrast.

VARIATIONS IN THE SECOND SOLUTION. In general, the greater the reward value of the second substance, the greater the anticipatory contrast effect. The data supporting this conclusion are as follows: (1) Contrast was obtained with 32% sucrose following 0.15% saccharin, but not with 2% sucrose as the second substance (Flaherty

& Checke, 1982). (2) Intake of a 2% sucrose solution is suppressed when it is followed by a 16% or 32% sucrose solution, but not when it is followed by an 8% sucrose solution. Suppression was greater in the 2-32 than in the 2-16 condition. These results occurred with a 15-second interval between solutions – there was no suppression with a 5-minute interval between solutions (Flaherty, Grigson, Checke & Hnat, 1991). (3) With a 4-minute delay between solutions, contrast was obtained with lab chow, 32% sucrose, and 64% sucrose as the second substance and 0.15% saccharin as the first substance, but not with chocolate milk, skim milk, or 5.8% Nutrasweet as the second substance (Lucas, Timberlake, Gawley & Drew, 1990). (4) With a 16-minute delay between solutions, contrast was obtained with chocolate milk, Nutrasweet, and both 32% and 64% sucrose solutions following 0.15% saccharin, but not with skim milk or lab chow (Lucas et al., 1990). (5) With a 32-minute delay, contrast was obtained only with a 64% sucrose solution, not with any of the other solutions used in the Lucas et al. study.

Although these data indicate that contrast is more likely when the second solution is of larger reward magnitude or quality, the data are too fragmentary to make any stronger statement – particularly when the complexity of variations in the intersolution interval is added to the equation. Lucas et al. summarized their data as suggesting that intake of the initial saccharin solution was an inverse function of the caloric value of the second substance when there was a 4-minute delay between solutions; with a 16-minute delay, however, the hedonic value of the second substance was more closely related to suppression than was the caloric value.

VARIATIONS IN THE FIRST SOLUTION. The data are quite orderly in studies in which the second solution has been held constant and the first solution varied. When 32% sucrose has been the second solution, the closer in value the first solution is, the *greater* the contrast is, within the ranges investigated. Examples of this are presented in Figures 5.4 and 5.5.

These data show that increasing the concentration of the initial saccharin or sucrose solution led to a more rapid development of contrast and a larger terminal contrast. Furthermore, when the initial substance had a low (or no) hedonic value, there was an initial period of facilitation of licking rather than contrast. As the hedonic value of the initial substance increased, this initial period of facilitation gave way to contrast (Flaherty, Turovsky & Krauss, 1994).

Independent assessments of the hedonic value of each solution may be obtained from the lick frequencies for the second solution available each day. These data, presented in Figures 5.6 and 5.7, show that 32% sucrose produced a higher lick frequency than any other solution. The lick frequencies for the lower-concentration sucrose solutions and for the saccharin solutions followed the concentration functions, so that the highest lick frequencies were for the 2% sucrose solution and for the 0.15% saccharin solution – the very solutions that led to the greatest *relative* suppression in first bottle intake.

These experiments suggest a direct relationship between the value of the initial substance and degree of contrast – the more closely the value of the initial substance approaches that of the second substance, the greater the contrast is.

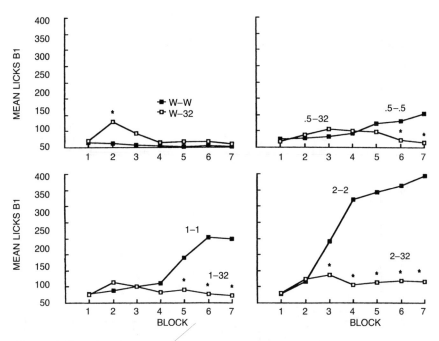

Figure 5.4 Effect of varying the hedonic value of the initial solution on anticipatory contrast with 32% sucrose as the second solution. Contrast was greatest when the most rewarding of these initial solutions (2% sucrose) preceded 32% sucrose. No contrast occurred when water (W) preceded 32% sucrose. Instead, a brief facilitation effect occurred. B1 = Bottle 1. (From Flaherty, Turovsky & Krauss, 1994.)

However, this relationship probably holds over only a limited range of values. One would expect that the relationship over the full range would be curvilinear. Some data obtained from an experiment in which different concentrations of saccharin served as the first and second substances support this suggestion. In this experiment, 0.15% was used as the second solution. For different groups of rats, the initial solution was 0.125%, 0.100%, 0.075%, or 0.05% saccharin. Contrast was obtained only in the last case – with the solution that was furthest away in concentration from the second solution; see Figure 5.8 (Flaherty & Rowan, 1986). These data appear to be inconsistent with the saccharin and sucrose series presented previously (Flaherty, Turovsky & Krauss, 1994). It could be the case that saccharin–saccharin pairings lead to different functional relationships than saccharin–sucrose or sucrose–sucrose pairings because the hedonic value of saccharin is not monotonically related to concentration, whereas that of sucrose is. It is also possible that the presence of calories in one of the solutions alters the contrast function – other studies have suggested that the caloric value of either the initial or the terminal substance does influence aspects of contrast (Flaherty, Grigson, Checke & Hnat, 1991; Lucas et al., 1990). An equally likely explanation is that different aspects of the hedonic value scale have been explored in these experiments. More parametric data are needed to fill in the gaps in these experiments.

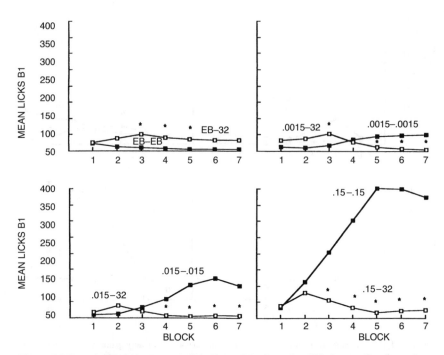

Figure 5.5 Data similar to those presented in Figure 5.4, except that different concentrations of saccharin were used as the initial solution and an empty bottle (EB) was used as the neutral condition instead of water. The pattern of results was similar to that reported in Figure 5.4. (From Flaherty, Turovsky & Krauss, 1994.)

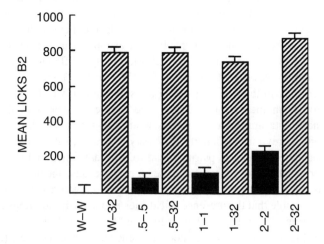

Figure 5.6 Mean lick frequency on the second bottle (B2) presented each day. The abscissa values represent both first- and second-bottle conditions of each group. Only the second-bottle lick data are presented here (the first-bottle data were presented in Figure 5.4). (From Flaherty, Turovsky & Krauss, 1994.)

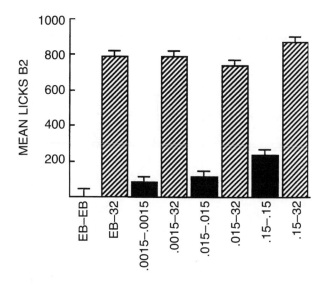

Figure 5.7. Second-bottle lick frequency data for the groups receiving saccharin. The abscissa values indicate both first- and second-bottle conditions for each group. Only the second-bottle lick data are illustrated here (the first-bottle data were presented in Figure 5.5). (From Flaherty, Turovsky & Krauss, 1994.)

Intersolution interval

Variations in the intersolution interval (ISI) in the anticipatory contrast procedure may serve as a means of assessing the time horizon over which animals make comparisons and judgments of relative food value in foraging (Lucas, Gawley & Timberlake, 1988). The data currently available suggest that anticipatory contrast diminishes as the interval between solutions increases, but a variety of factors may influence the details of this function.

One example of the ISI function is presented in Figure 5.9. In this experiment, reliable contrast was obtained with 1-, 5-, and 30-minute ISIs, but contrast was smaller with the longer interval (Flaherty & Checke, 1982). At the lower end, there is little or no difference in anticipatory contrast with ISIs of 0, 15 seconds, or 1 minute (Flaherty & Rowan, 1988, 1985).

The upper end of the ISI function is apparently modified by the relative novelty of the conditions under which the experiment is conducted. Thus, Lucas et al. (1988) obtained contrast over a 16-minute, but not a 32-minute interval, when the experiment was conducted in the animals' home cages, but contrast was obtained over 32 minutes when the experiment was conducted in a brightly illuminated, novel environment (which was the case in the Flaherty & Checke experiments). Another factor that influenced the ISI function in the Lucas et al. experiment was the delay time to the feeding of the daily ration following the

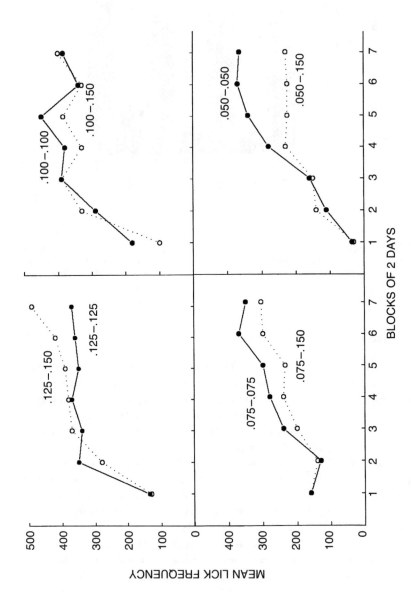

Figure 5.8 Effect of presenting different concentrations of saccharin in the first and second bottles in the anticipatory contrast procedure. Anticipatory negative contrast occurred only with the 0.050%-0.15% pairing. (From Flaherty & Rowan, 1986.)

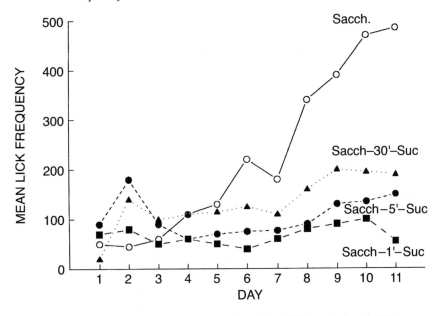

Figure 5.9 Anticipatory negative contrast produced by pairing 0.15% saccharin with 32% sucrose with different intersolution intervals (1, 5, or 30 minutes). The control group received only the initial saccharin solution. Contrast occurred in all conditions, but was reliably less with the 30-minute interval. (From Flaherty & Checke, 1982.)

end of the test session. When this ration was fed within 5 minutes after the end of the session, then contrast was obtained with a 32-minute ISI. However, when the ration was delayed for 90 minutes, no contrast was obtained with a 32-minute ISI (the postsession feeding time in the Flaherty and Checke experiments was approximately 20 minutes). This effect of postsession feeding suggests that the rats are able to integrate the relative value of three rewards/foods and adjust their behavior as a function of the temporal distribution of these substances.

Other factors that affect the ISI function include the deprivation condition of the animal and (apparently) the caloric value of the initial substance. Although contrast is readily obtained when there is a 30-minute interval between 0.15% saccharin and 32% sucrose, contrast is not obtained when there is a 5-minute interval between either 2% or 4% sucrose and 32% sucrose (Flaherty, Grigson, Checke & Hnat, 1991). Contrast is obtained with a 15-second ISI under both of these conditions. At first glance, it might seem that relative reward value is a factor in this result. However, the fact that 4% sucrose is preferred to 0.15% saccharin, but 0.15% saccharin is preferred to 2% sucrose (and yet the same ISI function is obtained with 2% and 4% sucrose in comparison with 0.15% saccharin), indicates that reward value is not the important factor in the ISI function in this case (Flaherty, Grigson, Checke & Hnat, 1991).

Deprivation condition, however, does influence the ISI function. When rats are food deprived (82% of free-feeding weight), contrast is obtained with a 15-second, but not a 5-minute, ISI with either 2% or 4% sucrose preceding 32% sucrose. However, if the rats are not deprived, contrast is obtained with a 5-minute ISI with either of these solutions preceding 32% sucrose. Deprivation condition does not influence the ISI function over the range of 15 seconds to 5 minutes when 0.15% saccharin precedes 32% sucrose (Flaherty, Grigson, Checke & Hnat, 1991). This effect of deprivation on sucrose–sucrose contrast, but not on saccharin–sucrose contrast, suggests that the animals may learn the caloric value of the initial substance, as well as relative hedonic value, and that the caloric value becomes important at long ISIs under conditions of food deprivation.

Access time

Contrast varies as a function of access time to the two solutions. When access times are equal in duration, then there is a curvilinear relationship, with greater contrast occurring with 2- or 3-minute access durations than with 1- or 10-minute access durations (Flaherty, Grigson, Coppotelli & Mitchell, 1996). These data are illustrated in Figure 5.10.

When access times are asymmetrical, the little data that are available suggest that long durations of access to the second substance enhance contrast, whereas long durations of access to the first substance decrease contrast. This pattern of results was obtained with access durations to the first and second solutions, respectively, of 3 minutes versus 3 minutes; 3 minutes versus 10 minutes; and 10 minutes versus 3 minutes (Flaherty, Grigson, Coppotelli & Mitchell, 1996).

Response contingency

If the availability of 32% sucrose is made contingent upon the performance of an instrumental response, such as running in a runway or pressing a lever, that response increases in probability. Why then does a contrast effect occur, rather than a reinforcement effect, in the .15-32 group compared to the .15-.15 group? Several experiments have suggested that contrast will occur only when there is a weak or nonexistent contingency.

The earliest anticipatory contrast experiments contained a nominal contingency between responding for the 0.15% saccharin and receipt of the 32% sucrose, in that a single lick on the bottle containing the saccharin was required to initiate the timer sequence that would eventually lead to the presentation of the second solution (see Flaherty & Checke, 1982). This minimal requirement was nonfunctional, however, because essentially the same results were obtained when a response-independent procedure was used (Flaherty & Grigson, 1988, experiment 1; Flaherty, Turovsky & Krauss, 1994).

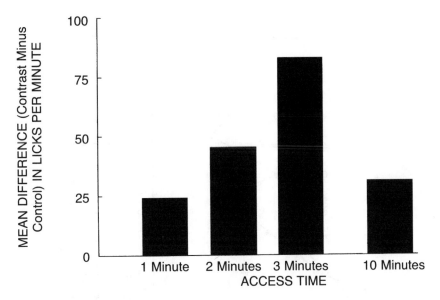

Figure 5.10 Degree of anticipatory contrast as a function of duration of access to the two solutions (0.15% saccharin versus 32% saccharin as the contrast group condition, and 0.15% saccharin versus 0.15% saccharin as the control group). Contrast was greatest with a 3-minute duration of access to each solution. (From Flaherty, Grigson, Coppotelli & Mitchell, 1995.)

In order to investigate the effects of contingency on contrast, a series of experiments was conducted with the imposition of a fixed lick requirement on the initial solution available (Flaherty & Grigson, 1988). One experiment compared a set of animals for whom an FR-200 lick contingency was in effect with a set of animals without a specific lick requirement (the first bottle was available for 3 minutes in this latter group). The results showed that the zero-contingency group showed a contrast effect in lick frequency (the .15-32 group licked less on the initial solution than did the .15-.15 control group) and also a contrast effect in latency to initiate licking on the first tube (the .15-32 group was slower than the .15-.15 group). A different result, facilitation rather than contrast, occurred in the FR-200 group. In this case, the .15-32 group initiated licking sooner than the .15-.15 group did. Similar results were obtained with lick contingencies of FR-10, FR-100, and FR-400 – the animals in the .15-32 groups initiated licking sooner than did the animals in the .15-.15 groups.

These experiments suggested that the imposition of a specific lick contingency would lead to reinforcement or facilitation rather than contrast. However, the comparison with the earlier, noncontingent experiments was not direct, because the initial solution was available for a considerably shorter time period in the lick-contingency experiments than in the duration experiments. In order to determine if time of availability was a factor, a yoked control procedure was

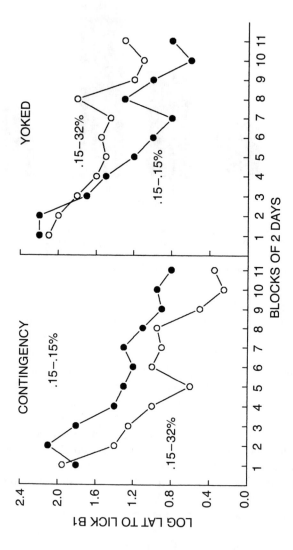

Figure 5.11 Log₁₀ latency to initiate licking on bottle 1 (0.15% saccharin) as a function of the following solution (more saccharin or 32% sucrose) and the contingency condition. The contingent group was required to make 200 licks before receiving the second solution. The animals in the yoked group received a duration of access to the first solution that was controlled by their yoked partners. These animals had no contingency requirement. The contingent group showed a facilitation (reinforcement) effect, whereas the yoked group showed a contrast effect. (From Flaherty & Grigson, 1988.)

used. In this experiment, one set of animals had an FR-200 lick requirement (.15-.15 and .15-32 groups). Animals in comparable solution conditions were yoked to animals in the FR-200 condition. Thus, the yoked animals had the same time of availability of the initial solution as the contingency animals, but without a specific lick requirement. The results of this experiment showed that the FR-200 group showed a reinforcement effect – shorter latency to initiate licking in the .15-32 group compared to the .15-.15 group; the yoked animals however, showed a contrast effect – longer latency to initiate licking in the .15-32 group than in the .15-.15 group. These data are illustrated in Figure 5.11.

Thus, the imposition of a specific lick contingency will override the rats' tendency to show contrast when a more palatable solution follows a less palatable solution in the absence of a response requirement.

Lesion effects

One study produced damage to the granule cells of the dentate area of the hippocampus by administration of the neurotoxin colchicine. This damage had no effect on the occurrence of anticipatory contrast (saccharin–sucrose, with a 1-minute ISI) or on the reversal of this contrast. This same lesion also did not affect successive negative contrast, although it did interfere with radial-maze learning (Flaherty, Rowan, Emerich & Walsh, 1989). Preliminary data also suggest that electrolytic lesions of the central nucleus of the amygdala do not affect anticipatory contrast (Coppotelli & Flaherty, 1994).

Drug effects

Anticipatory contrast has been relatively unexplored in terms of drug effects, but the available data are unanimous – the drugs investigated (chlordiazepoxide, cyproheptadine, buspirone, amphetamine, and fluoxetine) have not influenced contrast. Fluoxetine reduced both bottle 1 and bottle 2 sucrose intake (4% sucrose preceded 32% sucrose) but did not affect degree of contrast (Portugal et al., 1995). Conversely, chlordiazepoxide (6, 12, and 20 mg/kg) increased the intake of the initial saccharin solution, but this appetite-stimulating effect occurred equally in contrast and control groups – degree of contrast was not altered. Amphetamine tended to decrease intake of the saccharin, but there was no clear trend of an effect on contrast (Flaherty, Grigson & Rowan, 1986). The chlordiazepoxide data are illustrated in Figure 5.12.

The effects of both cyproheptadine and buspirone were assessed in the context of the hedonic series study previously described (Flaherty, Krauss & Turovsky, 1994). In this experiment, the effects of the drugs on contrast could be measured with both saccharin and sucrose as the initial substance. Cyproheptadine (3 and 6 mg/kg) increased lick frequency, but, generally, non-differentially in both contrast and control groups – it did not reduce contrast effects. This result was obtained with both saccharin and sucrose as the initial

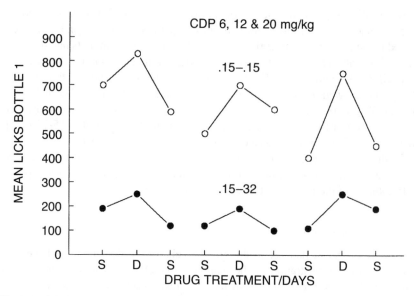

Figure 5.12 Effect of three doses of chlordiazepoxide (CDP) on anticipatory contrast. After contrast was established, the rats were given a series of 3-day cycles in which they received saline (S), CDP (D), and saline (S), in that order. The drug doses were given in ascending order. The CDP had an appetite-stimulating effect but did not influence contrast. (From Flaherty & Rowan, 1988.)

substance, but tended to be more pronounced at the higher concentrations of each substance (for example, 0.015% and 0.15% saccharin and 2% sucrose). Buspirone tended to decrease overall lick frequency, more so in the saccharin series than in the sucrose series, but the drug had no effect on contrast.

Of these four drugs investigated, two (chlordiazepoxide and cyproheptadine) were effective in reducing successive negative contrast, and two (buspirone and amphetamine) had no effect on successive negative contrast. The fact that none influenced anticipatory contrast suggests that the two types of contrast have a different psychopharmacology. The fact that neither the benzodiazepine anxiolytic (chlordiazepoxide) nor the nonbenzodiazepine anxiolytic (buspirone) affected anticipatory contrast suggests that this contrast model, unlike successive negative contrast, has nothing in common with animal models of anxiety.

Strain and species differences

The Maudsley Reactive (MR) and Maudsley Nonreactive (MNRA) rats differ in a variety of emotion-related tasks, with the MR strain typically the more responsive in these situations (Gray, 1987; also see Chapter 2). There was little difference, however, in the anticipatory contrast effects obtained in the two lines with lick frequency as the dependent variable (Rowan & Flaherty, 1991). There was, however, a substantial difference between the strains when latency to initiate licking was examined. In this case, the MNRA rats showed a contrast effect – longer latencies to initiate licking in the .15-32 group than in the .15-.15 group; however, the MR rats showed a reinforcement effect – shorter latencies to initiate licking in the .15-32 group than in the .15-.15 group. The reason for this difference in latency between the strains is unclear. To the extent that the typical differences between the strains represent a dimension of arousability (with the MR strain being more aroused than the MNRA strain – and this is not always clear; see Rowan & Flaherty, 1991), these results might suggest that inhibition or "patience" is involved in at least the latency measure of contrast.

The two lines selectively bred to differ in successive negative contrast in consummatory behavior (see Chapter 2) did not differ in anticipatory contrast under the parameters investigated – 4% sucrose followed by 32% sucrose with a 15-second ISI (Flaherty, Krauss, Rowan & Grigson, 1994).

Two selectively bred lines that did differ in anticipatory contrast were the Zucker lean and Zucker obese rats. In this case, the obese rats showed normal anticipatory contrast (4-32 versus 4-4) both when there was a 15-second and when there was a 5-minute ISI, but the lean rats showed contrast only with the 5-minute ISI. In this same experiment, the lean rats showed a slightly smaller successive negative contrast effect than did the obese rats (Flaherty, Krauss, & Hill, 1994).

There are virtually no comparative data using the anticipatory contrast paradigm. Goldfish, which show simultaneous contrast but not successive negative contrast, also do not show anticipatory contrast (Couvillon & Bitterman, 1985).

The strain and species comparison data are too fragmentary to permit any conclusions other than, perhaps, that there is no necessary relationship between SNC and negative anticipatory contrast (the Maudsley and Rutgers contrast rats differed in successive contrast, but not anticipatory contrast, at least in the consumption aspect of contrast, but the Zucker strains differed in both).

Theory of negative anticipatory contrast

Hedonic devaluation

The interpretation of negative anticipatory contrast in consummatory behavior was that the initial saccharin solution was devalued by its association with the subsequently occurring, and preferred, 32% sucrose solution (Flaherty & Checke, 1982; Flaherty & Rowan, 1985). Recent experiments, however, have cast doubt on this interpretation. The logic behind these experiments was that devaluation of the initial substance could be tested, in a within-S experiment, by pairing one cue with the initial substance when it predicted a better second substance and pairing a different cue with the initial substance when it did not predict a better second substance (e.g., $.15_{cue1}$-32 versus $.15_{cue2}$-.15). After contrast developed, devaluation of the initial substance could be tested in a preference test, in which the animals have a choice between the initial substances correlated with their respective cues.

If contrast is caused by devaluation, then the animals should consume less of the initial substance paired with the cue that predicts the better second substance.

This logic was used in a series of 14 experiments that provided no evidence in favor of the devaluation hypothesis (Flaherty, Coppotelli, Grigson, Mitchell & Flaherty, 1995). In 12 experimental conditions in which flavors or odors were used as signals for different reward conditions (.15-.15 versus .15-32, or .15-.15 versus .15-chocolate milk, or .15-no solution versus .15-chocolate milk), anticipatory contrast occurred in none, but a conditioned preference for the cue signalling 32% sucrose developed in 8 of the experimental conditions. Thus, this subset of experiments indicated that flavor/odor cues could not be used to test the devaluation hypothesis, because they seemed to preclude the occurrence of contrast, perhaps by conditioning flavor/odor preferences instead.

Anticipatory contrast did develop in all five experiments in which context, temporal alternation, or drinking-spout cues were used. There was a conditioned preference for the cue signalling 32% sucrose in one of four tests made in the three spout-cue studies. None of the studies in which contrast occurred provided evidence that the cue correlated with the saccharin solution that signalled 32% sucrose was devalued. Findings in general agreement with these were reported by Lucas and Timberlake (1992). The demonstration of contrast in the absence of any evidence of devaluation suggests that devaluation of the initial substance may not be the mechanism by which suppressed intake occurs in negative anticipatory contrast. The finding that the preference data did not reflect the acquisition behavior (that is, the cue/solution that was suppressed in acquisition may be preferred in the choice test) is consistent with a conclusion reached by Williams (1991, 1992a, 1992b) in regard to behavioral contrast. When a variable interval (VI) schedule was followed by extinction, Williams found a higher response rate than when the VI schedule was followed by another VI component; however, in a choice test, the animals preferred a cue correlated with a following VI schedule rather than one correlated with a following extinction schedule. Thus, there was a dissociation between response rate measures and choice.

As reasons for the dissociation between responding and choice, Williams speculated that choice (or value) is under the control of Pavlovian (predictive) contingencies, whereas response rate is under the control of operant contingencies (Nevin, Smith & Roberts, 1987). This perspective seems to be inapplicable to consummatory contrast data, because there is no explicit operant contingency involved in licking for the first solution and, if one is imposed, then contrast is replaced by a facilitation effect (Flaherty & Grigson, 1988). However, the hypothesis that performance in the choice test is governed by the signalling function of the cues paired with the solutions, rather than by the hedonic value of the solutions, is an appealing one. There is some support for the separability of these two functions in the taste aversion literature (Garcia and Hankins, 1977). However, a test for this hypothesis within the context of anticipatory contrast remains to be devised.

Although there are still some puzzles regarding the meaning of the preference test, studies using consummatory and operant techniques all lead to the same conclusion – devaluation is not the mechanism by which anticipatory contrast is produced (E. D. Capaldi & Sheffer, 1992; Flaherty, Coppotelli, Grigson, Mitchell & Flaherty, 1995; Lucas & Timberlake, 1992; Williams, 1991, 1992a, 1992b).

Response competition

A potential theoretical alternative to devaluation is response competition – the spatial separation of the first and second solutions may produce a lowered response rate for the initial solution because approach responses to the location of the impending higher-valued solution may interfere with consuming the less - valued solution. Indeed, informal observation of the rats in our experiments suggests that the animals do spend time in the vicinity of the second solution before it becomes available.

However, spatial competition correlated with environmental cues cannot account for all cases of anticipatory contrast, because contrast has occurred when both solutions were introduced via the same access hole (Flaherty & Checke, 1982, experiment 3). Furthermore, data from our laboratory (Flaherty, Grigson, Coppotelli, & Mitchell, 1996) have shown that contrast is reduced when both solutions are introduced in the same location, compared to when they are spa-

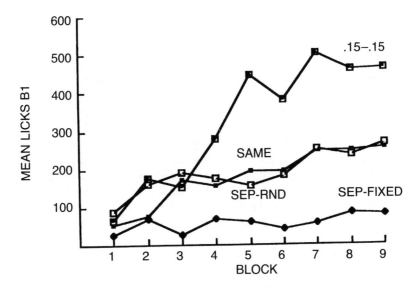

Figure 5.13 Degree of anticipatory contrast as a function of spatial separation of the first and second bottles. The three contrast groups received 0.15% saccharin followed by 32% sucrose. In Group "Same," the two solutions were presented sequentially through a center access hole; in Group "SEP-Fixed," the two solutions always appeared in the same locations on opposite sides of the cage; in Group "SEP-Random," the solutions also appeared on opposite sides of the cage, but whether the first bottle was on the left or right was varied randomly across days. The control group represents the average of these three conditions for the control (.15-.15) animals. (From Flaherty, Grigson, Coppotelli & Mitchell, 1996.)

tially separate, but contrast is still reliable and substantial in the former case. This effect is illustrated in Figure 5.13, which shows degree of contrast obtained when (a) the first and second solutions always occurred at the same, spatially separated, locations; (b) the first and second solutions occurred at spatially separated locations, but the location of the first and second solutions changed randomly from trial to trial; and (c) the two solutions occurred at the same location.

Although contrast was greatest with the consistent spatial separation of the two solutions, it occurred in all conditions. Thus, spatial separation is not necessary – an outcome also clearly indicated by the experiments in the laboratories of E. D. Capaldi, Timberlake, and B. Williams.

In another experiment, the two solutions were presented in opposite arms of a T-maze and the time that the animals spent in each arm was recorded. This experiment showed that reliable anticipatory contrast in the animals' approach behavior (to the arm containing the 32% solution) occurred, across trials, *prior to* contrast in lick frequency. However, there was no necessary relation between the two measures, because contrast in lick frequency developed within a 3-minute access period to the first bottle without a corresponding increase in approach to the alternative arm (where 32% sucrose would eventually appear) (Flaherty, Grigson, Coppotelli & Mitchell, 1996).

Overall, these data indicate that response competition may sometimes function to enhance anticipatory contrast (see also Timberlake, Gawley & Lucas, 1987), but it seems unlikely that it is the sole cause of such contrast.

Inhibition

An alternative interpretation is that the intake of the first substance may become inhibited when the presentation of an acceptable solution is followed by a preferred solution. One result that may indicate the presence of inhibition occurred when a series of different initial solutions were paired with 32% sucrose as the second solution. The largest degree of anticipatory negative contrast occurred when either 0.15% saccharin or 2% sucrose preceded the 32% sucrose, compared to lower concentrations of either sucrose or saccharin. The data suggesting that this suppression of intake of the initial solution might be related to inhibition occurred in consumption of the 32% sucrose that served as the second solution: The groups that showed the largest suppression of Bottle 1 intake consumed the most 32% sucrose in Bottle 2 (Flaherty, Turovsky & Krauss, 1994 – see Figures 5.6 and 5.7). This effect could be related to a rebound from inhibition mechanism (Nevin, 1973).

One potential test of the role of inhibition in anticipatory negative contrast is to use disinhibitory drugs. For example, anxiolytics such as the benzodiazepines are widely considered to be disinhibitory (see Sepinwall, 1985) in animal models of anxiety and conflict. However, chlordiazepoxide (8, 16, and 20 mg/kg) had no effect on between-S anticipatory negative contrast, even though it did have an appetite-stimulating effect – elevating the lick frequency of contrast and control groups equivalently (Flaherty & Rowan, 1988). This is quite different from the effect of chlordiazepoxide in successive negative contrast, where it, and other benzodiazepines, have potent disinhibitory effects (Flaherty, 1991b).

Chlordiazepoxide's lack of effect in anticipatory contrast parallels a similar failure of benzodiazepines to affect positive conditioned suppression (Miczek, 1973; Poling, Urbain & Thompson, 1977). Positive conditioned suppression bears some similarity to anticipatory contrast; behavior related to the attainment of a reward is suppressed by signals of an impending "free" reward (see, for example, Locurto, Norris, Cataldo & Laplace, 1981). Also, like anticipatory contrast, competing behaviors may account for at least some of the behavioral suppression (see Karpicke, 1978). However, also as in anticipatory contrast, if inhibition is involved, it is apparently of a type that is insensitive to the disinhibitory properties of the benzodiazepines.

A different pharmacological approach is suggested by the research of Soubrie and colleagues (for example, Soubrie, 1986). Soubrie has suggested that aspects of the serotonergic transmitter system may be involved in impulse control in situations not necessarily correlated with anxiety – a description that could apply to anticipatory negative contrast where the animals are essentially waiting for a better reward. However, the pharmacological evidence that is available is again negative. Neither cyproheptadine, a general serotonin antagonist, nor buspirone, a serotonin$_{1A}$ agonist, had an effect on anticipatory contrast (Flaherty, Turovsky & Krauss, 1994). Both drugs did affect consumption, with cyproheptadine producing an appetite-stimulating effect and buspirone tending to suppress intake, but neither drug differentially affected contrast and control conditions. The serotonin system is quite complicated, and it would be premature to draw any final conclusions based on the use of these two drugs. Nevertheless, the evidence suggests that inhibition mediated via a serotonergic pathway is probably not involved in anticipatory negative contrast.

Given the fairly strong evidence against both devaluation and competing responses as mediators of contrast, it is difficult to abandon the hypothesis of an inhibitory process as a causative agent in the behavioral suppression associated with anticipatory contrast. Perhaps inhibition associated with "waiting" for a preferred substance, *while in the presence of an acceptable substance,* has not been adequately conceptualized or characterized behaviorally and psychopharmacologically; further understanding of the mechanisms of anticipatory contrast await these advances.

Summary and conclusions

Negative anticipatory contrast is a robust phenomenon: (a) It develops quickly with a between-S design, within a few pairings of 0.15% saccharin and 32% sucrose; (b) it may be demonstrated statistically with a small number of rats; (c) it quite readily develops within-subjects when contextual stimuli are differentially paired with the contrast and control conditions; (d) it varies in an orderly and systematic fashion with changes in the reward characteristics of the two solutions, with the ISI, with access time, and, apparently, with the caloric value of the solutions; (e) it is readily replaced by a facilitation or reinforcement effect when a lick contingency is imposed; and (f) it is not altered by any drug or lesion treatment thus far investigated.

Anticipatory contrast may reflect processes normally used by a foraging animal – processes such as the relative evaluation of current and future food sources and the time/effort involved in obtaining the future food substance. Apparently analogous effects have also been obtained in the food consumption of children in laboratory situations (see, for example, Birch, 1991; Birch, Marlin & Rotter, 1984).

The fact that contrast is defined in terms of suppressed intake might seem to be *prima facie* evidence of devaluation as a mechanism by which contrast is produced. However, attempts to provide a deeper meaning to devaluation through the use of preference tests have produced data that do not support the hypothesis. Furthermore, if suppressed intake reflects devaluation, does enhanced intake seen with a lick contingency, and in some pairings of solution concentrations and ISIs (such as Flaherty, Grigson, Checke & Hnat, 1991), reflected enhanced valuation?

Some variation on the concept of inhibition may be the best current approach to understanding anticipatory contrast, but inhibition of behavior in the presence of a satisfactory substance while waiting for a better one will have a different psychology and neurobiology than inhibition produced by impending aversive events.

Positive anticipatory contrast

The story here is brief – there have been no demonstrations of positive anticipatory contrast in consummatory behavior. We have attempted to obtain positive anticipatory contrast by presenting a 4% solution that preceded a 2% solution. However, positive anticipatory contrast did not occur, even though a negative anticipatory contrast occurred in the same experiment when the 4% solution was followed by an 8% solution. Other experiments have examined 8% sucrose versus 2% sucrose, and 12% sucrose versus 0.15% saccharin, with similarly negative results.

Paradoxically, an operant version of positive anticipatory contrast is readily demonstrable with pigeons and may be obtained with rats, under certain specific conditions. These data will be considered when behavioral contrast is addressed in Chapter 6.

Simultaneous contrast

If rats are allowed brief, repeated access to two sucrose solutions of different concentrations, their consumption of both solutions may be altered compared to

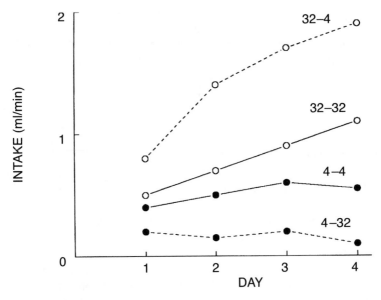

Figure 5.14 Simultaneous positive and negative contrast. Intake of 32% sucrose was greater when it was paired with 4% sucrose as the alternative solution than when it was paired with more 32% as the alternative solution, and intake of 4% sucrose was less when it was paired with 32% sucrose as the alternative solution than when it was paired with 4% as the alternative solution. The period of access was 6 minutes (total) per day in alternating 1-minute periods for each solution. (From Flaherty & Largen, 1975.)

when each solution is presented in isolation. The procedural difference between this paradigm and that of the anticipatory contrast effect paradigm, is that the animals are given repeated access to each solution within a short time period. As a consequence of this procedure, there is the possibility that intake of each solution may be influenced by peripheral taste factors, such as sensory adaptation, as well as by central mechanisms of contrast.

Use of this procedure permits the demonstration of rapidly developing positive and negative contrast effects, both between groups and within the same rats. Figure 5.14 illustrates intake when separate groups of rats were given 32% sucrose in both tubes, 4% sucrose in both tubes, or 32% in one tube and 4% in the other. Each tube was available for 1 minute and was then immediately replaced by the alternative tube (in a different spatial location) for 1 minute, and so on, until both tubes had been presented a total of three times. As illustrated, the rats that had access to both 32% and 4% sucrose consumed more of the 32% than rats that had only 32% (positive contrast) and consumed less of the 4% than rats that had only 4% (negative contrast) (Flaherty & Largen, 1975).

Contrast also develops rapidly with even briefer exposure to the two solutions on each presentation (15 seconds or 45 seconds) (Flaherty & Avdzej,

1974).[2] In addition to consumption measures, simultaneous contrast effects occur in latency to initiate intake, and they tend to increase in degree with repeated access to each solution (Flaherty & Avdzej, 1974; Flaherty & Largen, 1975). These data suggest that the simultaneous procedure may be more sensitive to contrast than either the successive or anticipatory contrast methods. This suggestion is supported by a study in which successive, simultaneous, and anticipatory contrast effects were investigated with four different pairs of saccharin concentrations. Negative anticipatory contrast developed with only one pair of concentrations (0.05%-0.05% versus 0.05%-0.15%) and successive negative contrast developed with two shift conditions (0.15% to either 0.075% or 0.05%), whereas simultaneous contrast developed to both of these pairs and also when 0.10% and 0.125% saccharin solutions were paired with 0.15% saccharin (Flaherty & Rowan, 1986).

This apparent greater sensitivity of simultaneous contrast to reward differences may reflect at least three aspects of this procedure: the opportunity for direct sensory interactions between the paired solutions (see, for example, Bartoshuk & Gent, 1984; Bartoshuk, McBurney & Pfaffman, 1964; Green & Lawless, 1991; Miller & Bartoshuk, 1991), the repeated opportunity for comparison of the two solutions within a short time period, and the reduced memory load necessary to make comparisons.

There has been little parametric research conducted with the simultaneous contrast procedure. Available data indicate that simultaneous contrast develops equivalently in free-fed and food-deprived rats (Flaherty, Lombardi, Kapust, & D'Amato, 1977); it is not influenced by chlordiazepoxide, imipramine, scopolamine, or sodium amobarbital (Flaherty, Becker & Driscoll, 1982; Flaherty, Lombardi, Kapust & D'Amato, 1977; Flaherty & Meinrath, 1979; Flaherty, Wrightson, Deptula & Duston, 1979); it is not subject to disinhibition by a novel stimulus (as is successive negative contrast – Lombardi & Flaherty, 1978); and it is present in very young rats (30 days) and does not change a great deal developmentally (30, 51, 72, 90 days of age), except that the positive contrast component tends to increase somewhat (Fagen & Shoemaker, 1979). A contrast effect that seems directly analogous to simultaneous contrast is present in human infants tested at an average age of 70 hours. In this study, 15% sucrose was alternated in 5-minute periods with either water or a sucking opportunity in which no fluid was present. In the case of the alternation with water, a negative contrast, but not a positive contrast, was present. Negative contrast also occurred in the case of alternation with the no-fluid condition, but positive contrast was not examined in this experiment (Kobre & Lipsitt, 1972). Thus, simultaneous contrast is present in very young humans and rats.

A close analysis of licking parameters indicates that two different behavioral mechanisms may underlie negative and positive simultaneous contrast. Under

[2]In these experiments, the same subjects were exposed to both contrast and control conditions, but on different days. Thus, on one day both tubes contained 32% sucrose, on another both contained 4% sucrose, and on a third and fourth day, one tube contained 4% sucrose and the other 32%, with the spatial location counterbalanced across days.

control conditions (when both available tubes have the same solution), the higher lick frequency for a 32% sucrose solution than for a 4% solution is mediated both by more licking bursts (3.95 versus 2.80 per 30-second access period) and a greater number of licks per burst. The decreased licking characteristic of negative contrast is mediated by a decrease in the number of bursts (2.80 to 1.99), a decrease in the number of licks per burst, and a decrease in burst duration. This is not the same licking microstructure that occurs in SNC. As reported in Chapter 2, the shift from high to low sucrose solutions produces an *increase* in the number of licking bursts, but a decrease in licks per burst (Grigson, Spector & Norgren, 1993). This difference in licking pattern supports the pharmacological data in suggesting that SNC and simultaneous negative contrast are different phenomena.

The enhanced licking characteristic of positive contrast was mediated by increased burst length, increased number of licks per burst, and decreased interburst interval. The number of bursts per se did not change – which may indicate that this parameter is maximal under absolute reward conditions for 32% sucrose and is not free to vary when the 32% is compared with a lower sucrose concentration (Fagen, Rycek, Ritz & Shoemaker, 1983).

Simultaneous contrast varies in an orderly fashion with the concentration of sucrose available for comparison. This orderliness is shown in three ways in Figures 5.15 and 5.16. In this experiment (Flaherty & Sepanak, 1978), rats were exposed to four different pairs of sucrose solutions (32% versus 2%; 32% versus

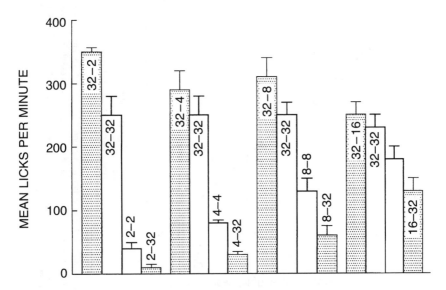

Figure 5.15 Simultaneous positive and negative contrast in lick frequency as a function of sucrose pairings (32-2 represents lick frequency for 32% sucrose when the alternative solution was 2% sucrose, etc.). The same animals experienced all sucrose conditions following a Latin-Square plan. Alternating 1-minute access periods were given within each solution pairing for a total of 3 minutes of each solution. Data for the last 4 minutes of each 6-minute session are presented. (From Flaherty & Sepanak, 1978.)

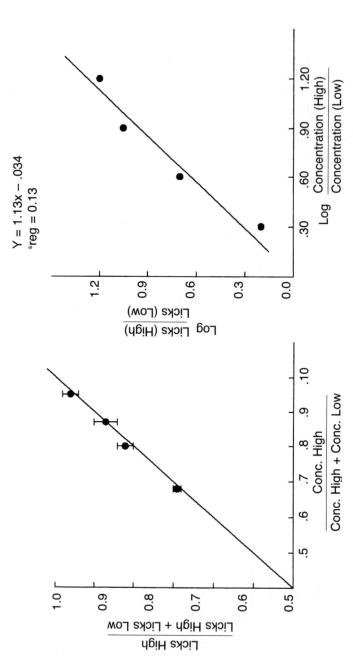

Figure 5.16 Left-hand panel: Same data as presented in Figure 5.15, analyzed in terms of the proportion of licks made to the higher concentration of each pair as a function of the proportion of total concentration available represented by the solution; (for example, the abscissa value for the 32 versus 2 condition would be 0.96 (32/([32 + 2])). Proportion of licks tended to match proportion of concentration available. The right-hand panel presents the same data, but plotted as $\log_{10}$ ratios of licks against concentrations. The regression equation indicates a good fit to a power function. (From Flaherty & Sepanak, 1978.)

4%; 32% versus 8%; and 32% versus 16%) in a within-subjects simultaneous contrast experiment. Figure 5.15 illustrates how contrast in lick frequency varies as a function of the concentration disparity. The left-hand panel of Figure 5.16 illustrates the same data plotted in terms of the proportion of total licks made to each solution as a function of the proportion of concentration available from the solution – proportion of intake matches proportion of concentration available even though the rats were free to lick or not lick at each tube.

Finally, the right-hand panel of Figure 5.16 illustrates the same data plotted in terms of $\log_{10}$ ratios of lick frequency to concentration ratios. The exponent of the antilog version of the linear regression function ($Y = 0.92X^{1.13}$) lies within the range (1.0–1.30) of exponents typically obtained in judgments of relative sweetness made by humans when the magnitude estimation procedure is used (Meiselman, 1971; Moskowitz, 1973; Stevens, 1969). Thus, the simultaneous contrast procedure may obtain estimates of sensory function parallel to those obtained in humans using magnitude estimation scaling techniques.

Another study in which different sucrose concentration pairs were examined (16% versus 2%; 16% versus 4%, 16% versus 8%; 16% versus 12%) found a similar exponent of the power function – 1.15 (Flaherty & Kaplan, 1979).

The similarity of these data to human sweetness judgments may be superficial or it may suggest similar psychophysical processes. The finding that simultaneous contrast is not influenced by any drug thus far tested, nor by a disinhibiting stimulus, is consistent with the possibility that contrast effects that occur in this procedure primarily reflect primitive sensory interactions. Indeed, recent unpublished data obtained from single-unit recordings in the nucleus tractus solitarious, the first relay station from the tongue in the taste system, indicate that negative and positive contrast effects may be obtained at that level, in single neurons, when an analogue of the simultaneous contrast procedure is used in anesthetized rats (Grigson and Norgren, unpublished data). However, the nucleus of the solitary tract has reciprocal connections with higher taste centers, including the amygdala; therefore, it is too early to exclude the involvement of higher centers in simultaneous contrast.

The application of this procedure to the analysis of contrast effects that might occur when different foods are mixed during meal consumption by humans remains to be determined.

Summary and conclusions

Simultaneous contrast may capture aspects of both successive contrast and anticipatory contrast, while also containing a unique component. Procedural considerations alone suggest that the simultaneous procedure provides the opportunity for both successive and anticipatory contrast. Also, there is evidence that an aspect of SNC can occur in the simultaneous negative contrast procedure (Flaherty & Largen, 1975). Some degree of commonality might also be suggested by the finding that the two Maudsley strains of rats differed in all three types of consummatory contrast (successive, anticipatory, and simultaneous), and in the same direction – the Reactive rats showing smaller contrast than the Nonreactive rats. The general similarity of reward disparity effects in all the paradigms[3] could also suggest common mechanisms. However, similarity in response to magnitude disparity may be a characteristic of *comparison,* whether it be in value in any of the three reward contrast procedures discussed thus far, or perhaps even in sensory contrast. Another way in which the three paradigms are similar is that, in all three, contrast seems to endure as long as animals are exposed to the different reward conditions.[4]

There is also evidence that each of the three reward contrast procedures contains an element of independence. For example, the finding that drugs (such as chlordiazepoxide) with potent effects on SNC do not influence either anticipatory contrast or simultaneous contrast argues strongly for a separation of mechanisms. Sodium amobarbital antagonizes SNC on both the first and second postshift days, but it does not affect simultaneous contrast. Also, cyproheptadine, which has potent effects on SNC, does not affect anticipatory contrast – suggesting different mechanisms in these two procedures.

There are other scattered items of evidence suggesting different mechanisms: A novel stimulus will disinhibit, to a degree, SNC, but not simultaneous contrast; rats selectively bred to show large or small SNC do not differ in anticipatory contrast; the Syracuse High Avoidance and Low Avoidance rats, which differ in SNC, do not differ in simultaneous contrast; and the three procedures seem differentially sensitive to reward disparity, with simultaneous contrast being more sensitive than SNC, which is more sensitive than anticipatory contrast, at least in the case of saccharin–saccharin shifts.

Curiously, no distinguishing lesion effects have been uncovered: Septal lesions do not affect SNC or simultaneous contrast; hippocampal lesions do not affect SNC in consummatory behavior or anticipatory contrast (but they do affect SNC in instrumental behavior); amygdala lesions and lesions of the parabrachial nucleus reduce SNC contrast, but their effects on other types of contrast have not been fully evaluated.

A reasonable, if tentative, conclusion at this stage of research would seem to be that there are at least three ways in which the comparison of rewarding stimuli may be made – retrograde, anterograde, or concurrently – and that different mechanisms may be involved in all three cases of reward relativity. The successive procedure may contain important search and emotional components; the anticipatory contrast procedure may contain an important associative component and lack an aversive emotional aspect; and the simultaneous procedure may be heavily influenced by sensory interactions.

[3] In general, the greater the disparity, the greater the contrast. However, anticipatory contrast may be more complex, with a curvilinear relationship, and simultaneous contrast seems to be the most orderly.

[4] It is true that SNC dissipates within 2 or 3 days following a shift. However, the repeated-shift studies show that repeatedly exposing the animals to different rewards will continue to produce SNC. Thus, SNC also endures as long as the animals have the opportunity to make frequent comparisons. This effect, though, may be more robust in consummatory contrast than in instrumental contrast.

6   Contrast with differential conditioning in runway and operant tasks

The increased [responding] characteristic of [positive behavioral] contrast that occurs during S⁺ [needs] an explanation because we cannot see the point of it. We must either find out what its point is, or discover that it has none, in which case we need some account of what has gone wrong with the animal's behavior.

– T. M. Bloomfield, 1969

Sometimes it seems as if animals are genetically programmed to puzzle human beings, especially psychologists.

– Lewis Thomas, 1983

Differential conditioning in runways

The successive and anticipatory contrast effects considered in earlier chapters were concerned with the extent to which animals compare rewards received at different times. Studies of contrast obtained in differential conditioning are largely concerned with the comparison of rewards received in different stimulus contexts – comparison over place (as well as time, in most experiments). The apparatus of choice in these experiments has been runways that differ in brightness. Thus, rats rewarded at the end of a black runway and not rewarded at the end of a white runway will soon demonstrate faster running in the black runway. The animals are not afforded a choice in differential conditioning experiments of this type – when placed in each alley they are faced with a go, no-go task. Differential responding also may develop if animals are rewarded in both alleys, but to different degrees. Contrast may occur under these conditions of differential reward amounts.

The first demonstration of such contrast was by Bower (1961). One group, the differential conditioning group, was rewarded with eight pellets in one alley and with one pellet in the alternative alley. One control group received one pellet in both alleys, and another control group received eight pellets in both alleys. The group that received eight pellets and one pellet eventually ran faster in the alley brightness correlated with the eight pellets. Their running speed in the alley in which they received one pellet was not only slower than the speed in the alley for eight pellets, it was also slower than that of the control group that received only the one-pellet reward. This result is termed simultaneous negative contrast (SimNC). The differential group did not run faster for eight pellets than did the control group that received only eight pellets. Thus, there was no evidence for simultaneous positive contrast (SimPC). Bower's results were illustrated in Figure 1.4. A study of contrast in differential conditioning by Ludvigson and Gay (1967) showed that this type of contrast is greatest in the start region of the run-way – where the differential cues are first encountered as the animals leave the neutral gray start box and enter the runways that are either black or white, each signalling different rewards. This result is illustrated in Figure 6.1. Similar results were obtained in an L-shaped maze in which the differential cues were not visible until the rats turned the corner of the "L." It was at this point that the neg-ative contrast became apparent (Chechile & Fowler, 1973). The rats running to the goal box took longer to get there for the small reward than did the small reward control group but, this was not simply because of slow running. The ani-mals, upon encountering the small-reward cue, would often turn back to the start box and scratch on the door. These competing or searching behaviors did not occur until after the animals had learned the discrimination (Chechile & Fowler, 1973). These behaviors are similar to those first noted by Crespi (1942 – see Chapter 1) in his SNC experiment and suggest a similarity in the mechanisms producing SNC and SimNC.

The topic of contrast in differential conditioning has been covered in several review papers (Black, 1968; Cox, 1975; Dachowski & Brazier, 1991; Dunham, 1968; Flaherty, 1982; Mackintosh, 1974). Perhaps because the procedure is time consuming, differential conditioning in runway behavior is not currently a method of choice for the study of contrast. An exhaustive review of the older lit-erature will not be presented here. Instead, the main issues, results, and theories will be briefly presented.

Both positive and negative simultaneous contrast?

Bower's study demonstrated SimNC but not SimPC. This is pretty much the state of the literature – negative contrast has been obtained frequently and reli-ably; positive contrast has been elusive (Flaherty, 1982, p. 412). The few stud-ies that have obtained SimPC used special techniques. Thus, positive contrast has been obtained when all rewards are delayed 20 seconds, perhaps eliminat-ing a "ceiling effect" artifact due to the large-reward control group's running at maximum speed (see Chapter 2; Calef, Calef, Maxwell & McHewitt, 1975; Mellgren, Wrather & Dyck, 1972). Another factor that may enhance the likeli-hood of detecting SimPC is the reduction in "decision time" afforded by hav-ing the differential alley cues present in the start box (rather than having both start boxes equal and neutral – the usual procedure) and by presenting the large- and small-reward trials in a predictable manner (regularly alternating or on separate days) (Mellgren et al., 1972; Mellgren & Dyck, 1974). These pro-

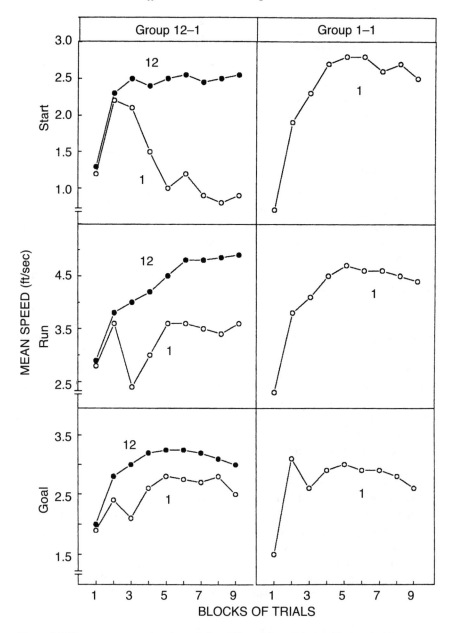

Figure 6.1 Mean start, run, and goal speeds in a differential conditioning, black and white runway study. The left column illustrates data for rats given 12 pellets correlated with one of the cues and 1 pellet correlated with the alternative cue. The right column presents data from control animals given 1 pellet in both cue conditions. The differential group (12 versus 1) ran slower for the 1-pellet reward than did the control group, but the difference occurred primarily in the start measure – where the animals first encountered the differential cues. (From Ludvigson & Gay, 1967.)

cedures may reduce any hesitancy that might occur in the differential conditioning groups related to determining which reward value is correlated with the
particular runway condition. The control groups would not be exposed to any
such retarding effects because they experience only one reward level.

These studies suggest that it is possible to obtain both SimPC and SimNC,
but there has been no systematic research other than demonstrations. Thus, the
following discussion of contrast in differential conditioning will be restricted to
issues related to SimNC.

Parameters

As is the case in all other forms of contrast, SimNC generally varies directly with
degree of reward disparity (see Davenport, 1962; Ludvigson & Gay, 1966;
Mackinnon, 1968; Matsumoto, 1969; Spear & Spitzner, 1966). Deprivation condition has not been systematically investigated.

The little data that exist suggest that degree of SimNC varies inversely with
intertrial interval (Haggbloom, 1979; Spear & Pavlik, 1966; Spear & Spitzner,
1966). This is a potentially interesting variable, because contrast must depend on
the comparison of the two rewards and this comparison should be influenced by
the time between rewards. As discussed in Chapter 2, SNC varies inversely with
retention interval, but the time parameter there is in days. Anticipatory contrast
also seems to vary inversely with the interval between the first and second solution (see Chapter 5), but, in this case, the effective range is in minutes. Because
contrast in differential conditioning might be composed of elements of both SNC
and anticipatory contrast, intertrial interval data might be a useful tool to investigate the relative contributions of the two processes (anterograde versus retrograde comparisons).

Use of either partial reward or varied magnitude of reward in the S+ condition (large-reward trials) reduces the degree of SimNC obtained on the small-
reward trials (McHose, 1970; McHose, McHewitt & Peters, 1972). These results
reflect the reward disparity factor and are consistent with the idea that negative
contrast is related to the average of the rewards experienced in the comparison
condition (see Chapters 2 and 4).

Simultaneous negative contrast may be obtained when the reward in the S-
condition is equivalent to that in the S+ condition but its delivery is delayed for
some time after the animal reaches the goal box (Beery, 1968; Chechile &
Fowler, 1973; Gavelek & McHose, 1970; Mackintosh & Lord, 1973; Sgro,
Glotfelty & Podlesni, 1969). This finding is consistent with the hypothesis that
delay reduces the incentive value of the reward.

The little evidence that is available suggests that discrepancies in percentage
of rewarded trials will also produce SimNC in runway behavior (McHose &
Peters, 1973).

Simultaneous negative contrast occurs in runway behavior when two different sucrose concentrations are used as S+ and S- (Flaherty, Riley & Spear, 1973).
This is noteworthy because SNC does not occur in runway behavior with differ-

ent sucrose rewards (see Chapter 2; Flaherty, 1982; Flaherty, Riley & Spear, 1973), suggesting that some form of immediate comparison is necessary to obtain instrumental contrast with variations in sucrose concentration – a condition that is not necessary for contrast in consummatory behavior.

In regard to comparative studies, SimNC seems to have more phylogenetic generality than SNC (see Chapter 2), occurring in goldfish and turtles, as well as in birds and mammals (see Burns, Woodard, Henderson & Bitterman, 1974; Gonzalez & Champlin, 1974; Gonzalez & Powers, 1973; Pert & Gonzalez, 1974).

Summary

Differential conditioning studies show that rewards received in one context affect the incentive value of rewards received in a somewhat different context. The factors affecting negative contrast in differential conditioning (contrast across context) seem to be largely the same as those affecting SNC (which is contrast across time). There is a suggestion, however, that the contrast in differential conditioning may be more general than SNC because (a) it apparently occurs across a broader phylogenetic spectrum; (b) it occurs with sucrose solutions as well as solid food; and (c) it seems to be more readily obtainable with differences in delay of reward than is SNC.

The degree to which contrast is trans-situational has not been tested in the extreme. Contrast in runway behavior will occur if rats are given 32% sucrose in a plastic box in one room and given 4% sucrose at the end of a runway in a different room (Flaherty & Avdzej, 1976), and contrast in lever-pressing behavior may be obtained if the reward for wheel running is changed (Premack, 1969). Chechile and Fowler (1973) found that contrast developed more slowly with a difficult discrimination (small difference between S+ and S- cues) than with an easy discrimination, but final degree of contrast was equivalent in both levels of difficulty. There is reason to think that there would be limits to the degree that rewards interact across space (as there is across time). However, these limits have not been widely explored for contrast with differential conditioning.

Behavioral contrast

Multiple schedules

The study of reward interactions using multiple schedules is, in principle, quite similar to the study of reward interactions using black and white runways. However, the data and theories that evolved around the two procedures are quite different.

Behavioral contrast was first recognized by Reynolds (1961) as an accompaniment of discrimination learning when pigeons were trained on multiple schedules. In a multiple schedule, there are usually two stimuli, each correlated with a particular schedule of reinforcement. These stimuli are presented alternately, and the rate at which the subject responds in the presence of each stimulus is measured. The acquisition of a discrimination is indicated when the subject responds at a higher rate in the presence of the stimulus correlated with the highest rate of available reinforcement. An example of behavioral contrast is presented in Figure 6.2 (Halliday & Boakes, 1971). In the first stage of this experiment, the response key was either blank or contained an angled line. Response rates were approximately equivalent in the first stage of the experiment (labelled VI-1, VI-1), when responding to either stimulus was reinforced at the same rate. In the second stage of the experiment, the reinforcement schedule in effect in the presence of the line was changed to extinction. Subsequently, response rate declined in the presence of the line stimulus. Of particular interest is the response rate during the blank stimulus – this response rate increased even though the reinforcement schedule had not changed. This increase above the previous baseline is termed positive behavioral contrast.

In general, positive behavioral contrast may be obtained by holding constant the density of reinforcement in one component of a multiple schedule (S+) and decreasing the density of reinforcement in the alternative component (S-). Positive behavioral contrast is defined in terms of an increase in response rate in the *unchanged* component above the baseline rate prevailing prior to the shift (or in terms of greater responding to the unchanged component in a shifted group, compared to an unshifted control group; for example, see Mackintosh, Little & Lord, 1972).

The initial demonstrations of behavioral contrast were of interest because positive behavioral contrast is contrary to what is predicted by Spence's theory of discrimination learning (Spence, 1937). Spence's model predicted that the generalization of inhibition from the S- stimulus should subtract from responses to S+. Thus, the rate of responding on the unchanged schedule should *decline* when the alternative schedule is shifted to extinction. Yet, very often, an enhancement (positive behavioral contrast), rather than a decrement, occurs.

As the discussion develops, it will become clear that there are two aspects of behavioral contrast. One of these, *local contrast*, refers to changes in response rate that occur just following a switch from S- to S+ or vice versa (see Malone, 1976; Nevin & Shettleworth, 1966; Rachlin, 1973). Local contrast tends to be transient, disappearing as the animal learns the discrimination (see, for example, Cleary, 1992; Vieth & Rilling, 1972). However, this is not always the case (Malone, 1976). The other aspect of contrast is variously referred to as *sustained contrast, overall contrast,* or *molar contrast* (Mackintosh, 1974; Williams, 1983). This aspect of contrast tends to be permanent, is not accounted for by response changes due to local contrast, tends to increase toward the termination of a schedule, and may account for the major portion of contrast in most experiments. The evidence suggests strongly that molar contrast is due to response changes in anticipation of the *impending* schedule of reinforcement – hence, sustained contrast is often referred to as anticipatory contrast (Williams, 1983). There is some evidence that local contrast may be a precursor of anticipatory contrast (Cleary, 1992; Marcucella & MacDonall, 1977; Rachlin, 1973). However, there is also evidence that this precursor rela-

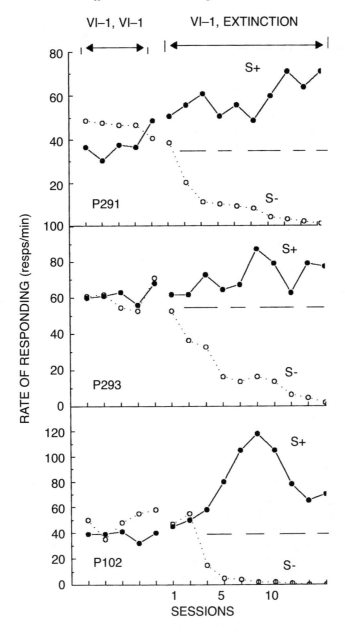

Figure 6.2 Multiple schedule performance of three pigeons shifted from a variable interval 1 minute, variable interval 1 minute schedule to a variable interval 1 minute, extinction schedule. Response rates in the changed component decreased, whereas response rates in the unchanged component increased to levels above the preshift baseline, demonstrating positive behavioral contrast. (Adapted from Halliday & Boakes, 1971.)

tionship is not necessary (Williams, 1974). Unfortunately, very few experiments have been concerned with isolating the conditions under which each aspect of contrast is maximized.

Determinants of behavioral contrast

REWARD DISPARITY. Behavioral contrast tends to be greater the greater the difference in reinforcement density between S+ and S- (see Bloomfield, 1967; McSweeney, 1975). One way of stating this relationship is to say that degree of contrast is a function of relative reinforcement rate in the unchanged component – the greater the relative reinforcement (in comparison to that available in the alternative schedule), the greater the contrast (see Williams, 1983, p. 347).

COMPONENT DURATION. When component durations are equal in length, then both positive and negative behavioral contrast[1] in key pecking are greater with shorter component durations (McSweeney, 1982; McSweeney & Melville, 1988; Williams, 1979, 1989). Short components increase the rate of alternation between the two schedules of reinforcement, and frequent opportunities to compare rewards may enhance reward interaction (Williams, 1989) – as do short ITIs in differential conditioning. In addition to providing more opportunities for comparison per unit time, short component duration decreases the time between comparison opportunities and may enhance reward interaction for this reason – as do short intersolution intervals in anticipatory contrast in consummatory behavior, and short retention intervals in SNC.

It is possible to vary exposure to the S- schedule while leaving exposure to the S+ schedule constant, and vice versa. The literature related to these experiments has been considered by Williams (1989) and by Aronson, Balsam, and Gibbon (1993). In general, given a constant duration of the *less*-valued component, rate of responding in the *more*-valued component is greater the shorter its duration. Also, given a constant duration of the *more*-valued component, rate of responding in this component is greater the longer the duration of the *less*-valued component. It is as if the value of the more-valued component is enhanced the shorter its duration relative to the less-valued component. In fact, Aronson et al. (1993) suggest that it is the ratio of duration of the two components that is critical for determining relative response rates.[2]

There is some evidence that component durations of 10 seconds for the ini-

---

[1] Negative behavioral contrast may be defined as a decrease in response rate from baseline in an unchanged component when the rate of reinforcement in a changed component is increased to a level greater than that prevailing in the unchanged component (see McSweeney & Norman, 1979, for a discussion of behavioral contrast definitions).

[2] McSweeney and Melville (1993) recently provided data that differ from this generalization. Variations in the extinction component, but not variations in the rewarded component, affected positive contrast (positive contrast was greatest at values of 30 and 60 seconds when the length of the extinction component was varied from 5 seconds to 960 seconds, but positive contrast was relatively unchanged when the length of the VI-2-minute component was varied from 5 to 960 seconds and the extinction component was held constant at 30 seconds).

tial component and 30 seconds for the following component maximize the anticipatory aspects of positive behavioral contrast (Williams, 1989, 1991). This relationship is notable because asymmetrical values of 3 minutes' access to the initial solution and 10 minutes' access to the following solution tend to produce very large anticipatory contrast effects in consummatory behavior (see Chapter 5; Flaherty, Coppotelli, Grigson & Mitchell, 1996).

Different component duration effects may be obtained when the response requirements are different – such as when pigeons press treadles rather than peck on keys (McSweeney, 1982) or when rats press a lever (McSweeney & Melville, 1991).

STIMULUS SIMILARITY. Another factor that influences degree of contrast is stimulus similarity and, consequently, the difficulty of the discrimination between the stimuli. Early evidence suggested that contrast was greater when the stimuli correlated with the two reinforcement conditions were similar (producing a difficult discrimination) (see, for example, Bloomfield, 1972; Blough, 1983). However, there are exceptions to this generalization (Mackintosh, 1974; Malone, 1976; Mackintosh, Little & Lord, 1972).

Recent studies have provided more detailed analyses of stimulus similarity. These studies have shown that *local* contrast and *overall* contrast are affected differently by stimulus similarity. Local contrast refers to an abrupt change in responding following a transition in reinforcement schedules (Mackintosh, 1974; Malone, 1976; Malone & Cleary, 1986; Nevin & Shettleworth, 1966; Rachlin, 1973; Williams, 1983). For example, in a multiple VI-2-minute, extinction schedule, there will often be a burst in responding following the transition from an extinction component to a VI-2-minute component.[3] This local contrast is influenced by stimulus similarity (Blough,1988). In Blough's study, dissimilarity between the S+ and S- reduced local contrast. The effects of stimulus similarity may be examined by using a measure of how well the animal behaviorally discriminates between the two stimuli and by then relating this measure to contrast. In general, there is a curvilinear relationship between the animals' discrimination performance and local contrast – contrast being largest at intermediate levels of discriminative responding (see also Blough & Blough, 1985; White, Pipe & McLean, 1984). These effects are illustrated in Figure 6.3.

Overall contrast effects are measured by averaging response rates over the entire duration of each component, rather than by simply focusing on transitions

Negative contrast was produced by shifting from a VI-2-minute VI-2-minute to a VI-2-minute VI-15-second schedule. Negative contrast was large and did not vary reliably as a function of changes in the more-valued (VI-15-second) component. When the less-valued (VI-2-minute) component was changed, contrast was largest with short durations of this component.

This experiment employed a "within-session" behavioral contrast procedure, whereas most behavioral contrast studies employ between-session procedures.

[3]This burst seems to be analogous to the induction effects reported by Pavlov (1927). He found that, in discrimination training, the magnitude of the conditioned response was often greater when a CS+ trial followed a CS- trial than when it followed another CS+ trial. Similar effects have also been reported in differential conditioning in runways (see Krane & Ison, 1971).

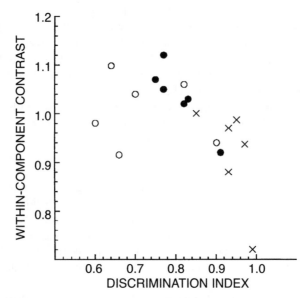

Figure 6.3 Degree of local positive behavioral contrast as a function of the discriminability of the S+ and S⁻ stimuli. (From P. Blough, 1988.)

periods or on just transition schedule components. Whereas local contrast effects may diminish with extended training, overall contrast effects tend to persist (see, for example, Mackintosh, 1974; Nevin & Shettleworth, 1966; Vieth & Rilling, 1972; Williams, 1983). According to Blough (1988), these overall contrast effects are not affected by stimulus similarity.

The implication of these data is that there is more than one mechanism involved in behavioral contrast. This theme has been developed most clearly in the work of Ben Williams, who has shown that the effects of an impending schedule of reinforcement differ from those of a preceding schedule of reinforcement. The remaining aspects of the differential effects of stimulus similarity, and certain other parametric effects, are most profitably considered in the context of theories of behavioral contrast.

Theories of behavioral contrast

> Any attempt to attribute all these results [from contrast experiments] to the operation of a single principle seems a singularly inappropriate theoretical goal.
>
> – N. J. Mackintosh, 1974

This section is not intended to be an exhaustive review of all the theories or all the evidence regarding behavioral contrast. It is intended to be a presentation of the major theories and essential points of evidence regarding those theories. The central thrust of this review is that there are two aspects of positive behavioral contrast: local contrast, which is an elevation in responding following the transition from S- to S+ and which tends to be transient, fading with extended training; and sustained contrast, which is an overall elevation in responding that tends to persist as long as the discriminative stimulus conditions exist. Current evidence suggests that the latter is due to control by the impending schedule of reinforcement – anticipatory contrast. This aspect of contrast has been most thoroughly investigated by Ben Williams and will be the first theory described here. Currently, the mechanism by which anticipatory contrast is produced is not known. Most alternative theories of contrast are actually concerned with local contrast, having been elaborated prior to Williams's demonstration of the major role played by anticipatory factors. For reviews, see Mackintosh (1974); McSweeney (1987); Nevin (1973); Rashotte (1979); Williams (1983); Williams & Wixted (1986).

It is possible that the same analysis applies to negative behavioral contrast, but this aspect of behavioral contrast has been investigated far less than positive contrast.

Anticipatory contrast

In a multiple schedule the S+ and S- stimuli alternate, each signalling their associated schedule of reinforcement. Is the elevated responding that occurs in S+ due to a comparison with the just past S- period (that is, a retrograde process like SNC)? Many theoretical interpretations of behavioral contrast have assumed this to be the case and, in fact, some data indicate that the transition from S- to S+ may be an important locus of one aspect of contrast – local contrast (Catania & Gill, 1964; Nevin & Shettleworth, 1966; Rachlin, 1973).

However, recent data obtained by Williams and his colleagues indicate quite strongly that it is the *following* schedule that is the major contributor to behavioral contrast. One of the items of evidence comes from a study in which Williams (1981) used a three-component multiple schedule. The first and third components, each signalled by a different stimulus, always had a VI-3-minute schedule of reinforcement associated with them. The reinforcement schedule of the middle component, which was signalled by a third stimulus, was varied. In some stages of the experiment, there was a VI-1-minute schedule in effect in the middle component; in other stages, there was a VI-6-minute middle component in effect. Of interest was the response rates in the components that followed or preceded the middle component. Williams (1981, 1983) reported that responding in the first component was more affected by changes in the middle component than was responding in the third component. In other words, contrast was primarily influenced by the impending reinforcement conditions rather than by the preceding reinforcement schedule. Other evidence regarding the role of impending rewards in operant tasks has been obtained by Bacotti (1976); Buck, Rothstein and Williams (1975); Farley (1980); Williams (1976, 1988, 1990a, 1992a); Williams and Wixted (1986); and Wilton and Gay (1969). Control of responding by anticipated rewards is compatible with the data collected with regard to anticipatory contrast in consummatory behavior (Chapter 5).

Stimulus similarity is one parameter that seems to separate local contrast from anticipatory contrast. Williams (1988) found that overall contrast (also termed *molar* contrast) was greatest toward the end of component presentation and was greatest with dissimilar stimuli (vertical line versus yellow key). Mackintosh, Little, and Lord (1972) also found greater contrast with an "easier" discrimination (vertical versus horizontal lines) than with a difficult discrimination (vertical versus 15° off vertical).

Williams found different results with contrast that occurred at the transition between schedules. It tended to be greatest just after the transition, and then diminish during the component. This local contrast was greatest with similar stimuli (vertical versus horizontal lines). Blough (1980, 1983) found similar stimulus similarity effects with local contrast; however, later studies relating local contrast to actual discriminative performance, rather than to physical stimulus similarity, obtained a curvilinear relationship between discriminability and local contrast (Blough, 1988; also see preceding section on "Stimulus similarity").

In a second experiment, Williams (1988) used a three-component schedule in order to separate more clearly the effects of anticipatory contrast from local contrast. The first and last components were always reinforced on a VI-90-second schedule, whereas the middle component was reinforced on either a VI-30-second or a VI-270-second schedule. Contrast in the first component (anticipatory contrast) was greater than contrast in the last component. Also, contrast in the first component increased during the session and was greatest with dissimilar stimuli – the same result obtained in the first experiment. The smaller contrast that occurred in the last component decreased within a component – that is, the further from the time of transition between stimuli, the smaller the contrast. Thus, contrast in the last component was local in nature. There was no effect of stimulus similarity on local contrast in this experiment.

In general, these results support the hypothesis that there are two types of contrast that occur in multiple schedules: (a) one generated by the transition between stimuli signalling different reward schedules and focused in the temporal vicinity of this transition – local contrast; and (b) one that is more enduring, that tends to increase during a session, and that is controlled by the impending schedule of reward – anticipatory contrast.

Pavlovian processes

Additivity theory

The data are compelling in favor of a strong causal role for the anticipated schedule of reinforcement in contrast, but there are other interpretations that place emphasis on the transition from a *preceding* schedule of low reinforcement to a current schedule of higher reinforcement as a major determinant of positive behavioral contrast. One of these interpretations, often termed *additivity theory*, emphasizes the role of Pavlovian-elicited responses as the cause of positive behavioral contrast.

Substantial evidence shows that presenting a cue for a schedule high in reinforcement density elicits responses directed toward that signal – a phenomenon termed *autoshaping* (Hearst & Jenkins, 1974). That is, without any response requirement, animals will direct behavior, such as pecking by pigeons, toward a signal correlated with reward. Often, this autoshaped behavior can be quite complicated, and its nature is influenced by characteristics of the signalling stimulus, the nature of the reward, and the species of animal (see Flaherty, 1985, Chapters 5 and 14; Timberlake, 1983; Timberlake & Grant, 1975). The autoshaping literature suggests that, in a multiple schedule, the onset of a cue signalling a reinforcement rate higher than the previous rate should increase responding (see Gamzu & Schwartz, 1973; Keller, 1974; Schwartz & Gamzu, 1977). For example, if an extinction schedule is correlated with a red key light and a VI-1-minute reinforcement schedule is correlated with a green key light, the transition from red to green should produce two types of responses: (a) elicited Pavlovian responses (because of the signalling properties of the green key light) and (b) operant responses controlled by the VI-1-minute reinforcement schedule. According to additive theory, it is the addition of these two classes of responses that accounts for the "extra" responses that occur to the S+ in a multiple schedule.

There was substantial early evidence that supported additivity theory. For example, Keller (1974) separated the operant response key from the signalling key and found that positive behavioral contrast did not occur when only responses on the operant key were examined, but the combination of responses to the signalling key (which were unnecessary for the receipt of reinforcement, but which were made by the pigeons anyway) and the responses to the operant key did produce the elevated responding characteristic of positive behavioral contrast. Similarly, contrast did not occur when pigeons were required to step on a treadle rather than peck on a key as the operant response (Hemmes, 1973). It was also argued that the difficulty of demonstrating behavioral contrast in rats, in comparison to the ease of such demonstrations in pigeons, was due to the difference in the likelihood that Pavlovian (autoshaped) responses would combine additively with operant responses.

Subsequent consideration of the additivity theory of behavioral contrast has not been favorable. McSweeney, Ettinger, and Norman (1981) distinguished among three versions of additivity theory and concluded that there is no strong evidence in favor of any. Williams (1983) concluded that there is negative evidence as well as a lack of positive evidence. Among the problems are the following: (a) Studies that superficially support the additivity theory have not included conditions in which the two types of responses (Pavlovian and operant) are trained separately and then tested for summation (McSweeney et al., 1981); (b) contrast has been demonstrated in rats and other species without the relationship between operant and consummatory (Pavlovian) responses that is required by the theory (see, for example, Beninger & Kendall, 1975; Dougan,

Farmer-Dougan & McSweeney, 1989; Gutman, Sutterer & Brush, 1975; Henke, Allen & Davison, 1972; Higa & McSweeney, 1987; Mackintosh, Little & Lord, 1972; McSweeney & Melville, 1991; Padilla, 1971; Wilkie, 1972); (c) contrary to the results obtained by Keller (1974), contrast has been obtained in several studies in which the signal source and the response key have been separated (see Williams, 1981 and 1983, for a discussion of this issue); (d) unlike the Hemmes (1973) result, contrast has been obtained in pigeons with a treadle-press response, although such contrast may be less sensitive than, and may have different parameters from, key-peck responses (McSweeney, 1978, 1983); (e) the important role demonstrated for the impending schedule (anticipatory contrast) described here is not consistent with the implications of additivity theory (which emphasize the signalling value of the current schedule for current reward); (f) additivity theory is limited as an explanation for behavioral contrast, because it accounts for positive behavioral contrast but not for negative behavioral contrast, in which there is a reduction in response rate (Schwartz, 1975).

Although the evidence suggests that additivity theory is not an adequate account of contrast, there is little doubt that the events described in the numerous investigations of the theory do occur and that, under some parametric conditions, these events constitute aspects of local positive contrast. Furthermore, the importance of the relationship between signalling stimuli and response requirements is an issue that arises in other learning situations, including discrimination learning, feature positive effects, learning set, and, possibly, drug addiction (Tomie, 1994).

Pavlovian processes and anticipatory contrast

Additivity theory was concerned with Pavlovian responses activated by the signalling value of the cue correlated with the *current* reinforcement schedule. It is also conceivable that Pavlovian responses could be elicited by the relationship between the current schedule and the following schedule. If that is the case, what is the role of Pavlovian processes in anticipatory contrast? Recall that in Chapter 5 the issue of Pavlovian processes in consummatory anticipatory contrast was raised (for example, see Flaherty & Rowan, 1985). There the concern was that the formation of an association between the initial substance (such as 0.15% saccharin) and the following substance (such as 32% sucrose) may lead to the devaluation of the initial substance. The spirit of this argument followed from demonstrations that devaluation of the reward (or unconditioned stimulus) can affect both Pavlovian and instrumental responding (see Colwill & Rescorla, 1986; Holland & Rescorla, 1979).

When operant researchers use the term *Pavlovian* they mean, by and large, elicited responses rather than "hidden" revaluation. Thus, the Pavlovian issue in the discussion of the operant literature is whether the sequential presentation of two schedules, with their correlated cues, will lead to elicited responses during the first schedule, responses that could be involved in behavioral contrast. Compare, for example, a VI-1-minute schedule followed by extinction versus a VI-1-minute schedule followed by a VI-2-minute schedule. If Pavlovian responses were elicited by such sequences, then responding should be higher in the latter VI-1-minute schedule (termed *facilitation*) than in the former. This is opposite to the pattern that would be expected if contrast occurred. Thus, Williams (1992a) has argued that contrast and Pavlovian processes must oppose one another. The data suggest that there are situations in which both patterns (facilitation and contrast) occur. Facilitation seems to occur when an initial signal has little or no reward value and precedes a signal of higher reward value. However, if the initial signal (event) itself has reward value, then contrast is likely to occur.

Thus, Brown et al. (1982) found that the availability of an unreinforced red key followed by a white key reinforced on a VI-30-second schedule led to a facilitation effect (responding on the red key) when the alternative components consisted of a nonreinforced green key followed by a nonreinforced white key (that is, there was greater responding on the red key than on the green key). If both red and green keys were nonreinforced and both were followed by white keys reinforced on the VI-30-second schedule, there was little responding to either red or green. Thus, facilitation occurs when one nonreinforced signal differentially predicts reward availability compared to another nonreinforced signal.

This result was confirmed by Hassin-Herman, Hemmes and Brown (1992), who found facilitation with the following conditions (Ext = extinction; RI = random interval):

Phase I	Phase 2
red (Ext.) – white (RI-30)	red (Ext) – white (Ext)
green (Ext) – white (RI-30)	green (Ext) – white (RI-30)

There was more responding to the green than to the red in Phase 2, but little responding to either in Phase I.[4] In another condition, the availability in Phase I of a lean reinforcement schedule (RI-150) instead of extinction reduced, but did not eliminate, the facilitation.

Williams (1992a) obtained similar results when there was no reinforcement available in the initial component, and differential reinforcement (VI-30-second versus Ext) in the second component.

Thus, greater responding (facilitation) clearly occurs to one of two available nonreinforced initial stimuli when that stimulus signals subsequent reinforce-

---

[4]There is evidence of a similar effect in anticipatory contrast in consummatory behavior. When the initial "substance" has little or no reward value (i.e., an empty drinking tube, or water for food-deprived rats), then presentation of a rewarding sucrose or saccharin solution as the second substance enhanced responding for the first substance (facilitation). However, if the first substance itself had reward value, then presentation of a preferred reward as the second substance reduced responding for the first substance (anticipatory contrast). The size of the facilitation effect was small compared to that of the contrast effect (Flaherty, Turovsky & Krauss, 1994).

ment but the alternative initial stimulus does not signal subsequent reinforcement. When neither stimulus signals subsequent reinforcement, there is little or no responding to either.

What if the initial stimuli are themselves reinforced but also signal differential subsequent reinforcement? This is the typical arrangement in behavioral contrast studies, but the occurrence of facilitation is more difficult to detect because the available contingencies in the initial components will themselves produce responding. As already described, Hassim-Herman et al. (1992) found less facilitation when an RI-150 schedule preceded an RI-30 schedule than when extinction preceded an RI-30 schedule. These results were not confirmed by Williams (1992a). In both Phase 1 and Phase 2 of Williams's experiment, one of the second components was reinforced on a VI-30-second schedule and the other was not reinforced. The initial components were changed between Phase 1 and Phase 2. In Phase 1, facilitation occurred to a blue signal that preceded the VI-30-second schedule, whereas a yellow signal preceded an extinction schedule. When both blue and yellow were reinforced on a VI-2-minute schedule in Phase 2, response rate on both increased, but the two rates did not differ.

In Phase 3, the same reinforcement conditions were maintained: blue (VI-2-minute) – VI-30-second; yellow (VI-2-minute) – Ext. However, the stimuli associated with the second component were changed. In Phases 1 and 2, the second components were not differentiated, both being signalled by a vertical line. In Phase 3, the second components were differentiated with separate cues, and anticipatory contrast (reduced responding) appeared on the initial blue component (a VI-2-minute schedule that signalled an impending VI-30-second schedule).

Although this result might suggest that differential signals for the second schedule are critical in determining whether facilitation or contrast occurs, this is apparently not the case. After obtaining contrast in Phase 3 of his experiment, Williams returned to the Phase 2 conditions in which there were no differential signals for the second components. Anticipatory contrast remained. Furthermore, the Hassim-Herman et al. (1992) study included a condition in which the second components (RI-30 versus Ext) were differentially signalled and the initial components had the same conditions (red – RI-150, green – RI-150). Unlike in the Williams study, in this study facilitation, rather than contrast, occurred in the component that preceded the RI-30 schedule.

What is clear is that facilitation occurs when there is differential prediction of reinforcement by nonreinforced stimuli. Whether facilitation or contrast occurs when there is a lean schedule in the initial component and a richer schedule in the second component may be a parametric issue. This state of affairs is quite similar to that which occurs with consummatory anticipatory negative contrast. As reviewed in Chapter 5, when an empty tube or a tube containing water is followed by access to 32% sucrose, facilitation occurs. When an initial substance is a weak reinforcer, such as 0.0015% saccharin, there is a reduced period of facilitation followed eventually by contrast. In general, as the value of the initial substance increases and approaches that of the second substance, within limits, facilitation gives way to contrast. This function, however, is curvilinear – facilitation is seen again as the initial substance passes some threshold in regard to its closeness in value to the second substance. This parameter has not been fully explored in the behavioral contrast literature.

Summary

Overall, the evidence suggests that elicited responses, controlled either by signals for the current reinforcement schedule (additivity theory) or by the subsequent reinforcement schedule, may occur when multiple schedules are used. However, such elicited responses seem not to be a major determinant of contrast in the additivity sense, and they may actually oppose contrast when elicited by the following schedule, given certain parameters. Generally, sustained contrast seems to be accounted for by anticipatory factors that are not related to these elicited responses.

Response competition

There have been several variations on the idea that the elevation in responding in the unchanged component of a multiple schedule is related to (or caused by) the decline in responding to the shifted component. In general, the hypothesis is that animals allocate their responses in accordance with available reinforcements, and, the more alternative reinforcement schedules available (both programmed by the experiment and nonprogrammed reinforcements, (such as grooming), the fewer responses available for any one alternative. Thus, when a VI-1-minute, VI-1-minute multiple schedule is shifted to a VI-1-minute, extinction schedule, the responses originally allocated to the shifted component are now available for the unchanged component – hence, an elevation in responding to this component.

The initial variation of this theory was simply that the decline in responding to S- causes the positive behavioral contrast in S+ (Freeman, 1971). The data, however, clearly show that decline in response rate is neither a necessary nor a sufficient condition for the occurrence of contrast in S+. One experiment showing that such a decline is not a sufficient condition was done by Halliday and Boakes (1971). In this experiment, pigeons were given initial training on a multiple VI-1-minute schedule with a blank disc and an angled line as the stimuli. After responding had stabilized, the schedule in effect during presentations of the angled line was shifted from a VI-1-minute to a variable-time (VT) 1-minute. On a VT-1-minute schedule, reward is delivered on the average every minute – *without the necessity of a response*. Thus, a VT schedule is like a VI schedule except that the animals do not have to make an instrumental response to get a reward. The results obtained following this shift are illustrated in Figure 6.4.

It is clear that rate of responding in the presence of the line stimulus fell, but there was no corresponding increase in responding during S+, meaning that there was no behavioral contrast (compare Figure 6.4 with Figure 6.2). Thus, a decline

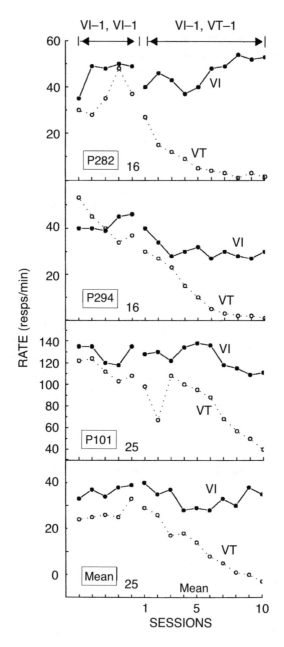

Figure 6.4 Response rates before and after a shift from a variable interval 1 minute, variable interval 1 minute schedule to a variable interval 1 minute, variable time 1 minute schedule. In the variable time component, "free" access to food was given on the average of every minute. Response rates declined in this component, but there was no increase in the unchanged component. (After Halliday & Boakes, 1971.)

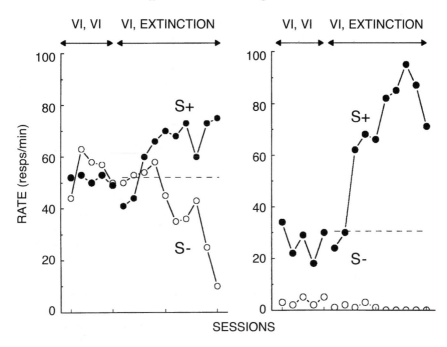

Figure 6.5 Response rates following a shift from a variable interval, variable interval schedule to a variable interval, extinction schedule (left-hand panel), and following a shift from a variable interval, variable time schedule to a variable interval, extinction schedule (right-hand panel). Contrast occurred in both cases, without the necessity of a decline in response rate in the latter condition. (After Halliday & Boakes, 1974.)

in response rate in the presence of one stimulus is not *sufficient* to produce behavioral contrast.

Another study by Halliday and Boakes (1974) shows that a decline in response rate is not a necessary condition for the occurrence of behavioral contrast. This experiment also involved a VT schedule, but it was a more complex experiment than the one just described. The general procedure was as follows. Pigeons were first trained to peck at a response disc illuminated by white light. The birds were then separated into two groups. One group was shifted to a multiple VI-1-minute, VT-1-minute schedule with red illumination indicating S+ and green illumination indicating S- (the VT component). As was mentioned in the earlier discussion of a VT schedule, there is a decline in response rate to S⁻ but there is no evidence of contrast. During this stage of the experiment, the second group of pigeons was maintained on a VI-1-minute schedule when the keys were illuminated both red and green.

When responses had stabilized in this stage of the experiment, comparison of the two groups showed that in the group with the VT component, responses to S- had declined almost to zero and the response rate to S+ was somewhat *lower* than the average response rate of the group maintained on the VI-1-minute schedule for both red and green stimuli (see Figure 6.5).

In the next, and most interesting, stage of the experiment, both groups were shifted to a *multiple* VI-1-minute extinction schedule with the red illumination as S+. Examination of response rates to S+ showed that behavioral contrast occurred in both groups (note the sudden rise in S+ response rates in Figure 6.5).

The occurrence of contrast is not surprising in the group given standard training. However, note that in the group shifted from the multiple VI, VT schedule the contrast occurred *without a decline in responding*. That is, contrast was produced by a decline in reinforcement frequency without the usually correlated decline in response rate. Thus, a reduction in response rate is neither a necessary nor a sufficient condition for the occurrence of behavioral contrast.

More subtle variations of the response competition hypothesis have been proposed (see, for example, Hinson & Staddon, 1978; McLean, 1992; McLean & White, 1983; Staddon, 1982; White, 1978). A focus in these alternative versions is the locus of reinforcement interactions in multiple schedules and the locus of the reinforcement for alleged competing responses. The simpler view of reinforcement interactions is that they occur between the two schedules in effect in the two components of the multiple schedule (such as VI-1-minute versus extinction). According to this simpler view, contrast is due to the enhanced *relative* value of the VI-1-minute schedule in comparison to the extinction schedule. A more complex view is that there are more reinforcers involved than just the two programmed by the multiple schedule. Evidence for this is that behaviors other than responding to the manipulandum – behaviors such as grooming, sniffing, or rearing in rats, or "misdirected" pecking, wing flapping, preening, and other interim behaviors in pigeons – occur regularly (Manabe, Kuwata & Kurashige, 1992; Staddon & Simmelhag, 1971). The presumption is that there are reinforcers for these behaviors.

The behavioral competition theory argues that the relative value of these "other" reinforcers is altered within a component of the multiple schedule, and it is this within-component alteration that is responsible for behavioral contrast. Competition might operate in the following way (Williams & Wixted, 1994). A high density of reinforcement in one component of a multiple schedule controls behavior to a degree that precludes extraneous ("unmeasured") behaviors from obtaining reinforcement (that is, there will be relatively little grooming, etc.). Then, during the less dense reinforcement schedule, these alternative behaviors become more likely, because the value of their reinforcers is enhanced relative to what is provided by the schedule, and therefore these behaviors compete with the operant behavior.

Contrast is due, therefore, to the relative value of the reinforcements for the operant behaviors and those of the extraneous behaviors. Aspects of this argument are reminiscent of an issue that arose in regard to the effects of deprivation state on runway behavior. Rats under greater deprivation run faster in runways. The question was whether they actually run *faster* or whether their behavior is interrupted less by competing responses because, perhaps, the more extreme deprivation conditions may enhance the reward value of the goal object. The answer to that question is a little bit of both – competing responses are reduced by increases in deprivation, but, accounting for measurable competing responses, rats also run faster when deprived more (Porter, Madison & Senkowski, 1968).

The answer is similar in the case of behavioral contrast. Although there is some evidence to support the idea that reinforcement of alternative behaviors affects degree of contrast (McLean, 1992), these effects are not sufficient to explain contrast (Williams & Wixted, 1994). Furthermore, approximately equivalent degrees of contrast occur when there is a substantial change in behavior in the shifted component (as in a typical shift from VI, VI to VI, Ext) and when there is little change in behavior in the shifted component (as in a shift from VI, VT to VI, Ext [see the Halliday & Boakes 1974 experiment discussed previously] and in a shift from a VI, signalled VI to a VI, Ext schedule [Williams, 1980]). Furthermore, when extraneous behaviors are measured, the time allocated to them does not account for behavioral contrast. Instead, when it is not pecking the key, most of the pigeon's time is spent in inactivity (Manabe et al., 1992). To quote from Williams and Wixted (1994, p. 111) "the controlling variable [in contrast] is changes in relative rate of reinforcement independent of changes in level of behavior maintained by the reinforcement" – a view consistent with that expressed by Williams in 1980.

Other considerations of this issue may be found in Boakes, Halliday, and Mole (1976); Dougan, McSweeney, and Farmer (1985); Dougan, McSweeney, and Farmer-Dougan (1986); Nevin (1973); and Williams (1980, 1983).

Relative value

An issue that arose in the consideration of anticipatory contrast in consummatory behavior (Chapter 5) was whether an initial saccharin solution that preceded a subsequent 32% solution was devalued by this conjunction. Furthermore, the possibility that negative anticipatory contrast was due to such a devaluation was considered. The evidence reviewed indicated that devaluation of the initial solution did not occur and, thus, relative value, measured in this way, could not be an explanation of anticipatory contrast.

The same issue arises in the case of behavioral contrast (Williams, 1979). A study by Williams (1991) illustrates an approach to determine whether the occurrence of positive behavioral contrast results from an increase in the *value* of the schedule that leads to the higher response rate (that is, contrast). Williams obtained behavioral contrast by training pigeons on a four-component multiple schedule. The four components were arranged in two pairs such that a VI-2 minute schedule correlated with stimulus A was followed by a VI-30-second schedule correlated with stimulus B, whereas a VI-2-minute schedule correlated with stimulus C was followed by an extinction schedule correlated with stimulus D.

As illustrated in Figure 6.6, response rates were considerably greater for the

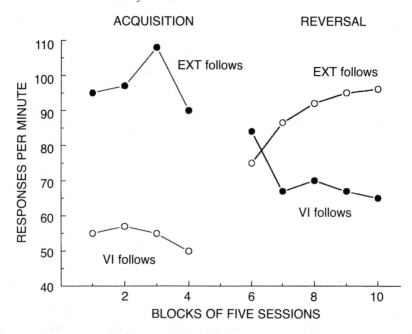

Figure 6.6 Response rates on a variable interval 2-minute schedule were higher when extinction followed the current schedule than when a VI-30-second schedule followed the current schedule – a typical pattern demonstrating positive anticipatory behavioral contrast. The cue pairings were reversed between the two phases. (After Williams, 1991.)

VI-2-minute schedule that was followed by extinction than for the VI-2-minute schedule that was followed by the VI-30-second schedule. When the signal–consequent relationships were reversed in the second stage of the experiment (for example, VI-2-minute followed by extinction shifted to VI-2-minute followed by VI-30-second), behavior also reversed – the animals shifted to respond more when the extinction schedule followed the VI-2-minute schedule.

Do the higher response rates preceding the extinction component indicate that the animals place a higher *value* on a VI-2-minute schedule when it precedes extinction than they place on a VI-2-minute schedule when it precedes a VI-30-second schedule? In order to answer this question, Williams provided choice trials in which the pigeons were confronted with both VI-2-minute signals (stimulus A and stimulus C) simultaneously – thus providing them with a choice of responding on either VI-2-minute signal. The results of this preference test, illustrated in Figure 6.7, show that the birds responded more on the stimulus that signalled that the VI-30-second schedule was to follow. This response pattern reversed when the cues were reversed – just as did response rates (Figure 6.6).

These results show that choice does not mirror response rate – in fact, they are the inverse of each other. Thus, the fact that pigeons respond at a higher rate for a VI-2-minute schedule that signals a subsequent extinction period than for a

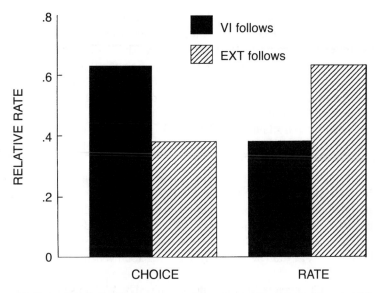

Figure 6.7 Choice data obtained in the same experiment that was illustrated in Figure 6.6. When the cues signalling that the extinction schedule would follow and that the VI-30-second schedule would follow were presented concurrently, the pigeons responded more on the current VI-2-minute schedule when the cue was for an impending VI-30-second schedule than for an impending extinction schedule. Thus, the choice data were the inverse of the response rate data. (Williams, 1991.)

VI-2-minute schedule that signals a subsequent VI-30-second schedule does not mean that they value the VI-2-minute schedule that precedes extinction more than the VI-2-minute schedule that precedes a VI-30-second schedule. In fact, the preference test suggests that they value it less. Williams's data indicate a clear dissociation between response rate and choice as a measures of value.

In a second experiment, Williams (1991) interspersed choice trials at various stages in the acquisition of contrast. The results of this study showed that pigeons preferred the VI-2-minute cue that preceded a VI-30-second schedule over a VI-2-minute cue that preceded an extinction schedule at all stages of training. In fact, the preference was evident long before contrast developed in response rate – another indication of a dissociation between response rate and choice as indicators of reward value.

Whereas the 1991 study by Williams was clear in its dissociation of response rate and preference in regard to contrast, it did not provide specific information regarding the relative contributions of positive and negative contrast. This is because the design of the experiment was such that a multiple VI-2-minute, Ext schedule (which should produce positive contrast) was compared to a multiple VI-2-minute, VI-30-second schedule (which should produce negative contrast). There were no multiple VI-2-minute, VI-2-minute control conditions against which to assess relative enhanced responding compared to the VI-2-minute, Ext condition (positive contrast) or to assess depressed responding compared to the

VI-2-minute, VI-30-second schedule (negative contrast). A related study (Williams, 1992b) included these controls, but there were a number of other procedural differences from the 1991 experiments. The basic finding of the 1992 study was consistent with the general conclusion from the 1991 studies – response rates and choice behavior in a preference test do not provide the same answer to the question of relative value. In this case, there was a reliable anticipatory positive contrast effect (responding on a VI-2-minute schedule was greater when it was followed by extinction than when it was followed by another VI-2-minute schedule), but there was no reliable preference for either of the cues correlated with the initial VI-2-minute components.

The situation was reversed in the case of negative contrast. There was no reliable anticipatory negative contrast effect – response rates for the initial VI-2-minute component were not different when that schedule was followed by another VI-2-minute schedule or by a VI-30-second schedule. However, there was a reliable difference in the choice test – the pigeons preferred the cue correlated with the VI-2-minute schedule that was followed by the VI-30-second schedule.

These results suggest that the pattern obtained by Williams in his 1991 study reflected the combined effects of both positive and negative anticipatory contrast. Although the results of these two studies (Williams, 1991, 1992b) leave some questions unanswered, they do show that contrast and preference measures tend to be inversely related. A similar pattern is obtained in the case of anticipatory contrast in consummatory behavior (Chapter 5).

The conclusion for this section would seem to be that contrast in response rate is not due to a change in the relative value of the reinforcement, or at least not due to a change that reflects the change in the same direction as response rate. One caveat here concerns the choice test. Perhaps this test does not measure preference at all. Perhaps it reflects a perceived act–outcome contingency on the part of the animal – something corresponding to the anthropomorphic idea that "responding when cue A is present produces reward X." This interpretation would be particularly interesting if it could be argued that the choice situation (presentation of both stimuli concurrently) was considered to be a higher-order stimulus that functioned as an occasion-setter or discriminative stimulus (Holland, 1989; Rescorla, 1992) supporting a different pattern of responding from that obtained when only a single stimulus was present on the training trials. The problem with this view is that some degree of learning should be necessary before the choice situation functions as a hierarchical stimulus; Williams (1992b) found that preference developed early in training and did not change. Also, Flaherty, Grigson, Coppotelli, Mitchell, and Flaherty (1995) found that preference did not change as a function of access time on the first choice test in a consummatory anticipatory negative contrast experiment.

Perhaps the best conclusion is that the evidence does not favor a change in relative value as an explanation for contrast, but performance on the preference test remains to be understood before a final conclusion is drawn.

Emotional response

An explanation of behavioral contrast in terms of emotional processes has been entertained by many. For example, Terrace (1966a, 1966b, 1966c) argued that contrast was related to the aversiveness of S-. Bower (1966) believed that behavioral contrast might be explained in terms of Amsel's frustration theory, just as he offered an explanation for SimNC in these terms (see this chapter's section on "Differential conditioning in runways"). Mackintosh (1974) also stated that local positive contrast was probably a reflection of the energizing effects of frustration. In this regard, Gray and Smith (1969) had noted that rats given partial reward for running in a runway sometimes run faster than rats given continuous reinforcement. They suggested that this apparent energizing effect of nonreward (or reduced reward) might account for positive behavioral contrast. Gray and Smith further suggested an interaction between stimulus similarity and frustration: Decreasing stimulus similarity should decrease contrast when there are low levels of frustration, but it should increase contrast, within limits, when there is a high level of frustration. This fairly specific prediction (assuming that degree of frustration could be related to degree of reward disparity between S+ and S-) has not been given a systematic test.

In an analysis of "ordinary language" interpretations of emotion and positive behavioral contrast, Bloomfield (1969) distinguished between *relief,* which he proposed was elicited by the onset of S+, and *elation,* which occurred following the receipt of a reward for responding in S+. These distinctions, in a sense, parallel those considered in this chapter's section on "Pavlovian processes but, in this case, the distinction is in terms of hypothetical emotional states rather than overt responses. There is a notable absence of data regarding Bloomfield's hypothesis. Nevertheless, the idea is interesting because it touches upon other potentially relevant uses of these terms. For example, Crespi (1942, 1944) interpreted SPC in runway behavior as being due to an elation effect (Chapters 1 and 4). The difference between the SPC procedure and positive behavioral contrast is that the onset of S+ in the behavioral contrast paradigm is preceded by an S- period; thus the concept of "relief" upon presentation of S+ prior to "elation" at the receipt of reward is appropriate for behavioral contrast, but not for SPC. The concept of "relief" as a reward has also been used in the explanation of avoidance behavior (Denny, 1991). A further interesting relationship is that there is some evidence that SPC in runway behavior may be enhanced if the shift to large reward is made after a downshift in reward (see Chapter 2). This might be interpreted as reflecting an additive effect of two positive emotions (relief + elation) in the spirit of conditioning model theories (for example, Amsel, 1991, 1992; Mowrer, 1960).

Bloomfield's conceptualization of relief may also be related to the interpretation of the transition from S- to S+ as an example of the energizing effect of frustration. Bloomfield proposed a parallel emotional structure for negative behavioral contrast. A switch from S+ to S- may elicit *disappointment,* and responding in the presence of S- may elicit *frustration.* Both of these concepts have been used in considering SNC. It could be the case that local negative behavioral contrast is closely related to SNC (in Amsel's terms, it could reflect a disruptive effect of primary frustration).

What are the data in regard to these theories? Some aspect of behavioral contrast is related to the aversiveness of the S-. Evidence in support of this statement includes the following:

(a) Degree of behavioral contrast is correlated with degree of aversiveness of the S-, as measured by the subjects' tendencies to escape from S- given the opportunity (Gonzalez & Champlin, 1974) or to turn away from the S- immediately after its onset (Manabe, 1992).

(b) Adding an aversive electric shock to S- without changing the reinforcement schedule will produce a contrast effect (Farley & Fantino, 1968, cited in Williams, 1983; Terrace, 1968).

(c) Damage to the amygdala, which tends to produce a tame animal by reducing fear and stress (see, for example, Davis, 1992; LeDoux, 1990; Schulkin, McEwen & Gold, 1994), also reduces contrast (Henke; 1972; Henke, Allen & Davison, 1972), whereas damage to the ventromedial hypothalamus, which produces an emotionally reactive and "finicky" animal, enhances behavioral contrast (Jaffe, 1973).

(d) Lesions of the septal area, which heighten emotional reactivity but to a considerably lesser degree than ventromedial hypothalamic lesions do, have been reported both to enhance positive behavioral contrast (Caplan & Graefe, 1980) and to have no effect (Davison, Lowther & Allen, 1975; Dickinson, 1972; Henke, 1976).

(e) Level of corticosterone (a hormone released under conditions of stress, among other occasions) is elevated following a shift in schedules that produce contrast (Goldman, Coover & Levine, 1973; Hart & Coover, 1982). The study by Hart and Coover (1982) showed that the shift from baseline (VI-30 seconds, VI-30 seconds) to contrast conditions (VI-30 seconds, extinction) or reduced reinforcement (VI-60 seconds, VI-60 seconds) produced approximately equivalent transient elevations in corticosterone; however, the two groups subsequently did not differ even though contrast continued to develop in the VI-30-second, extinction group. This suggests that, under some conditions, the *maintenance* of positive behavioral contrast is not stressful.

(f) In a positive behavioral contrast analogue using 3-month-old human infants, fussing and crying accompanied the extinction component, whereas "cooing" and smiling often accompanied the presentation of S+ (Rovee-Collier & Capatides, 1979). The babies in these studies also tended to look away from the S- when it was presented but stared at the S+ when it was available.

(g) Using a variant of multiple schedules in which a probe stimulus signalling either higher or lower reward than that prevailing in the background condition, Ridgers and Gray (1979) found that the barbiturate amylobarbitone reduced negative contrast but not positive contrast. Using a similar procedure, Baltzer, Huber, and Weiskrantz (1979) found that chlordiazepoxide and diazepam (Librium and Valium), as well as amylobarbitone, reduced both positive and negative contrast, but the effect was greater on negative contrast. Antidepressants were generally ineffective in this paradigm. It is difficult to relate the effects obtained in these two experiments to other studies of behavioral contrast because the procedures were so atypical. However, the best assumption is that the drugs were affecting local contrast because the probe stimuli were brief intrusions onto a background reinforcement schedule.

In a more conventional experiment, Bloomfield (1972) found that the neuroleptic chlorpromazine and the antidepressant desmethylimipramine both diminished positive behavioral contrast that occurred following a shift from VI-1-minute, VI-1-minute to VI-1-minute, Ext. Bloomfield also reported that degree of positive behavioral contrast was directly related to the difficulty of the discrimination and that the drugs were considerably more effective when there was a difficult discrimination than when there was an easy discrimination. The evidence in regard to stimulus similarity previously reviewed would suggest that the contrast obtained in Bloomfield's experiment was primarily local contrast. Given that this may be true, the effectiveness of the drugs used by Bloomfield is still somewhat surprising, because neither is considered to be an anti-anxiety agent and neither antidepressants nor neuroleptics are particularly effective in animal models of anxiety (Flaherty, 1991a; Flaherty, Becker, Checke, Rowan, & Grigson, 1992; Howard & Pollard, 1991). An alternative interpretation of these data is that the effects of chlorpromazine and desmethylimipramine may have been due to motoric effects, causing a lowered response rate, or a rate-dependent lowered response rate, rather than due to emotional effects per se.

Overall, these data suggest that emotional reactions play some role in behavioral contrast, but the data are also nonspecific in regard to what that role is. One problem is that behavioral analysis has suggested that there are two components to contrast – local and sustained. The evidence is quite strong that sustained contrast is related to anticipatory factors. Local contrast, on the other hand, seems clearly to be related to the effects of the transition between signalling stimuli – that is, it is controlled by the influence of just past events on current events. It seems quite likely that emotional aspects of contrast come into play in local contrast. Some time ago, Mackintosh (1974) argued that the Amsel Frustration Effect (FE) is a type of local positive contrast (see Chapter 4). The FE is usually considered an example of the energizing effect of frustration. The prototypical demonstration involved two runways (and associated goal boxes) that rats traversed in sequence. In the basic procedure, animals were rewarded intermittently in the first goal box and consistently in the second goal box. The behavior of most interest occurs in the second alley, where animals run faster following a nonrewarded trial in the first goal box than following a rewarded trial there (see Amsel & Roussel, 1952; Davenport, Flaherty & Dyrud, 1966; Davenport &

Thompson, 1965; Wagner, 1959). This faster running (or shorter latency to press a lever) *following* a nonrewarded versus a rewarded trial is assumed to reflect an energizing influence of frustration; this is referred to as the FE.

Apparently, the same effect has been demonstrated utilizing a multiple schedule procedure (Scull, Davies & Amsel, 1970). This study employed a type of multiple, FI-30-second, Ext schedule and found that the rats responded faster to S+ when the previous "trial" was nonrewarded than when it was rewarded. The same effect occurred when a "mixed" schedule was used (that is, a schedule without discriminative stimuli signalling the reward conditions). The authors interpreted these results as examples of positive behavioral contrast (we would now say local positive behavioral contrast) – contrast due to the sequential effect of S+ following a nonrewarded response.

The facts that (a) subjects turn away from the S- immediately after its onset; (b) contrast does not occur with a long interval between S- and S+ (Wilton & Clements, 1972); (c) corticosterone elevation seems most prominent just after a schedule shift; (d) some drugs are most effective with difficult discriminations – the condition that seems to maximize local contrast; and (e) amygdala lesions reduce positive behavioral contrast and the FE (see previous discussion; Henke & Maxwell, 1973), whereas lesions of the ventromedial hypothalamus increase both (see previous discussion, and Henke, 1974), are all consistent with attributing a role to emotional responses in local positive contrast. Consistent also is the often expressed view that local positive contrast reflects a rebound from inhibition (of responses during S-) (see, for example, Coelho De Rose, 1986; Mackintosh, 1974; Malone & Cleary, 1986; Nevin, 1973; Terrace, 1966c). Underlying this view may be the assumption that the animals are inhibiting their responses because of the aversive consequences of responding without reinforcement (Amsel, 1992).

One major problem with assuming that local contrast is causally related to an emotional response (and that the FE is a type of local contrast) is that anxiolytic drugs that reduce behavioral contrast (such as barbiturates) do not affect the FE (Ison, Daly & Glass, 1967; see Gray, 1982, 1987, for reviews).

The role of emotion in behavioral contrast would be greatly clarified if pharmacological and neurobiological manipulations were incorporated into studies that use behavioral parameters designed to maximize the contributions of either local or anticipatory factors. The previous review suggests several steps that might be taken. For example, difficulty of the discrimination could be varied to emphasize one or the other aspect of contrast; temporal parameters optimal for anticipatory contrast could be utilized; the Williams three-ply multiple schedule, with systematically varied parameters, could be used to investigate concurrently the effects of neurobiological treatments on local versus anticipatory contrast; drug treatments could be applied either early in training (during the presence of local contrast) or after local contrast has faded but anticipatory contrast remains (see Cleary, 1992).

A reasonable interpretation of current knowledge might be that emotional reactions may play a significant role in local contrast, but anticipatory contrast may reflect the operation of other psychological factors. It is not clear if emotional reactions are necessary for the initial development of anticipatory contrast. Also not clear is exactly how emotional reactions act on a behavioral and neurobiological basis to produce contrast. For example, why should an emotional reaction be expected to facilitate the behavior (operant response) that produces positive contrast and interfere with that same behavior in the negative contrast situation?

Inhibition

The concept of inhibition has been used in two principal ways with regard to behavioral contrast. First, local positive contrast has often been described in terms of a rebound from inhibition that presumably exists during S- (see, for example, Malone, 1976; Nevin, 1973). This interpretation is often indistinguishable from an interpretation in terms of emotional reactivity other than it is perhaps more neutral in terms of mechanism. There is no more evidence in favor of, or opposed to, this theory than there is for the emotional response theory (for detailed discussions of inhibition in contrast, see Mackintosh, 1974; Nevin, 1973; and Williams, 1983). Among the principal items of difficulty for an explanation of positive contrast in terms of rebound from inhibition are the following: the data from Williams's previously cited experiments that show contrast occurs primarily toward the end of the S+ period (anticipatory contrast), rather than at the beginning; the lack of a relationship between responding during S- and degree of contrast (Kodera & Rilling, 1976); the occurrence of contrast after time-out periods (absence of discriminative cues), when there can be no responding to an S- (see Mackintosh, Little & Lord, 1972; Taus & Hearst, 1970).[5] However, as discussed when interpreting behavioral contrast in terms of an emotional response, the various demonstrations of local contrast under some parameters (see Malone, 1976; Malone & Cleary, 1986; Nevin & Shettleworth, 1966; Vieth & Rilling, 1972; Yarczower, 1970) suggest that a process like inhibition, or withdrawal from S-, does play some role in local contrast, but it is almost certainly not the cause of overall (sustained) contrast. What is currently lacking is any understanding of a mechanism – neurobiological or behavioral – by which inhibition would produce contrast.

The second way in which the concept of inhibition has been used is in terms of the performance of the control group/condition against which contrast is measured. Catania showed that reinforcement of one response inhibits other reinforced responding on a concurrent schedule (Catania, 1969) and that reinforced responding can be self-inhibiting (Catania, 1973). Catania suggested that this may be an issue related to the occurrence of behavioral contrast on multiple schedules,

---

[5] Malone (1976) failed to find contrast with time-out periods, and Vieth and Rilling (1972) found greater contrast with S- presentation than with time-out periods.

which are typically measured after a shift from reinforced responding in the presence of either of two stimuli to reinforced responding in the presence of only one of those stimuli. In a variation on this theme, McSweeney (1987) has argued that behavior in the first component of a multiple schedule could be suppressed by the delayed reinforcement to the same response when reinforcers occur in the second component of the schedule (for example, in a VI, VI schedule). If this schedule is now shifted to VI, Ext, as is often done in contrast studies, then a source of suppression is removed and responding in the unchanged component should be elevated, as is the case in positive behavioral contrast. This view of contrast is consistent with aspects of the following schedule's being the major determinant of sustained contrast (anticipatory contrast), but, as McSweeney notes, it does not provide a mechanism for the occurrence of contrast.

Summary

Behavioral contrast occurs in multiple schedules when animals are switched from equivalent reinforcement schedules in the presence of two stimuli to differential reinforcement schedules in the presence of those same stimuli. There are two aspects to contrast – local and sustained. Local contrast occurs at transitions zones between S+ and S- stimuli; it may diminish with extended training; and it seems most likely to be related to emotional responses activated by the changes in reward schedules signalled by S+ and S-. The more enduring aspects of contrast are anticipatory in nature, being controlled by characteristics of the impending schedule relative to the current schedule. Thus, animals respond to the current schedule in comparison both to the one that they have just left and to what will be coming next. Both aspects of contrast are controlled by relative rates of reinforcement in the two schedules, whereas relative rates of responding per se are not an important determinant of contrast.

Summary: incentive contrast and behavioral contrast compared

There are a number of procedural characteristics that differentiate the usual behavioral contrast experiment from the discrete-trial incentive contrast experiments.

Thus, behavioral contrast studies generally

(a) use response rate as the dependent variable rather than use the latency measures characteristic of discrete-trial studies;
(b) vary reinforcement schedule rather than reinforcement magnitude;
(c) use pigeons rather than rats as subjects;
(d) employ a zero "intertrial interval," whereas the interval is considerably greater in discrete-trial experiments;
(e) utilize a period of nondifferential reinforcement prior to a shift to differential reinforcement;

    (f) have a much greater total time in experimental training than do incentive contrast studies; and

    (g) use preshift baselines rather than unshifted control groups for comparison purposes.

There are exceptions to all these generalizations, but they characterize the typical behavioral contrast experiment. Even though these procedural differences exist, there are many similarities between behavioral contrast and discrete-trial incentive contrast effects. Both differential conditioning experiments in runways and behavioral contrast studies are best considered as representing a combination of successive and anticipatory contrast (see Dachowski & Brazier, 1991, for a "taxonomy of contrast"). (In this regard, simultaneous contrast, differential conditioning, and behavioral contrast all represent variations on the same design.)

    Two studies provide clear examples of the similarity between behavioral contrast and contrast in differential conditioning. Gonzalez and Champlin (1974) used pigeons on a multiple schedule and measured response rate (characteristic of behavioral contrast studies), but they varied reward magnitude (1 versus 10 pellets) on a VI-1-minute, VI-1-minute schedule, had a brief intertrial interval (ITI) (2 seconds), used independent control groups at the two reward levels, and did not have a period of nondifferential reinforcement (all characteristic of discrete-trial contrast studies).

    Under these conditions, negative contrast was obtained but not positive contrast – typical results in differential conditioning studies. In a second study in the same paper, Gonzalez and Champlin eliminated the ITI and instituted a period of nondifferential reinforcement (10 pellets) prior to the shift. Under these conditions, both positive and negative contrast occurred – results characteristic of the behavioral contrast procedure. It is not known whether it was the elimination of the ITI or the nondifferential preshift period that led to the enhancement of the positive contrast effect. But the use of the nondifferential preshift period does have one clear implication – it sets the occasion for a successive contrast effect, as well as the discriminative contrast to occur. That is, if the nondifferential period is with the large reward (as in this study), then SNC should occur under the S– condition, and if the nondifferential period is with the small reward, then SPC could occur under the S+ condition. In the usual positive behavioral contrast study, the period of nondifferential reinforcement is with the large reward (for example, VI-1-minute, VI-1-minute shifted to VI-1-minute, Ext). The Gonzalez and Champlin study indicates that this condition may enhance positive contrast – and, of course, positive contrast is readily obtained in behavioral contrast experiments.

    In the other study of interest, Padilla (1971) used rats and black and white runways (typical of discrete-trial studies), but he varied schedule of reinforcement, had no ITI, and had the rats freely shuttling between the alleys, thereby creating rate of shuttling as a dependent variable. These last three conditions are all characteristic of behavioral contrast experiments. Padilla obtained evidence of both positive and negative contrast with schedule variations (and also with reward magnitude variations). These two studies indicate that different research traditions (operant and runway) are being used to study the same basic phenomenon, but the differential behavioral contrast procedure emphasizes comparison of rewards over time, whereas the differential conditioning procedure emphasizes comparison of rewards over context, as well as over time.

Given this, there are many functional similarities between behavioral contrast and discrete-trial contrast. For example, contrast is inversely related to ITI in both; contrast can be produced with differences of delay of reinforcement, as well as with differences in schedule and magnitude of reinforcement, in both (see previous discussion and Keller, 1970); variations in stimulus similarity affect both, and similar theoretical interpretations have arisen in both traditions. It is also possible that behavioral contrast and contrast in differential conditioning may be grouped together and separated from successive contrast by phylogenetic considerations – the former being more general than the latter (Bitterman, 1975; Pert and Gonzalez, 1974).

7   Summary and epilogue

Tell the world how much you earn and all who earn less will dis-
like you for being outrageously overpaid, while all who earn
more will hold you in contempt for being worth so little.
                                          – Russell Baker, 1989

Summary

Several isolated studies beginning in 1928 and ranging through the late 1950s
showed that rats and monkeys were capable of responding to rewards in terms
of their relative value as well as their absolute value. These reward relativity
effects were observed as exaggerations in behavior when rats were shifted from
one reward to another or experienced two different rewards in two different
stimulus contexts. The behavioral exaggerations are typically measured in
comparison to a separate group of animals that experiences only one level of
reward.

Successive contrast

As research activity in this area increased, it became apparent that relativity
effects (contrast effects) occurred in several different paradigms. The first effect
discovered occurs when animals are trained with one level of reward and then
shifted to a lower level. Compared to unshifted control animals, shifted animals
show an abrupt decrement in goal-directed behavior and perform more poorly in
this regard than unshifted controls. The decrement in goal-directed behavior is
accompanied by increases in various activity-related behaviors and hormonal
indicants of stress. Within several days, the shifted rats typically recover back to
baseline levels represented by unshifted controls. This successive negative contrast effect (SNC) is robust, but it is affected by a number of parameters. In general, SNC varies directly with degree of reward disparity between preshift and
postshift levels; it diminishes with increasing retention intervals between the last
experience with the preshift reward and the first experience with the postshift
reward; it tends to be enhanced by increased motivation (increased food deprivation); and it may be diminished by prior experience with the eventual postshift
reward (perhaps because of incentive averaging) – but this effect is limited,
because SNC will also occur repeatedly when rats are exposed to repeated
reward reductions.

167

The current evidence indicates that SNC is restricted phylogenetically – it occurs in mammals, birds, and bees, but not in fish or amphibians. Different lines of rats selectively bred for other purposes also differ in degree of SNC, and it is also possible to selectively breed rat lines that differ in degree of SNC.

Successive negative contrast occurs in complex feeding situations, in complex environments, and with aversive events as reinforcers. It also occurs even if there is a substantial change in context between the preshift and postshift phases of the experiment, indicating that animals readily compare rewards across different contexts.

Although behaviorally simple, SNC may involve several psychological processes: sensory detection of a reward change; evaluative comparison of the current reward with the memory of past rewards; searching for the "missing" reward if the new reward is valued less than the original reward; a stress/emotional reaction if the original reward is not obtained; and eventual recovery. The robustness and ubiquity of SNC suggest that it represents an important part of mammalian behavior (or at least rat behavior). A tendency toward "dissatisfaction" may prove adaptive in foraging situations, perhaps by biasing a "giving-up-time" function toward leaving when a current foraging patch falls below expectation.

Pharmacological evidence suggests that SNC has an element of aversiveness; recovery is promoted by anxiolytics but not, in general, by drugs with other effects. It is possible that this aversiveness arises because of a conflict created by the confinement of rats in restricted areas, as is typical of laboratory studies, and would not necessarily be the case in a natural setting where an animal was free to leave, perhaps to discover greener fields. Preliminary psychopharmacological profiles also indicate that SNC shows a pattern of drug responsiveness that shares commonalities with animal models of fear and anxiety, but these data also indicate that SNC is not totally congruent with fear and anxiety. The emotional reaction that accompanies reward reduction may have distinctive characteristics, even in the emotional repertoire of lower mammals.

Little is known regarding the neurobiology of SNC. Current evidence suggests that instrumental (appetitive) behaviors that reflect SNC rely on systems involving the hippocampus, entorhinal cortex, and cingulate cortex, whereas consummatory contrast effects (and perhaps the basic reward comparison process) involve at least amygdala and parabrachial nucleus systems. There is also evidence that a GABA system mediates aspects of recovery from contrast, but the localization of this system (systems?) and its interaction with other transmitter networks has not been uncovered.

When reward level is increased, shifted rats may perform at a higher level than unshifted rats receiving the same level of reward. This successive positive contrast effect (SPC) is much less robust than SNC – so much so that some early reviews dismissed it as a nonreliable phenomenon. However, the weight of evidence suggests that SPC is real, but special procedures (such as delay of reward) may be necessary for a clear demonstration. Part of the difficulty in observing

SPC may be artifactual: Performance limitations ("ceiling" effects) may obscure SPC, and generalization decrement resulting from changed stimulus conditions (that is, different reward) may antagonize whatever behavior-enhancing effects the reward increase has. (Therefore, generalization decrement should enhance SNC.) It is also possible that SPC is less robust than SNC because there is a true asymmetry in nature. It could be the case, for example, that excess "satisfaction""(SPC) is not particularly adaptive, as compared to a tendency for dissatisfaction (SNC), given the environment in which mammals evolved.

Anticipatory contrast

The suppression of intake of a valued substance when it is followed, in once-daily pairings, by a preferred substance is also a robust type of contrast. This anticipatory negative contrast effect (ANC) develops within a few pairings and, current evidence indicates, will be maintained as long as the differential reward conditions are maintained.

Anticipatory negative contrast in consummatory behavior also develops within-subjects when contextual stimuli are differentially paired with the contrast (such as 0.15% saccharin followed by 32% sucrose) and control (such as 0.15% saccharin followed by 0.15% saccharin) conditions, but ANC does not develop when flavor or odor cues are used as differential signals for impending solutions. ANC varies in an orderly fashion with changes in the reward characteristics of the two solutions (curvilinear relationship), with the intersolution interval (inverse relationship), with access time (curvilinear relationship when access is equal to the two solutions; inverse when only the initial solution increases in duration; direct when only the second solution increases in duration), and, apparently, with both the caloric value and hedonic value the of solutions. In addition, ANC is readily replaced by a facilitation or reinforcement effect when a lick-contingency is imposed; it is not altered by any drug or lesion treatment thus far investigated.

Anticipatory negative contrast may reflect processes normally used by a foraging animal – processes such as the relative evaluation of the nutritional/hedonic properties of current compared to future food sources and of the time/effort involved in obtaining the future food substance. Apparently analogous effects have also been obtained in the food consumption of children in laboratory situations.

Current evidence suggests that hedonic devaluation of the initial solution is not the mechanism by which ANC is produced. Inhibition may be the best approach to understanding ANC, but inhibition of behavior in the presence of a satisfactory substance while waiting for a better one will have a different psychology and neurobiology than inhibition produced by impending aversive events. In this regard, it is likely that ANC is psychologically and neurobiologically quite different from SNC.

There is, thus far, no evidence that anticipatory positive contrast occurs in consummatory behavior.

Simultaneous contrast in consummatory behavior

If the anticipatory contrast procedure is extended so that animals receive more than one exposure to each of two solutions each day, then what is termed (somewhat misleadingly) simultaneous contrast occurs. In most published studies of consummatory simultaneous contrast, the same subjects receive the two control conditions (for example, 4% sucrose in each of two bottles on some days and 32% sucrose in each of two bottles on other days) and the contrast conditions (that is, 32% sucrose in one bottle and 4% sucrose in the alternative bottle). Other designs have used independent groups in each control condition, leaving only the contrast condition as a within-subject manipulation. Simultaneous contrast may capture aspects of both successive contrast and anticipatory contrast, while also containing a unique component.

When the within-subject design is used, degree of overall contrast (positive plus negative) varies systematically with reward disparity, following a power function with an exponent above 1.00. Degree of contrast seems unaffected by degree of deprivation and by the few drug and lesion manipulations conducted thus far. There is the suggestion that sensory interaction between the two solutions may contribute substantially to simultaneous contrast.

In considering only consummatory behavior, some degree of commonality among successive, anticipatory, and simultaneous contrast is suggested by the finding that the two Maudsley strains of rats differed in all three types of consummatory contrast and in the same direction – the Reactive rats showed smaller contrast than the Nonreactive rats. Contrary evidence, however, is provided by the finding that rats selectively bred to differ in SNC do not differ in anticipatory contrast, and by the finding that Syracuse High and Low avoidance rats differ in SNC but do not differ in simultaneous contrast. Also, the finding that chlordiazepoxide promotes recovery from SNC but does not affect ANC contrast or simultaneous contrast argues strongly for the existence of separate mechanisms. Similarly, sodium amobarbital antagonizes SNC, but it does not affect simultaneous contrast; and cyproheptadine antagonizes SNC, but does not affect ANC.

A tentative conclusion regarding contrast in consummatory behavior is that there are at least three ways in which the comparison of rewarding solutions may be made – retrograde (SNC), anterograde (ANC), or concurrently – and that different mechanisms may be involved in all three cases of reward relativity. The successive procedure may contain important search and emotional components, the anticipatory contrast procedure may contain an important associative component and lack an aversive emotional aspect, and the simultaneous procedure may be heavily influenced by sensory interactions.

Contrast in discrimination learning

Relativity effects are also readily apparent when rats are trained in different contexts (for example, black and white runways) with a different level of reward in each. The factors affecting negative contrast in differential conditioning (contrast across context) seem to be largely the same as those affecting SNC (which is contrast across time). There is a suggestion, however, that the contrast in differential conditioning may be more general than SNC because it apparently occurs across a broader phylogenetic spectrum; it occurs with sucrose solutions as well as solid food; and it seems to be more readily obtainable with differences in delay of reward than is SNC.

Contrast may develop more slowly with a difficult discrimination (small difference between S+ and S- cues) than with an easy discrimination, but final degree of contrast is apparently equivalent. However, very little research has been done on this issue in runway studies with rats. There is reason to think that there would be limits to the degree that rewards interact across space (as there is across time). However, these limits have not been widely explored for contrast with differential conditioning.

As was the case with SPC, positive contrast in differential conditioning is a rare event and its demonstration may require special considerations, such as introducing a constant delay of reinforcement in order to remove potential "ceiling" effects created by control rats' running at the maximum possible speed.

Behavioral contrast is the term historically applied to contrast effects that occur in discrimination training when free-operant procedures, such as multiple schedules, are used. These experiments typically differ procedurally from runway differential conditioning studies in that pigeons are usually the subjects, reward is usually varied in density over time (for example, multiple variable interval schedules) rather than in terms of amount of pellets, and many long daily training sessions are given rather than a few trials per day for two or three weeks.

The operant procedures have revealed two aspects to contrast in discrimination learning – local and sustained. Local contrast occurs at transitions zones between S+ and S- stimuli, it may diminish with extended training, and it seems most likely to be related to emotional responses activated by the changes in reward schedules signalled by S+ and S-. Local contrast effects may be examples of successive contrast effects.

The more enduring aspects of contrast are anticipatory in nature, being controlled by characteristics of the impending schedule relative to the current schedule. Thus, animals respond to the current schedule in comparison both to the one that they have just left and to what will be coming next. Both aspects of contrast are controlled by relative rates of reinforcement in the two schedules, whereas rate of responding per se is not an important determinant of behavioral contrast.

Duration of the two components (S+ and S-) affects degree of contrast – the ratios of the two components seem to be the important parameter and, in general, the shorter the S+ component compared to the S- component, the greater the response rate in the presence of S+. Stimulus similarity also affects behavioral contrast. Current evidence suggests that local contrast is related to stimulus similarity in a curvilinear fashion, whereas anticipatory contrast may be greatest with dissimilar stimuli.

Many theorists have suggested an emotional aspect to behavioral contrast , and there is substantial evidence in favor of this position. However, current analysis suggests that the emotional reaction may be restricted primarily to local contrast. Anticipatory contrast apparently does not involve a change in the value of the initial reward, even though response rate controlled by that reward changes as the animal's behavior comes under the influence of the following reward. In the anticipatory aspects of behavioral contrast, just as in anticipatory contrast in consummatory behavior, there seems to be an inverse relationship between response rate and preference – a paradox that remains to be resolved.

Psychologically, successive contrast and local contrast are probably fundamentally the same process – a process that enhances reward differences at the temporal border of reward transitions. Anticipatory contrast may contain less of an emotional element and a substantial associate component. It may be involved in longer-term adjustments to reward disparities and provide adaptive behaviors related to forgoing a current reward while "waiting" for a better one (anticipatory negative contrast) or to capitalize on a current limited availability of a preferred reward (anticipatory positive contrast).

Contrast in discrimination learning tasks may involve elements of both of these fundamental types of contrast. Indeed, the influence of successive contrast effects may appear even in the simpler aspects of anticipatory contrast described in Chapter 5; cross-day transitional effects may occur and thereby modulate the degree of anticipatory contrast present (Timberlake & Engle, 1995).

The simultaneous contrast that occurs in the consumption of sweet solutions is procedurally similar to contrast that occurs in discrimination training, but there may be a special sensory interaction, due to the nature of the reward and the solutions' rapid juxtaposition, that adds a unique element to this type of contrast. Possibly, this "unique" element is nothing more than the additive effects of contrast in a sensory system and contrast in a more abstract, higher-order, value system.

The ubiquity of contrast in rewarded behavior suggests that relativity is a fundamental aspect of animal motivation. Certainly, the regularity characterizing the occurrence of both successive negative contrast and recovery from SNC suggests a process of fundamental importance in evolution – a regularity of nature.

Epilogue

If reward relativity effects are pervasive in the behavior of lower animals and if there are at least superficial resemblances between aspects of contrast effects in animals and human behavior in similar situations (for example, the Russell Baker epigram), it may be worth the time to speculate a little on these parallels.

Although it is "simple," successive negative contrast may have multiple stages. The observations of the first investigators of contrast were perspicacious in that subsequent evidence supports the involvement of both searching behavior and emotional reactions in successive negative contrast. Furthermore, there may be an orderly sequence of psychological processes triggered by reward reductions (Chapter 4), a sequence that, while differing in detail, may be quite similar in events as diverse as reward shifts in rats, material loss in humans (or thwarted expectations), and loss of a valued person. Thus, successive negative contrast bears a resemblance to disappointment in humans. In rats, the resemblance is in terms of the sequence of events – reduction from the usual level of reward – and, additionally, in terms of the evidence that negative contrast is stressful and in terms of the regularity of recovery. A description of a more persuasive similarity in a chimpanzee was provided by Sue Savage-Rumbaugh. The chimp, Sherman, carried an issue of *National Geographic* with a cover picture of Koko, the gorilla, over to Dr. Savage-Rumbaugh and typed "outdoor" on his keyboard. Once outside, Dr. Savage-Rumbaugh realized that Sherman was leading her to the gorilla cages, where he was generally not allowed to go. Dr. Savage-Rumbaugh then indicated that they could not go there. Sherman then "became very despondent, dropping the picture of Koko which he had been hugging tightly for the last 15 minutes. He whimpered and gestured in the direction of the gorilla cages he then moped about for some time" (Sue Savage-Rumbaugh, personal communication).

Although disappointment is a condition of life and disappointments normally abate over time,[1] there are those that lead to more serious psychological and social consequences. Successive negative contrast in animals may provide a model for the characterization of the neurobiology and psychopharmacology of disappointment and, perhaps more important, an understanding of individual differences in "disappointability." The paradigm may also be useful for further understanding of dissatisfaction as a driving force in cultural or evolutionary change. As suggested in Chapter 4, a phenomenon as robust as successive negative contrast probably has had some adaptive value, perhaps in shaping the process of foraging. Carrying the foraging argument to a perhaps extreme position, the "behavioral dispersion" and searching produced by reward reduction may also be analogous to (or homologous with) migration patterns in humans when rewards fall below expectations.

The sustained contrast that occurs with discrimination training is also robust, but it is subject to modification by many parameters and less clearly accounted for than successive contrast. One of the relevant issues is that behavioral contrast is influenced by the degree of similarity between the S+ and S- stimuli; current data suggest that local contrast and anticipatory contrast may show different functional relationships with stimulus similarity. This could be both a point of attack for further understanding the two processes in animal research and a fruitful area for research on human applications of contrast with concurrently experienced differential rewards.

Apparent instances of such contrast in humans are numerous. For example,

---

[1] F. Scott Fitzgerald referred to the "abortive sorrows and shortwinded elations of men" in *The Great Gatsby*.

as the quote from a *New York Times* column by Russell Baker suggests, salaries are a frequent source of comparison and irritation. In contemporary society, it is common to read of this issue in the sports pages where athletes, given enormous compensation in absolute terms, are often unsatisfied because they compare their salaries to those of teammates or other athletes viewed as equal in ability.[2]

A common problem in business is how to deal with rising costs through salary reductions. Implicitly aware of potential problems arising from salary reductions, a number of corporate executives have sought to curtail salary expenses by adopting a lower salary scale, but only for new employees. However, this strategy is not particularly effective because the new employees tend to compare their responsibilities to the older employees' and, seeing that they do the same work, are not happy with the arrangement.[3]

Although there are the occasional grumble and various attempts to "reform" the health care system, most people do not begrudge physicians a reasonably high level of income. This is probably because physicians are not viewed as directly comparable by most people when the cost and length of their education, the time demands placed on many physicians, and the potential importance of their profession for each of us, are all taken into account.

Thus, the issue of stimulus similarity in sustained contrast in animals may translate into the issues of comparability and relevance in determining whether or not contrast occurs, and the extent of irritation or disturbance elicited by the contrast, in the daily social behavior of humans. This question of comparability may also be related to "frames of reference" in human judgments. Tversky and Kahneman have shown that many judgments are influenced by the way in which people categorize their comparisons. For example, someone who has paid $10 for a theater ticket and then loses it would be unlikely to purchase another ticket – because he or she would not want to pay twice for the same ticket. However, if the same person discovered that he or she had lost a $10 bill just before paying $10 for the ticket, that person would go ahead and buy the ticket. Apparently, the "lost" $10 is coded as not relevant to the price of the ticket and, therefore, the price of the ticket is not annoying. Tversky and Kahneman have uncovered many other examples of relativity in "rational" judgments (Kahneman & Tversky, 1984). The relevance of animal research on incentive relativity, particularly on the role of stimulus context in comparison and contrast, to these various context effects in human behavior remains to be explored.

---

[2] A ballplayer for the New York Mets was involved in a fight with a teammate and threatened to leave the team after signing a contract for $7.2 million dollars and then learning that he was still only the sixth highest paid player on the team. The fight involved one of those paid more (*New York Times*, 1989). A football player for the Dallas Cowboys threatened to leave when they signed a new player at a salary higher than his $450,000. He stated that he was "not second to anyone" (*New York Times*, 1986). Numerous examples of related problems can be found in the sports pages.

[3] See, for example, "Two Tier Wage Systems," *New York Times* (1987). This problem was also illustrated in a 1986 "Agatha Crumm" cartoon in which the supervisor (Agatha) informs an employee (Perkins) that his work is very good and that he will get another gold star. When Perkins is not pleased, Agatha notes that gold stars used to make him happy. Perkins responds that this was before he learned that other people received bonuses.

Local contrast may also play a role in human behavior. For example, it is not uncommon for divorced or separated couples to share their children. It is conceivable that any aberrant behaviors that might occur at the transition period from one parent to the other may be examples of local contrast. Indeed, some behaviors such as dependency or noncompliance have been interpreted in just this way (Gross, 1982). Considered in this way, any regularly occurring transition period between differential levels of reward might contain a component of contrast. Thus, the "Thank God It's Friday" and the "Blue Monday" attitudes may represent local contrast in those who do not find sufficient rewards in their work.

There is another aspect of contrast with potential relevance to human behavior. The nature of the suppression produced in the anticipatory negative contrast procedure is not understood. One possibility is that an acceptable substance (or event) that precedes a preferred substance (or event) is devalued through the development of an association between the two valued substances. An interpretation along these lines has the advantage of explaining how a "future" event can influence current behavior without an animal's having the ability actually to anticipate the future in a cognitive sense. As reviewed in Chapters 5 and 6, however, there is no evidence thus far supporting the devaluation interpretation. Furthermore, there is a lack of agreement on what role Pavlovian associative processes play in this type of learning. Researchers in the operant tradition focus on *responses* elicited by such an association, and such responses should interfere with anticipatory contrast (see Chapter 6). However, researchers in the tradition of general associationism consider that Pavlovian CSs may have signal value and emotion-eliciting properties, as well as response-eliciting properties. It is possible that the signalling or emotional aspects of associative learning alter responding to the initial substance (considered to be the CS in this paradigm).

Anticipatory contrast, considered in this fashion, has several areas of potential relevance. For example, delay of gratification is often considered to be a desirable trait and a method of individual and cultural advancement. One way in which an analogue of delay of gratification is studied in animal research is choice between large delayed rewards versus immediate small rewards – sometimes termed the study of impulsiveness (see, for example, Logue & King, 1991). The anticipatory contrast procedure may be related to this delay of reward research, but it is not identical; in the anticipatory contrast procedure, the animals are free to have both the immediately available substance and the delayed substance. Yet, they "choose" to forgo the immediate substance and wait for the preferred substance.

Anticipatory contrast may also enhance our understanding of drug addiction. One of the socially and individually deleterious aspects of addictive behavior is that addicted individuals often lose interest in other activities that are normally rewarding. It is as if the great reward value of addictive drugs suppresses interest in normally acceptable rewards. But this bears a resemblance to anticipatory contrast where, for example, a subsequent 32% sucrose solution will cause a rat to largely ignore a current 4% sucrose solution – something that would normally be acceptable and even consumed with a degree of avidity. Is it useful to consider this suppressive effect of addictive behavior to be a form of anticipatory contrast? To what degree are rats (or humans) able to compare reward value in the abstract – independent of sensory modality?

Contrast undoubtedly exerts an influence in a variety of animal and human behaviors – sharpening the borders between reward alternatives, promoting dissatisfaction (or excessive satisfaction), redirecting behaviors, and biasing judgments in a nonrational fashion. However, we are far from understanding exactly the degree to which contrast effects are important in the behavior of lower animals and humans, and exactly how and why they occur.

Appendix:
Psychopharmacology of selected animal
models of anxiety

... fear on one side,
... on another anxiety,
... here pain for the thing that was loved and lost,
... there grief for an injury received ...

– St. Augustine
City of God

Successive negative contrast and selected
anxiety models

Table 4.1 listed the effects of various drugs in several animals models of anxiety – three of the models involved shock as an aversive stimulus (potentiated startle, punished drinking, potentiated startle), one involved novelty and open space (elevated plus maze), and one involved reward reduction (successive negative contrast). The data suggested that these diverse situations had much in common, at least as far as commonality of drug effects was concerned, but there were also differences. The idea behind analyses such as that presented in Table 4.1 is that insight into the diversity of emotional states/physiological processes in rats may be gained from the combined examination of behavioral tasks and psychopharmacological profiles. This Appendix presents the references used to construct Table 4.1.

Excellent reviews of the effects of anxiolytics and other agents on a wide range of proposed animal models of anxiety are presented in File (1991), Treit (1985), and Willner (1991). An analysis of degree of commonality among several animal models of anxiety is presented by Belzung and Le Pape (1994). Presented here will be more detailed documentation of the material considered in relation to Table 4.1 in Chapter 4.

Benzodiazepines, ethanol, and barbiturates

The benzodiazepines are highly effective in all models; barbiturates are generally effective; ethanol tends to be effective, but there are exceptions.

Punishment-suppressed drinking is alleviated by CDP (6–40 mg/kg) and other benzodiazepines (see Colpeart, Meert, Niemegeers & Janssen, 1985; Goldberg, Salama, Patel & Malick, 1983; Howard & Pollard, 1991; Kilts, Commissaris &

Rech, 1981; Vogel, Beer & Clody,1971); by sodium amobarbital (3–10 mg/kg) and other barbiturates (Kilts et al., 1981; Vogel et al., 1971); but not by ethanol in a dose range of 30–2,000 mg/kg of a 10% solution (Kilts et al., 1981).

Benzodiazepines (CDP, diazepam) have anticonflict activity in the Geller–Seifter procedure, with CDP being effective at doses as low as 2.5 mg/kg p.o. (Cook & Sepinwall, 1975) and diazepam at 1.0 mg/kg i.p. (Kilts et al., 1981). Both of these agents and midazolam are also effective in the Davidson–Cook modification of operant conflict (Green & Hodges, 1991; Howard & Pollard, 1991). Barbiturates also have antipunishment effects (Cook & Davidson, 1973; Geller & Seifter, 1960; Howard & Pollard, 1991; Kilts et al., 1981); the effects of ethanol are inconsistent (Cook & Davidson, 1973; Geller, Bachman & Seifter, 1963; Sepinwall & Cook, 1978), although there are some situations in which ethanol is clearly effective (see Cook & Davidson, 1973, p. 333).

Potentiated startle is reduced by the benzodiazepines diazepam, flurazepam (Davis, 1979, 1991), and midazolam (Hijzen & Slangen, 1989), by sodium amytal (Chi, 1965), and by ethanol (Williams, described in Miller & Barry, 1960).

In the plus maze, diazepam (0.5–2 mg/kg), CDP (5 and 7.5 mg/kg), and midazolam (2.5 mg/kg) had anxiolytic effects (Cruz, Frei & Graeff, 1994; Dunn, Corbett & Fielding, 1989; File & Aranko, 1988; File & Johnston, 1989; Lister, 1991; Moser et al., 1990; Pellow, Chopin, File & Briley, 1985). Acute phenobarbitone (25 and 35 mg/kg) had a nonreliable anxiolytic effect in one study (Pellow et al., 1985), and a reliable anxiolytic effect (35 mg/kg) in another study (Johnston & File, 1989). In mice, CDP (7.5 and 10 mg/kg), sodium pentobarbital (30 mg/kg), and ethanol (1.6 g/kg) were all reported to have anxiolytic effects (Hale, Johnston & Becker, 1990; Lister, 1987).

Thus, the benzodiazepines and barbiturates have generally consistent anxiolytic effects in contrast and in the comparison models, whereas the effects of ethanol are somewhat model specific. However, nothing has been reported in these other models that is comparable to the finding that CDP and ethanol are ineffective on the first postshift day in contrast, but sodium amobarbital is effective on both the first and second postshift days.

Morphine

The antipunishment effects of morphine in punished drinking and operant conflict are limited or nonexistent (Leaf & Muller, 1965; Sepinwall & Cook, 1978), but the drug is effective in reducing potentiated startle (Davis, 1979, 1991). As in the contrast procedure, naloxone antagonized the effect of morphine but did not itself affect potentiated startle (Davis, 1979). There are apparently no reports of morphine in the plus maze.

Considering that the effects of morphine in contrast, although reliable, are small, and that they are marginal at best in punished drinking and operant conflict, current evidence indicates that a morphine-related endogenous opiate system may not be strongly involved in conflict situations, although it may have some role to play in nonconflict fear systems.

Serotonergic agents

The serotonergic system(s) have proven to have a complex pharmacology (Whitaker-Azmitia & Peroutka, 1990), and complex effects for serotonergic agents have been reported within and between the models considered here. In addition, many of the serotonergic agents under consideration affect other transmitter systems as well as serotonin; thus for many studies it is not clear if the reported effects are "purely" serotonergic or involve a complex of transmitter effects.

Serotonin antagonists

The general antagonists cyproheptadine (10 and 30 mg/kg), cinanserin (3 and 30 mg/kg), and methysergide (3 and 30 mg/kg) were all reported to have anticonflict effects in a punished drinking procedure (Boast, Popick, Stone, & Kalinsky, 1985). However, contrary results have been obtained. Kilts et al. (1981) reported that methysergide (1–10 mg/kg) was ineffective in their modification of the Vogel et al. procedure, and that cinanserin (10–100 mg/kg) was also ineffective except for a 56 mg/kg dose. In other studies, cyproheptadine, methysergide, and cinanserin were found ineffective in alleviating punished drinking (Kilts, Commissaris, Gordon & Rech, 1982; Petersen & Lassen, 1981).

The results obtained with serotonin antagonists in operant conflict have also been mixed. Cinanserin has been reported to have an anxiolytic effect at doses of 15 mg/kg (the same dose that is effective in contrast), but not at higher and lower doses (Cook & Sepinwall, 1975). However, Geller, Hartmann, and Croy (1974; reported in Gardner, 1986) found that a 60 mg/kg dose was effective, but lower doses were not. Also, low doses of methysergide have been reported effective, but a 10 mg/kg dose ineffective (Cook & Sepinwall, 1975). However, using different procedural parameters, Stein, Wise, and Beluzzi (1975) reported that a 10 mg/kg dose of methysergide had an antipunishment effect. In a variation of the Geller–Seifter procedure (for example, an FR- rather than a VI-reinforced period with interspersed periods of signaled CRF punishment), cinanserin (10–56 mg/kg) and methysergide (1–18 mg/kg) were found to be ineffective (Kilts et al., 1981). In a different modification of the basic Geller–Seifter procedure, Hodges, Green, and Glen (1987) found anxiolytic effects with both peripheral (2.5 and 5.0 mg/kg) and intra-amygdala administration of methysergide. Cyproheptadine has been found to have small but reliable anticonflict effects (Sepinwall & Cook, 1980), but Gardner (1985, p. 297) suggests that these could be due to direct effects of the drug on a chloride ionophore linked to GABA, rather than through a serotonergic mechanism. Another study failed to find an anticonflict effect of cyproheptadine (10 mg/kg p.o.) in a variant of the operant conflict test (Deacon & Gardner, 1986).

The variations among these and other studies (see Gardner, 1985, 1986; Kilts et al., 1981; Thiebot, 1986) in the effectiveness of 5-HT antagonists suggests that procedural factors, such as the schedules used, shock intensity, and preinjection time, may interact with drug and drug dose in determining the anticonflict activities of these 5-HT antagonists. In addition, the different antagonists used in these studies may be active in different brain regions (see Moret, 1985) and/or on different 5-HT receptor subtypes (see Ogren & Fuxe, 1985; Sills, Wolfe & Frazier, 1984).

One outcome is clear – the general 5-HT antagonists are not as effective as the benzodiazepines or barbiturates in punished drinking and operant conflict models. Furthermore, the specificity or quirkiness of their effectiveness suggests that the agents may be influencing some local behavior related to the demand characteristics of the experiment rather than a global anxiety mechanism.

It is also of interest that nothing like the powerful effects of cyproheptadine on contrast has been obtained in punished conflict procedures.

In the case of potentiated startle, the antagonists cinanserin (10 mg/kg) and cyproheptadine (5 mg/kg) are ineffective (Davis, Cassella & Kehne, 1988). There is some evidence that methysergide attenuates potentiated startle, but it also affects baseline response to the startle stimulus itself (Mansbach & Geyer, 1988). Reduction of serotonin with the synthesis inhibitor PCPA enhanced potentiated startle and baseline responding (Davis et al., 1988).

In the plus maze, cyproheptadine (0.5 mg/kg) had a nonreliable anxiogenic effect (Kshama, Hrishikeshava, Shanbhogue & Munonyedi, 1990). However, metergoline, a nonspecific serotonin antagonist that has not been used in contrast, had an anxiolytic effect (at 4 mg/kg, but not 2 or 10 mg/kg) (Pellow, Johnston & File, 1987). The administration of PCPA (200 mg/kg, three days prior to test) also has been reported to have an anxiolytic effect, greater than that of diazepam (Kshama et al., 1990). This anxiolytic effect of serotonin depletion on plus maze behavior was supported by the finding that major destruction of serotonergic innervation of the cortex and hippocampus by the neurotoxin 5,7-dihydroxytryptamine led to a substantial increase in the percentage of open-arm entries (Briley, Chopin, & Moret, 1990).

Specific 5-HT$_2$ antagonists

Specific antagonists of the 5-HT$_2$ receptor have not proven to be effective in the models under review here. Thus, ritanserin had no effect in a variant of the Geller–Seifter procedure (Deacon & Gardner, 1986) and ketanserin (2 mg/kg) was reported to have no effect on fear-potentiated startle (unpublished data cited in Davis, 1991). In the elevated plus maze, ritanserin (0.25, 1.25, and 10 mg/kg) reduced the percentage of open-arm entries and the percentage of time spent in the open arm – an anxiogenic rather than anxiolytic effect (Pellow et al., 1987).

Buspirone and gepirone

Buspirone and gepirone are 5-HT$_{1A}$ agonists. Because the 5-HT$_{1A}$ receptor functions as an autoreceptor, the increased activity of which reduces serotonin release, agonists at this receptor should decrease serotonin function, thereby acting like inhibitors of the system. The effects of buspirone on punished drinking are unclear. Buspirone has been found effective in several studies (see Eison, Eison, Stanley & Riblet, 1986; Moser et al., 1990; Riblet, Taylor, Eison & Stanton, 1982; Taylor et al., 1984; Weissman et al., 1984), but totally ineffective (in the same dose ranges) in others (see Gardner, 1986; Goldberg et al., 1983; Johnston & File, 1986; Sepinwall, 1985). There is some indication that buspirone might be more likely to be found effective under conditions of a reversed light/dark cycle (Eison et al., 1986) and when subjects that lick at a low rate are removed from the experiment. The data reviewed by Howard and Pollard (1991) also suggest that buspirone is more likely to be effective in tests using unsignalled shock than in tests using signalled shock.

Buspirone is largely ineffective in operant conflict when rats are used (see Gardner, 1986; but see Porter, Johnson & Jackson, 1985, and Young et al., 1987, for contrary evidence, and Soubrie, 1986, for a discussion of the issue); it may or may not be effective in monkeys (Sepinwall, 1985; Weissman et al., 1984); and in pigeons, buspirone, as well as gepirone, may have anxiolytic properties (Barrett, Witkin & Mansbach, 1984; Barrett, Witkin, Mansbach, Skolnick & Weissman, 1986), which are probably not due to dopaminergic actions in the case of buspirone (Witkin & Barrett, 1986).

Both buspirone and its analogue gepirone reduced the magnitude of potentiated startle (Kehne, Cassella & Davis, 1988; Mansbach & Geyer, 1988). However, the effects of buspirone in this paradigm may not be related to its effects on serotonergic systems (Davis, 1991; Davis, Cassella & Kehne, 1988; Davis, Hitchcock & Rosen, 1988).

The weight of the evidence suggests that systemically administered buspirone does not have an anxiolytic effect in the elevated plus maze. In one study, buspirone (0.5–8 mg/kg) had no reliable effect on arm entries and, at the highest doses, tended to decrease the percentage of time in the open arms – an anxiogenic effect (Pellow Johnston et al., 1987). Two other studies found no effect with low doses of buspirone, and anxiogeniclike effects with higher doses (1 and 2 mg/kg) (Moser, 1989; Moser et al., 1990). A nonreliable tendency for buspirone (2 mg/kg) to increase the percentage of time in open arms (an anxiolytic effect) was obtained in still another study (Kshama et al., 1990). However, contrary evidence – an anxiolytic effect of both buspirone (1 mg/kg) and gepirone (1 and 2.5 mg/kg) – was reported by Dunn et al. (1989). The latter paper seems to differ little from those finding negative results: There were minor handling differences prior to testing and the walls on the closed arms were lower (30 versus 50 cm) than in the other experiments.

There is a report that intra-hippocampal administration of buspirone (into the dentate gyrus) increased the time spent in the open arms (Kostowski, Plaznik & Stefanski, 1989).

Imipramine

The antidepressant imipramine affects adrenergic and serotonergic neurotransmitter systems. Its serotonergic effects are principally to block re-uptake of serotonin at presynaptic sites (Briley, 1985).

As in negative contrast, imipramine has been found to be ineffective (1–10 mg/kg) in the drinking-conflict procedure (Kilts et al., 1981, 1982) and, over a wide range of doses, in operant conflict (Cook & Davidson, 1973) as are (in general) other antidepressants with serotonergic activity (Gardner, 1985, p. 303).

Imipramine also did not reduce potentiated startle when given acutely (5 or 10 mg/kg), chronically (10 mg/kg), or both (Cassella & Davis, 1985), nor did imipramine (5–15 mg/kg) affect behavior in the elevated plus maze (Pellow et al., 1985).

Dopaminergic agents

The neuroleptic haloperidol has been found to have an anticonflict effect in punished drinking in low doses (0.05 and 0.10 mg/kg) (Pich & Samanin, 1986), but the neuroleptic chlorpromazine (0.1–3.0 mg/kg) does not alleviate punished drinking (Kilts et al., 1981). Amphetamine has been found to have no effect (Vogel et al., 1971) or to increase suppression in the punished-drinking procedure (Ford, Rech, Commissaris & Meyer, 1979).

Amphetamine is generally ineffective in selectively alleviating punishment-suppressed responding in the operant conflict task (see Cook & Davidson, 1973; Geller & Seifter, 1960; Pollard & Howard, 1979). There are, however, a few circumstances in which small anticonflict effects of amphetamine have been observed. These include situations in which shock intensity was low or situations in which the animals were not food deprived (see Sepinwall and Cook, 1978, for a review).

Promazine, chlorpromazine, and haloperidol are ineffective in alleviating punished responding; in fact, they generally decrease overall responding (Cook & Davidson, 1973; Geller & Seifter, 1960; Howard & Pollard, 1991; Morse, 1964). The failure of these three compounds and the failure of amphetamine to have clear and consistent effects suggests a negligible role for dopaminergic mechanisms in conflict-related behavior.

Haloperidol (0.1–0.25 mg/kg) had no effect in the elevated plus maze (Pellow et al., 1985).

Noradrenergic agents

Clonidine has been reported to have an anxiolytic effect on punished drinking when administered in a low dose (6.25 µg/kg), but it has a propunishment effect at higher doses (12.5 and 25.0 µg/kg) in a modified Vogel test (Soderpalm & Engel, 1988). However, these data should be interpreted with caution, because the rats were offered a glucose solution in this experiment; a study of simple intake of an 8% sucrose solution revealed parallel effects of clonidine (increase with a 6.25 µg/kg dose and decreases with the two higher doses) in a situation that involved no shock or apparent conflict (Flaherty & Grigson, 1989).

In the operant conflict procedure, the results obtained with noradrenergic agents other than imipramine have been mixed. For example, the alpha$_2$ agonist clonidine has been reported to be effective in this model (Bullock, Kruse &

Fielding, 1978; Handly & Mithani, 1984b; Kruse, Theurer, Dunn, Novick & Shearman, 1980), but the β-adrenergic antagonist propranolol is ineffective (McMillan, 1973; Robichaud, Sledge, Heffner & Goldberg, 1973; Sepinwall, Grodsky, Sullivan & Cook, 1973; Wise, Berger & Stein, 1973). However, as was the case with buspirone, there is some evidence that propranolol may be effective as an anxiolytic in pigeons (Dural, Krantz & Barrett, 1986). Although noradrenergic agents do not have major effects in contrast or operant conflict situations, they may be effective in some other anxiety or "panic-attack" models (see Chopin, Pellow & File, 1986; Mason & Fibiger, 1979; Soderpalm & Engel, 1988).

Clonidine (10–40 ug/kg) decreased potentiated startle but propranolol (20 mg/kg) had only a partial antagonistic effect (Davis, Redmond & Baraban, 1979).

In the elevated plus maze, clonidine has been reported to have anxiolytic effects (Handley & Mithani, 1984a) or no consistent effects at all (Pellow, 1986).

Cholinergic agents

As was the case in contrast, the anticholinergic scopolamine (0.2–0.8 mg/kg) has no effect on punished drinking (Vogel et al., 1971).

Other data are too fragmentary for meaningful comparisons. The general conclusions derived from these data were presented in Chapter 4.

Extinction

A comparison of contrast with extinction was presented in Flaherty (1991a). The general conclusions in that paper were as follows:

(a) By and large, anxiolytics retard the course of extinction. The effects of antidepressants are less certain, but the little evidence that is available suggests minimal effects in both paradigms.

(b) Although anxiolytics retard extinction, extinction does take place under the influence of the drugs and, in fact, the retardation is often not a major effect. Even the moderate effect demonstrated in these studies may overstate the case, because a consistently nonreinforced group injected with the drug is usually not included in these experiments. The inclusion of such a control group would allow for an estimate of the rate-enhancing effect of the drugs independently of any specific effects that the agents may have on extinction.

(c) The moderate effect of emotion-related drugs no doubt reflects the likelihood that extinction is primarily an associative process. That is, extinction may consist largely of disconfirmation learning – learning that a specific stimulus or response is no longer followed by a reward (see Mackintosh, 1974) or by a reward in the specific extinction context (Bouton, 1991). The emotional response that accompanies extinction may serve to hasten the process, but it is not the prime mover. In a natural setting, the animals would presumably go elsewhere in search of sustenance; in this sense, an anxiolytic effect would be maladaptive if it enhanced persistence in an unprofitable endeavor. This might be demonstrated by the use of multiple reward locations, such as in a radial-arm maze, as suggested by Devenport's results obtained with ethanol (Devenport, 1984).

(d) The procedural similarity between extinction and negative contrast is paralleled in the effectiveness of the anxiolytics in moderating both and in the failure of antidepressants to influence either substantially. A difference between extinction and negative contrast is that there is still a reward available in the contrast paradigm and, in the usual restricted experimental setting, an orderly endogenous recovery process seems to drive deprived animals to the acceptance of the postshift reward (Chapters 2, 3, and 4).

(e) The data showing that antidepressants do not systematically affect contrast or extinction complement other data showing that such agents also do not influence exploratory behavior or the reward value of food and water (see review by File & Tucker, 1986). If it may be concluded that the data suggest a lack of a disinhibitory effect of antidepressants in extinction, contrast, DRL responding, and discrimination training (although the evidence is less clear in the last case), then three elements important for extinction and contrast (reward value, tendency to explore when reward value is decreased, and inhibition of behaviors leading to the reduced reward) are all apparently unaffected by antidepressants. However, *extended* chronic treatment (such as 25 days) of treatment with imipramine (2.5 mg/kg), DMI (10 mg/kg), or amitriptyline (10 mg/kg) yields some, perhaps small, degree of anxiolytic activity in other animal models of anxiety, such as punished drinking and novelty suppressed feeding (see Bodnoff et al., 1988; Fontana & Commissaris, 1988); therefore, more chronic studies in the extinction paradigm may be needed before the book is closed on this issue.

Other conclusions suggested by the data regarding extinction and contrast are as follows:

(a) The extinction of consummatory behavior seems to share a common pharmacological profile with the extinction of instrumental behavior.

(b) The evidence suggests that anxiolytics administered during acquisition of an intermittent reinforcement schedule reduce or eliminate the partial reinforcement extinction effect, but these effects are not simple – they are dependent on parametric considerations such as the number of acquisition trials, the intertrial interval, and the location in a runway in which the dependent measures are taken.

(c) Behaviors that are "energized" in extinction have a different pharmacological profile from the behaviors that decline in extinction.

(d) Responding to the unrewarded stimulus in a discrimination learning paradigm is affected by anxiolytics in a fashion similar to standard extinction, but there are not enough data to make a clear statement regarding the effects of antidepressants in this paradigm.

References

Abram, M. (1984, June 10). What constitutes a civil right? *New York Times*, pp. 52–64.

Ader, R. (1970). The effect of early experience on the adrenalcortical response to different magnitudes of stimulation. *Physiology & Behavior, 5*, 837–59.

Ammon, D., Abramson, C. I., & Bitterman, M. E. (1986). Partial reinforcement and resistance to extinction in honeybees. *Animal Learning & Behavior, 14*, 232–40.

Amsel, A. (1958). The role of frustrative nonreward in noncontinuous reward situations. *Psychological Bulletin, 55*, 102–19.

(1962). Frustrative nonreward in partial reinforcement and discrimination learning: Some recent history and a theoretical extension. *Psychological Review, 69*, 306–28.

(1971). Positive induction, behavioral contrast, and generalization of inhibition in discrimination learning. In H. H. Kendler & J. T. Spence (Eds.), *Essays in neobehaviorism* (pp. 217–36). New York: Appleton-Century-Crofts.

(1990). Arousal, suppression, and persistence: Frustration theory, attention, and its disorders. In J. A. Gray (Ed.), *Psychobiological aspects of relationships between emotion and cognition* (pp. 239–68). Hillsdale, NJ: Erlbaum.

(1991). *Behaviorism, neobehaviorism, and cognition in learning theory: Historical and contemporary perspectives*. Hillsdale, NJ: Erlbaum.

(1992). *Frustration theory: An analysis of dispositional learning and memory*. Cambridge: Cambridge University Press.

Amsel, A., & Roussel, J. (1952). Motivational properties of frustration: I. Effect on a running response of the addition of frustration to the motivation complex. *Journal of Experimental Psychology, 43*, 363–8.

Amsel, A., & Stanton, M. (1980). Ontogeny and phylogeny of paradoxical reward effects. In J. S. Rosenblatt, R. A. Hinde, C. Beer, & M. Busnel (Eds.), *Advances in the study of behavior* (pp. 227–74). New York: Academic Press.

Amsel, A., Work, M. S., & Penick, E. C. (1962). Activity during and between periods of stimulus change related to feeding. *Journal of Comparative and Physiological Psychology, 55*, 1114–17.

Archer, J. (1973). Tests for emotionality in rats and mice: A review. *Animal Behavior, 21*, 205–35.

(1975). Rodent sex differences in emotional and related behavior. *Behavioral Biology, 14*, 451–79.

Aronson, L., Balsam, P. D., & Gibbon, J. (1993). Temporal comparator rules and responding in multiple schedules. *Animal Learning & Behavior, 21*, 293–302.

Asbury Park Press (1983, August 27), p. 1.

Ashida, S., & Birch, D. (1964). The effects of incentive shift as a function of training. *Psychonomic Science, 1*, 201–2.

Associated Press (1984, April) reprinted in *The Daily Targum,* Rutgers University, 19 April 1984, p. 6.

Bacotti, A. V. (1976). Home cage feeding time controls responding under multiple schedules. *Animal Learning & Behavior, 4*, 41–4.

Bagshaw, M. H., & Benzies, S. (1968). Multiple measures of the orienting reaction and their dissociation after amygdalectomy in monkeys. *Experimental Neurology, 20*, 175–87.

Bagshaw, M. H., Mackworth, N. H., & Pribram, K. H. (1972). The effect of resections of the inferotemporal cortex of the amygdala on visual orienting and habituation. *Neuropsychologia, 10*, 153–62.

187

Bain, A. (1855). *The senses and the intellect*. London: Parker (cited in Boakes, 1984).

Balleine, B. (1992). Instrumental Performance following a shift in primary motivation depends on incentive learning. *Journal of Experimental Psychology: Animal Behavior Processes, 18*, 236–50.

Baltzer, V., Huber, H., & Weiskrantz, L. (1979). Effects of various drugs on behavioral contrast using a double crossover procedure. *Behavioral and Neural Biology, 27*, 330–41.

Barnes, W., & Tombaugh, T. (1973). Another failure to obtain negative contrast following reductions to sucrose reward. *Psychological Reports, 33*, 801–2.

Barrett, J. E., Witkin, J. M., & Mansbach, R. S. (1984). Behavioral and pharmacological analysis of buspirone. *Federation Proceedings, 43*, 931.

Barrett, J. E., Witkin, J. M., Mansbach, R. S., Skolnick, P., & Weissman, B. A. (1986). Behavioral studies with anxiolytic drugs. III. Antipunishment actions of buspirone in the pigeon do not involve benzodiazepine receptor mechanisms. *Journal of Pharmacology and Experimental Therapeutics, 238*, 1009–13.

Bartoshuk, L. M., & Gent, J. F. (1984). Taste mixtures: An analysis of synthesis. In D. Pfaff (Ed.), *Taste, olfaction and the central nervous system* (pp. 210–32). New York: Rockefeller University Press.

Bartoshuk, L. M., McBurney, D. H., & Pfaffman, C. (1964). Taste of sodium chloride solutions after adaptation to sodium chloride: Implications for the "water taste." *Science, 143*, 967–8.

Beatty, W. W., & Schwartzbaum, J. S. (1967). Enhanced reactivity to quinine and saccharin solutions following septal lesions in the rat. *Psychonomic Science, 8*, 483–4.

(1968). Commonality and specificity of behavioral dysfunctions following septal and hippocampal lesions in rats. *Journal of Comparative and Physiological Psychology, 66*, 60–8.

Becker, H. C. (1986). Comparison of the effects of the benzodiazepine midazolam and three serotonin antagonists on a consummatory conflict paradigm. *Pharmacology, Biochemistry, & Behavior, 24*, 1057–64.

Becker, H. C., & Anton, R. F. (1990). Valproate potentiates and picrotoxin antagonizes the anxiolytic action of ethanol in a nonshock conflict task. *Neuropharmacology, 29*, 837–43.

Becker, H. C., & Flaherty, C. F. (1982). Influence of ethanol on contrast in consummatory behavior. *Psychopharmacology, 77*, 253–8.

(1983). Chlordiazepoxide and ethanol additively reduce gustatory negative contrast. *Psychopharmacology, 80*, 35–7.

Becker, H. C., & Hale, R. L. (1991). Ro 15–4513 antagonizes the anxiolytic effects of ethanol in a non-shock conflict task at doses devoid of anxiogenic activity. *Pharmacology, Biochemistry, & Behavior, 39*, 803–7.

Becker, H. C., Jarvis, M., Wagner, G., & Flaherty, C. F. (1984). Medial and lateral amygdala lesions differentially influence contrast with sucrose solutions. *Physiology & Behavior, 33*, 707–12.

Beery, R. G. (1968). A negative contrast effect of reward delay in differential conditioning. *Journal of Experimental Psychology, 77*, 429–34.

Benefield, R., Oscos, A., & Ehrenfreund, D. (1974). Role of frustration in successive positive contrast. *Journal of Comparative and Physiological Psychology, 86*, 648–51.

Beninger, R. J., & Kendall, S. B. (1975). Behavioral contrast in rats with different reinforcers and different response topographies. *Journal of the Experimental Analysis of Behavior, 24*, 267–80.

Belzung, C., & Le Pape, G. (1994). Comparison of different behavioral test situations used in psychopharmacology for measurement of anxiety. *Physiology & Behavior, 56*, 623–8.

Berridge, K. C. (1996). Food reward: Brain subtrates of wanting and liking. *Neuroscience and Biobehavoral Reviews, 20*, 1–25.

Bevan, W. (1968). The contextual basis of behavior. *American Psychologist, 23*, 701–13.

Biggio, G., & Costa, E. (Eds.) (1986). *Gabaergic transmission and anxiety*. New York: Raven Press.

Bindra, D. A. (1974). A motivational view of learning, performance, and behavior modification. *Psychological Review, 81*, 199–213.

Birch, L. L. (1991). Obesity and eating disorders: A developmental perspective. *Bulletin of the Psychonomic Society, 29*, 265–72.

Birch, L. L., Marlin, D., & Rotter, J. (1984). Eating as the "mean" activity in a contingency: Effects on young children's food preferences. *Child Development, 55,* 432–9.

Bitterman, M. E. (1975) The comparative analysis of learning. *Science, 188,* 699–709.

    (1988). Vertebrate-invertebrate comparisons. In H. J. Jerrison & I. Jerrison (Eds.), *Intelligence and evolutionary biology.* NATO ASI Series (Vol. G17, pp. 251–76). Berlin: Springer-Verlag.

Black, R. W. (1968), Shifts in magnitude of reward and contrast effects in instrumental and selective learning: A reinterpretation. *Psychological Review, 75,* 114–26.

    (1969). Incentive motivation and the parameters of reward in instrumental conditioning. In W. J. Arnold & D. Levine (Eds.), *Nebraska Symposium on Motivation* (pp. 85–141). Lincoln: University of Nebraska Press.

Blanchard, D. C., & Blanchard, R. J. (1972). Innate and conditioned reactions to threats in rats with amygdaloid lesions. *Journal of Comparative and Physiological Psychology, 81,* 281–90.

Bloomfield, T. M. (1967). Behavioral contrast and relative reinforcement frequency in two multiple schedules. *Journal of the Experimental Analysis of Behavior, 10,* 151–8.

    (1969) Behavioral contrast and the peak shift. In R. M. Gilbert & N. S. Sutherland (Eds.), *Animal Discrimination Learning* (pp. 215–41). London: Academic Press.

    (1972). Contrast and inhibition in discrimination learning by the pigeon: Analysis through drug effects. *Learning & Motivation, 3,* 162–78.

Blough, P. M. (1980). Behavioral and dimensional contrast in rats. *Journal of the Experimental Analysis of Behavior, 33,* 345–57.

    (1983). Local contrast in multiple schedules: The effect of stimulus discriminability. *Journal of the Experimental Analysis of Behavior, 39,* 427–35.

    (1988). Overall and local contrast in multiple schedules: Effects of stimulus similarity and discrimination performance. *Animal Learning & Behavior, 16,* 395–403.

Blough, P. M., & Blough, D. S. (1985). Sequential effects in dimensional contrast. *Journal of the Experimental Analysis of Behavior, 39,* 427–35.

Boakes, R. (1984). *From Darwin to behaviorism: Psychology and the minds of animals.* Cambridge: Cambridge University Press.

Boakes, R. A., Halliday, M. S., & Mole, J. S. (1976). Successive discrimination training with equated reinforcement frequencies: Failure to obtain behavioral contrast. *Journal of the Experimental Analysis of Behavior, 26,* 65–78.

Boast, C., Popick, F., Stone, G., & Kalinsky, H. (1985). Positive correlation between serotonin antagonism and anticonflict activity. *Society for Neuroscience Abstract,* #128.9.

Bodnoff, S. R., Suranyi-Cadotte, B., Aitken, D. H., Quirion, R., & Meaney, M. J. (1988). The effects of chronic antidepressant treatment in an animal model of anxiety. *Psychopharmacology, 95,* 298–302.

Bolles, R. C. (1967). *Theory of motivation.* New York: Harper & Row.

Bolles, R. C. (Ed.) (1991). *The hedonics of taste.* Hillsdale, NJ: Erlbaum.

Bouton, M. E. (1991). Context and retrieval in extinction and in other examples of interference in simple associative learning. In L. Dachowski & C. F. Flaherty (Eds.), *Current topics in animal learning: Brain, emotion, and cognition* (pp. 25–53). Hillsdale, NJ: Erlbaum.

Bower, G. H. (1961). A contrast effect in differential conditioning. *Journal of Experimental Psychology, 62,* 196–9.

    (1966). Recent Developments II: Discrimination Learning and Attention. In E. R. Hilgard & G. H. Bower (Eds.), *Theories of learning.* New York: Appleton-Century-Crofts.

Bower, G. H., Fowler, H., & Trapold, M. A. (1959). Escape learning as a function of amount of shock reduction. *Journal of Experimental Psychology, 58,* 482–4.

Bowlby, J. (1973). *Attachment and loss.* Vol. 2, *Separation: Anxiety and anger.* New York: Basic Books.

Brazier, M. M., & Dachowski, L. (1991). Consummatory contrast effects in nondeprived rats following shifts in sucrose concentration. *The Psychological Record, 41,* 125–32.

Briley, M. (1985). Imipramine binding: Its relationship with serotonin uptake and depression. In A. R. Green (Ed.); *Neuropharmacology of serotonin* (pp. 50-78). Oxford: Oxford University Press.

Briley, M., Chopin, P., & Moret, C. (1990). Effect of serotonergic lesion on "anxious" behavior measured in the elevated plus-maze test in the rat. *Psychopharmacology, 101*, 187–9.

Brillat-Savarin, J. A. (1825). *The physiology of taste*. M. F. K. Fisher (Translator). San Francisco: North Point Press, 1986.

Broadhurst, P. L. (1975). The Maudsley Reactive and Nonreactive strains of rats: A survey. *Behavior Genetics, 5*, 299–319.

Brogden, W. J. (1951). Animal studies of learning. In S.S. Stevens (Ed.), *Handbook of Experimental Psychology* (pp. 568–612). New York: Wiley.

Brown, B. L., Hemmes, N. S., Coleman, D. A., Jr., Hassin, A., & Goldhammer, E. (1982). Specification of the stimulus-reinforcer relation in multiple schedules: Delay and probability of reinforcement. *Animal Learning & Behavior, 10*, 365–76.

Brush, F. R. (1985). Genetic determinants of avoidance learning: mediation by emotionality? In F. R. Brush & B. Overmier (Eds.), *Affect, conditioning and cognition* (pp. 27–42). Hillsdale, NJ: Erlbaum.

Bryce, G. F., & Jacoby, J. H. (1979). Paradoxical short-term effects of cyproheptadine on insulin and glucagon release in the rat. *European Journal of Pharmacology, 54*, 349–57.

Buck, S. L., Rothstein, B., & Williams, B. A. (1975). A re-examination of local contrast in multiple schedules. *Journal of the Experimental Analysis of Behavior, 24*, 291–303.

Bullock, S. A., Kruse, H., & Fielding, S. (1978). The effect of clonidine on conflict behavior in rats: Is clonidine an anxiolytic agent? *Psychopharmacologist, 20*, 223.

Burns, R. A. (1984). The goal units dimension in negative contrast failures with sucrose. *Journal of General Psychology, 111*, 9–23.

Burns, R. A., & Burns, D. P. (1978). Reduction in sucrose reward magnitude without generalization decrement. *Bulletin of the Psychonomic Society, 12*, 196–8.

Burns, R. A., Dupree, E. S., & Lorig, T. S. (1978). Successive reductions of liquid and solid rewards. *Bulletin of the Psychonomic Society, 12*, 351–4.

Burns, R. A., Lorig, T. S., & McCrary, M. D. (1986). Reduction of sucrose reward to smaller and nonreward levels without contrast effects. *The Journal of General Psychology, 113*, 97–102.

Burns, R. A., Woodard, W. T., Henderson, T. B., & Bitterman, M. E. (1974). Simultaneous contrast in the goldfish. *Animal Learning & Behavior, 2*, 97–100.

Calef, R. S. (1972). The effect of large and small magnitudes of intertrial reinforcement on successive contrast effects. *Psychonomic Science, 29*, 309–12.

Calef, R. S., Calef, R. A., Maxwell, F. R., & McHewitt, E. R. (1975). Positive discrimination contrast with delay of reward or low drive. *Bulletin of the Psychonomic Society, 6*, 120–2.

Calef, R. S., Calef, R. A., Prochaska, A. D., & Geller, E. S. (1978). Negative contrast as a function of reinforcement location and consistent vs. varied reward magnitude. *Bulletin of the Psychonomic Society, 12*, 471–4.

Calef, R. S., Hopkins, D. C., McHewitt, E. R., & Maxwell, F. R. (1973). Performance to varied reward following continuous reward training in the runway. *Bulletin of the Psychonomic Society, 2*, 103–4.

Campbell, D. E., Crumbaugh, C. M., Knouse, S. B., & Snodgrass, E. (1970). A test of the "ceiling effect" hypothesis of positive contrast. *Psychonomic Science, 20*, 17–18.

Candido, A., Maldonado, A., Megias, J. L., & Catena, A. (1992). Successive negative contrast in one-way avoidance learning in rats. *The Quarterly Journal of Experimental Psychology, 45B*, 15–32.

Capaldi, E. D. (1971). Simultaneous shifts in reward magnitude and level of food deprivation. *Psychonomic Science, 23*, 357–9.

(1978). Effects of changing alley color on the successive negative contrast effect. *Bulletin of the Psychonomic Society, 12*, 69–70.

Capaldi, E. D., & Sheffer, J. D. (1992). Contrast and reinforcement in consumption. *Learning & Motivation, 23*, 63–9.

Capaldi, E. D., & Singh, R. (1973). Percentage body weight and the successive negative contrast effects in rats. *Learning & Motivation, 4*, 405–16.

Capaldi, E. D., Smith, N. S., & White, L. A. (1977). Control of reward expectancies by drive stimuli. *Journal of Experimental Psychology: Animal Behavior Processes, 3*, 178–88.

Capaldi, E. J. (1966). Partial reinforcement: A hypothesis of sequential effects. *Psychological Review, 73*, 459–79.

(1972). Successive negative contrast effect: Intertrial interval, type of shift, and four sources of generalization decrement. *Journal of Experimental Psychology, 96*, 433–8.

(1974). Partial reward either following or preceding consistent reward: A case of reinforcement level. *Journal of Experimental Psychology, 102*, 954–62.

Capaldi, E. J., & Lynch, D. (1967). Repeated shifts in reward magnitude: Evidence in favor of an associational and absolute (noncontextual) interpretation. *Journal of Experimental Psychology, 75*, 226–35.

Capaldi, E. J., & Ziff, D. R. (1969). Schedule of partial reward and the negative contrast effect. *Journal of Comparative and Physiological Psychology, 68*, 593–6.

Caplan, M., & Graefe, J. (1980). Punishment-induced suppression and the occurrence of behavioral contrast in rats with septal lesions. *Behavioral and Neural Biology, 30*, 278–91.

Cassella, J. V., & Davis, M. (1985). Fear-enhanced acoustic startle is not attenuated by acute or chronic imipramine treatment in rats. *Psychopharmacology, 87*, 278–82.

Catania, A. C. (1969). Concurrent performances: Inhibition of one response by reinforcement of another. *Journal of the Experimental Analysis of Behavior, 12*, 731–44.

Catania, A. C. (1973). Self-inhibiting effects of reinforcement. *Journal of the Experimental Analysis of Behavior, 19*, 517–26.

Catania, A. C., & Gill, C. A. (1964). Inhibition and Behavioral contrast. *Psychonomic Science, 1*, 257–8.

Chechile, R., & Fowler, H. (1973). Primary and secondary negative incentive contrast in differential conditioning. *Journal of Experimental Psychology, 97*, 189–97.

Chen, J., Gross, K., & Amsel, A. (1981). Ontogeny of successive negative contrast and its dissociation from other paradoxical effects in preweanling rats. *Journal of Comparative and Physiological Psychology, 95*, 146–9.

Chi, C. C. (1965). The effect of amobarbital sodium on conditioned fear as measured by the potentiated startle response in rats. *Psychopharmacologia, 7*, 115–22.

Chopin, P., Pellow, S., & File, S.E. (1986). The effects of yohimbine on exploratory and locomotor behavior are attributable to its effects on noradrenaline and not benzodiazepine recaptors. *Neuropharmacology, 25*, 53–57.

Ciszewski, W. A., & Flaherty, C. F. (1977). Failure of reinstatement treatment to influence negative contrast. *American Journal of Psychology, 90*, 219–29.

Cleary, T. L. (1992). The relationship of local to overall behavioral contrast. *Bulletin of the Psychonomic Society, 30*, 58–60.

Cleland, E. A., Williams, M. Y., & DiLollo, V. (1969). Magnitude of negative contrast effect in relation to drive level. *Psychonomic Science, 15*, 121–2.

Coelho De Rose, J. C. (1986). Behavioral contrast in fixed interval components: Effects of extinction component duration. *Journal of the Experimental Analysis of Behavior, 45*, 175–88.

Cole, L. W. (1911). The relation of strength of stimulus to rate of learning in the chick. *Journal of Animal Behavior, 1*, 111 (cited in Simmons, 1924).

Collier, G., Knarr, F. A., & Marx, M. H. (1961). Some relations between the intensive properties of the consummatory response and reinforcement. *Journal of Experimental Psychology, 62*, 484–95.

Collier, G., & Marx, M. H. (1959). Changes in performance as a function of shifts in the magnitude of reinforcement. *Journal of Experimental Psychology, 57*, 305–9.

Colpeart, F. C., Meert, T. F., Niemegeers, C. J. E., & Janssen, P. A. G. (1985). Behavioral and 5–HT antagonist effects of ritanserin: A pure and selective antagonist of lsd discrimination in rat. *Psychopharmacology, 86*, 45–54.

Colwill, R. M., & Rescorla, R. A. (1986). Associative Structures in instrumental learning. In G. H. Bower (Ed.), *The psychology of learning and motivation* (Vol. 20, pp. 55–104. New York: Academic Press.

Commissaris, R. L., & Rech, R. H. (1982). Interactions of metergoline with diazepam, quipazine, and hallucinogenic drugs on a conflict behavior in the rat. *Psychopharmacology, 76*, 282–5.

Cook, L., & Davidson, A. B. (1973). Effects of behaviorally active drugs in a conflict procedure in rats. In S. Garattini, E. Mussini & L. O. Randall (Eds.), *The Benzodiazepines* (pp. 327–45). New York: Raven Press.

Cook, L., & Sepinwall, J. (1975). Psychopharmacological parameters and methods. In L. Levi (Ed.), *Emotions—Their Parameters and Measurement* (pp. 379–404). New York: Raven Press.

Cooper, S. J., & Estall, L. B. (1985). Behavioral pharmacology of food, water, and salt intake in relation to drug actions at benzodiazepine receptors. *Neuroscience & Biobehavioral Reviews, 9*, 5–19.

Coppotelli, C., & Flaherty, C. F. (1993). Effect of serotonergic drugs on negative contrast. Paper delivered at Eastern Psychological Association meeting, Arlington, VA.

Costa, E. (Ed.) (1983). *The Benzodiazepine: From Molecular Biology to Clinical Practice*. New York: Raven Press.

Couvillon, P. A., & Bitterman, M. E. (1984). The overlearning extinction effect and successive negative contrast in honeybees *(Apis mellifera)*. *Journal of Comparative Psychology, 98*, 100–9.

(1985). Effects of experience with a preferred food on consummatory responding for a less preferred food in goldfish. *Animal Learning & Behavior, 13*, 433–8.

Cowles, J. T., & Nissen, H. W. (1937). Reward-expectancy in delayed responses of chimpanzees. *Journal of Comparative Psychology, 24*, 345–58.

Cox, W. M. (1975). A review of recent incentive contrast studies involving discrete-trial procedures. *Psychological Record, 25*, 373–93.

Crawley, J. N., Glowa, J. R., Majewska, M. D., & Paul, S. M. (1986). Anxiolytic activity of an endogenous adrenal steroid. *Brain Research, 398*, 382–5.

Crespi, L. P. (1942). Quantitative variation in incentive and performance in the white rat. *The American Journal of Psychology, 40*, 467–517.

(1944). Amount of reinforcement and level of performance. *Psychological Review, 51*, 341–57.

Cruz, A. P. M., Frei, F., & Graeff, F. G. (1994). Ethopharmacological analysis of rat behavior on the elevated plus-maze. *Pharmacology, Biochemistry, & Behavior, 49*, 171–6.

Dachowski, L., & Brazier, M. M. (1991). Consummatory incentive contrast: Experimental design relationships and deprivation effects. In L. Dachowski & C. F. Flaherty (Eds.), *Current topics in animal learning: Brain, emotion, and cognition* (pp. 245–70). Hillsdale, NJ: Erlbaum.

Daly, H. B. (1974). Reinforcing properties of escape from frustration. In G.H. Bower (Ed.), *The psychology of learning and motivation* (pp. 187–232). New York: Academic Press.

(1991). Changes in learning about aversive nonreward accounts for ontogeny of paradoxical appetitive reward effects in the rat pup: A mathematical model (DMOD) integrates results. *Psychological Bulletin, 109*, 325–39.

Daly, H. B., & Rosenberg, K. M. (1973). Infantile stimulation and its effects on frustration- and fear-motivated behavior in rats. *Learning & Motivation, 4*, 381–96.

Davenport, J. W. (1962). The interaction of magnitude and delay of reinforcement in spatial discrimination. *Journal of Comparative and Physiological Psychology, 55*, 267–73.

Davenport, J. W., Flaherty, C. F., & Dyrud, J. P. (1966). Temporal persistence of frustration effects in monkeys and rats. *Psychonomic Science, 6* , 411–12.

Davenport, J. W., & Thompson, C. I. (1965). The Amsel frustration effect in monkeys. *Psychonomic Science, 3*, 481–2.

Davis, M. (1979). Diazepam and flurazepam: Effects on conditioned fear as measured with the potentiated startle paradigm. *Psychopharmacology, 62*, 1–7.

(1991). Animal models of anxiety based on classical conditioning: The conditioned emotional response and the fear-potentiated startle effect. In S. E. File (Ed.), *Psychopharmacology of anxiolytics and antidepressants* (pp. 187–212). New York: Pergamon.

(1992). The role of the amygdala in conditioned fear. In J. P. Aggleton (Ed.), *The amygdala: Neurobiological aspects of emotion, memory, and mental dysfunction* (pp. 255–305). New York: Wiley-Liss.

Davis, M., Cassella, J. V., & Kehne, J. H. (1988). Serotonin does not mediate anxiolytic effects of buspirone in the fear-potentiated startle paradigm: Comparison with 8–OH-DPAT and ipsapirone. *Psychopharmacology, 94*, 14–20.

Davis, M., Hitchcock, J. M., & Rosen, J. B. (1988). Anxiety and the amygdala: Pharmacological and anatomical analysis of the fear-potentiated startle paradigm. In G. Bower (Ed.), *The psychology of learning and motivation* (Volume 21, pp. 263–305). New York: Academic Press.

Davis, M., Redmond, D. E., Jr., & Baraban, J. M. (1979). Noradrenergic agonists and antagonists: Effects on conditioned fear as measured by the potentiated startle paradigm. *Psychopharmacology, 65*, 111–18.

Davis, S. F., Harper, W. E., & Seago, J. D. (1975). Runway performance of normal, sham, and anosmic rats as a function of magnitude of reward and magnitude shift. *Bulletin of the Psychonomic Society, 6*, 367–9.

Davis, S. F., & North, A. J. (1967). The effect of varied reinforcement training on behavior following incentive reduction. *Psychonomic Science, 9*, 395–6.

Davison, C., Lowther, W. R., & Allen, J. D. (1975). Effects of septal lesions on behavioral contrast. *Physiological Psychology, 3*, 179–82.

Deacon, R., & Gardner, C. R. (1986). Benzodiazepine and 5HT ligands in a rat conflict test. *British Journal of Pharmacology, 88*, 330P.

Denenberg, V. H., & Grota, L. J. (1964). Social-seeking and novelty-seeking behavior as a function of differential rearing histories. *Journal of Abnormal and Social Psychology, 69*, 453–6.

Denny, M. R. (1991). Relaxation/relief: The effect of removing, postponing, or terminating aversive stimuli. In M. R. Denny (Ed.), *Fear, avoidance, and phobias.* (pp. 199–229). Hillsdale, NJ: Erlbaum.

Devenport, L. D. (1984). Extinction-induced spatial dispersion in the radial arm maze: Arrest by ethanol. *Behavioral Neuroscience, 98*, 979–85.

Dickinson, A. (1972). Septal damage and response output under frustrative nonreward. In R. A. Boakes & M. S. Halliday (Eds.), *Inhibition and learning* (pp. 461–96). London: Academic Press.

DiLollo, F. D., & Beez, V. (1966). Negative contrast effect as a function of magnitude of reward decrement. *Psychonomic Science, 5*, 99–100.

Dodson, J. D. (1917). Relative values of reward and punishment in habit formation. *Psychobiology, 1*, 231–76.

Domjan, M. (1976). Determinants of the enhancement of flavored water intake by prior exposure. *Journal of Experimental Psychology: Animal Behavior Processes, 2,* 17–27.

Donovick, P. J. (1968). Effects of localized septal lesions on hippocampal EEG activity and behavior in rats. *Journal of Comparative and Physiological Psychology, 66*, 569–78.

Dougan, J. D., Farmer-Dougan, V. A., & McSweeney, F. K. (1989). Behavioral contrast in pigeons and rats: Comparative analysis. *Animal Learning & Behavior, 17*, 247–55.

Dougan, J. D., McSweeney, F. K., & Farmer, V. A. (1985). Some parameters of behavioral contrast and allocation of interim behavior in rats. *Journal of the Experimental Analysis of Behavior, 44*, 325–35.

Dougan, J. D., McSweeney, F. K., & Farmer-Dougan, V. (1986). Behavioral contrast in competitive and noncompetitive environments. *Journal of the Experimental Analysis of Behavior, 46*, 185–97.

Dunham, P. J. (1968). Contrasted conditions of reinforcement: A selective critique. *Psychological Bulletin, 69*, 295–315.

Dunham, P. J., & Kilps, B. (1969). Shifts in magnitude of reinforcement: Confounded factors or contrast effects. *Journal of Experimental Psychology, 79*, 373–4.

Dunlap, W. P., & Frates, S. D. (1970). Influence of deprivation on the frustration effect. *Psychonomic Science, 21*, 1–2.

Dunn, R. W., Corbett, R., & Fielding, S. (1989). Effects of 5–HT$_{1A}$ agonists and NMDA receptor antagonists in the social interaction test and the elevated plus maze. *European Journal of Pharmacology, 169*, 1–10.

Dural, L. A., Krantz, D. S., & Barrett, J. E. (1986). The antianxiety effect of beta blockers on punished responding. *Pharmacology, Biochemistry, & Behavior*, 25, 371–4.

Ehrenfreund, D. (1971). Effect of drive on successive magnitude shift in rats. *Journal of Comparative and Physiological Psychology*, 76, 418–23.

Ehrenfreund, D., & Badia, P. (1962). Response strength as a function of drive level and pre- and postshift incentive magnitude. *Journal of Experimental Psychology*, 63, 468–71.

Eison, A. S., Eison, M. S., Stanley, M., & Riblet, L. A. (1986). Serotonergic mechanisms in the behavioral effects of buspirone and gepirone. *Pharmacology, Biochemistry, & Behavior*, 24, 701–7.

Elliott, M. H. (1928). The effect of change of reward on the maze performance of rats. *University of California Publications in Psychology*, 4, 19–30.

Ettenberg, A., & Camp, C. H. (1986a). Haloperidol induces a partial reinforcement extinction effect in rats: Implications for dopamine involvement in food reward. *Pharmacology, Biochemistry, & Behavior*, 25, 813–21.

  (1986b). A partial reinforcement extinction effect in water reinforced rats intermittently treated with haloperidol. *Pharmacology, Biochemistry, & Behavior*, 25, 1231–5.

Everitt, B. J., & Robbins, T. W. (1992). Amygdala-ventral striatal interactions in reward-related process. In J. Aggleton (Ed.), *The amygdala: Neurobiological aspects of emotion, memory, and mental dysfunction* (pp. 401–29). New York: Wiley-Liss.

Fagen, J. W., & Prigot, J. A. (1993). Negative affect and infant memory. In C. Rovee-Collier & L. P. Lipsitt (Eds.), *Advances in Infancy Research* (Vol. 8, pp. 169–216). Norwood, NJ: Ablex.

Fagen, J. W., & Rovee, C. K. (1976). Effects of quantitative shifts in a visual reinforcer on the instrumental response of infants. *Journal of Experimental Child Psychology*, 21, 349–60.

Fagen, J. W., Rycek, R. F., Ritz, E. G., & Shoemaker, G. E. (1983). Effect of varying sucrose concentration on macrobehavioral aspects of licking in the rat. *The Journal of General Psychology*, 109, 181–7.

Fagen, J. W., & Shoemaker, G. E. (1979). Contrast effects in the rat: A developmental study. *Developmental Psychobiology*, 12, 83–92.

Farley, J. (1980). Automaintenance, contrast, and contingencies: Effects of local vs. overall and prior vs. impending context. *Learning & Motivation*, 11, 19–48.

Feierabend, I. K., Feierabend, R. L., & Nesvold, B. A. (1969). Social change and political violence: Cross-national patterns. In H. D. Graham & T. R. Gurr (Eds.), *Violence in America: Historical and comparative perspectives*. New York: Signet.

Feldon, J., Katz, Y., & Weiner, I. (1988). The effects of haloperidol on the partial reinforcement extinction effect (PREE): Implications for neuroleptic drug action on reinforcement and nonreinforcement. *Psychopharmacology*, 95, 528–33.

File, S. E. (1987). The contribution of behavioral studies to the neuropharmacology of anxiety. *Neuropharmacology*, 26, 877–86.

File, S. E. (Ed.) (1991). *Psychopharmacology of anxiolytics and antidepressants*. New York: Pergamon.

File, S. E., & Aranko, K. (1988). Sodium valproate and chlordiazepoxide in the elevated plus-maze test of anxiety in the rat. *Neuropsychobiology*, 20, 82–86.

File, S. E., & Johnston, A. L. (1989). Lack of effects of $5HT_3$ receptor antagonists in the social interaction and elevated plus-maze tests of anxiety in the rat. *Psychopharmacology*, 99, 248–51.

File, S. E., & Tucker, J. C. (1986). Behavioral consequences of antidepressant treatment in rodents. *Neuroscience & Biobehavioral Reviews*, 10, 123–34.

Flaherty, C. F. (1982). Incentive contrast: A review of behavioral changes following shifts in reward. *Animal learning & behavior*, 10, 409–40.

  (1985). *Animal learning and cognition*. New York: Knopf/McGraw-Hill.

  (1991a). Effect of anxiolytics and antidepressants on extinction and negative contrast. In S. E. File (Ed.), *Psychopharmacology of anxiolytics and antidepressants* (pp. 213–30). New York: Pergamon.

(1991b). Incentive contrast and selected animal models of anxiety. In L. Dachowski & C.F. Flaherty (Eds.), *Current topics in animal learning: Brain, emotion and cognition* (pp. 207–43). Hillsdale, NJ: Erlbaum.

Flaherty, C. F., & Avdzej, A. (1974). Bidirectional contrast as a function of rate of alternation of two sucrose solutions. *Bulletin of the Psychonomic Society, 4*, 505–7.

(1976). Transsituational negative contrast. *Animal Learning & Behavior, 4*, 49–52.

Flaherty, C. F., Becker, H., & Checke, S. (1983). Repeated contrast in consummatory and open field behaviors with repeated reward shifts. *Animal Learning & Behavior, 11*, 407–14.

Flaherty, C. F., Becker, H. C., Checke, S., Rowan, G. A., & Grigson, P. S. (1992). Effect of chlorpromazine and haloperidol on negative contrast. *Pharmacology Biochemistry & Behavior, 42*, 111–17.

Flaherty, C. F., Becker, H., & Driscoll, C. (1982). Conditions under which amobarbital sodium influences consummatory contrast. *Physiological Psychology, 10*, 122–8.

Flaherty, C. F., Becker, H. C., & Osborne, M. (1983). Negative contrast following regularly increasing concentrations of sucrose solutions: Rising expectations or incentive averaging? *The Psychological Record, 33*, 415–20.

Flaherty, C. F., Becker, H. C., & Pohorecky, L. (1985). Correlation of corticosterone elevation and negative contrast varies as a function of postshift day. *Animal Learning & Behavior, 13*, 309–14.

Flaherty, C. F., Blitzer, R., & Collier, G. H. (1978). Open field behaviors elicited by reward reduction. *American Journal of Psychology, 91*, 429–43.

Flaherty, C. F., Capobianco, S., & Hamilton, L. W. (1973). Effect of septal lesions on retention of negative contrast. *Physiology & Behavior, 11*, 625–31.

Flaherty, C. F., & Caprio, M. (1976). Dissociation between instrumental and consummatory measures of incentive contrast. *American Journal of Psychology, 89*, 485–98.

Flaherty, C. F., & Checke, S. (1982). Anticipation of incentive gain. *Animal Learning & Behavior, 10*, 177–82.

Flaherty, C. F., Ciszewski, W. A., & Kaplan, P. S. (1979). Retention of taste quality following brief exposure to sucrose. *Chemical Senses and Flavour, 4*, 73–8.

Flaherty, C. F., Clarke, S., & Coppotelli, C. Lack of tolerance to the contrast-reducing actions of chlordiazepoxide with repeated reward reductions, in press, *Physiology and Behavior.*

Flaherty, C. F., Coppotelli, C. Are the anti-content actions of cyproheptadine due to serotonergic mechanisms? Unpublished data.

Flaherty, C. F., & Coppotelli, C., Grigson, P. S., Mitchell, C., & Flaherty, J. E. (1995). Investigation of the devaluation interpretation of anticipatory negative contrast. *Journal of Experimental Psychology: Animal Behavior Processes, 21*, 229–47.

Flaherty, C. F., Coppotelli, C., King, L., & Portugal, P. Effect of fluoxetine on anticipatory and successive contrast, submitted.

Flaherty, C. F., Coppotelli, C., & Potaki, J. (in press). Effect of chlordiazepoxide in free-fed rats exposed to repeated reward reductions. *Physiology and Behavior.*

Flaherty, C. F., & Driscoll, C. (1980). Amobarbital sodium reduces successive gustatory contrast. *Psychopharmacology, 69*, 161–2.

Flaherty, C. F., & Grigson, P. S. (1988). From contrast to reinforcement: Role of response contingency in anticipatory contrast. *Journal of Experimental Psychology: Animal Behavior Processes, 14*, 165–76.

(1989). Effect of clonidine on sucrose intake varies as a function of dose, deprivation condition, and duration of exposure to sucrose. *Pharmacology, Biochemistry, & Behavior, 32*, 383–9.

Flaherty, C. F., Grigson, P. S., Checke, S., & Hnat, K. C. (1991). Deprivation state and temporal horizons in anticipatory contrast. *Journal of Experimental Psychology: Animal Behavior Processes, 17*, 503–18.

Flaherty, C. F., Grigson, P. S., Coppotelli, C., & Mitchell, C. (1996). Anticipatory contrast as a function of access time and spatial location of saccharin and sucrose solutions, *Animal Learning and Behavior, 24*, 68–81

Flaherty, C. F., Grigson, P. S., & Demetrikopoulos, M. K. (1987). Effect of clonidine on consummatory negative contrast and on novelty-induced stress. *Pharmacology, Biochemistry, & Behavior*, 27, 659–64.

Flaherty, C. F., Grigson, P. S., Demetrikopoulos, M. K., Weaver, M. S., Krauss, K. L., & Rowan, G. A. (1990). Effect of serotonergic drugs on negative contrast in consummatory behavior. *Pharmacology, Biochemistry, & Behavior*, 36, 799–806.

Flaherty, C. F., Grigson, P. S., & Lind, S. (1990). Chlordiazepoxide and the moderation of the initial response to reward reduction. *The Quarterly Journal of Experimental Psychology*, 42B, 87–105.

Flaherty, C.F., Grigson, P.S., & Rowan, G.A. (1986). Chlordiazepoxide and the determinants of contrast. *Animal Learning & Behavior*, 14, 315–21.

Flaherty, C. F., Hrabinski, K., & Grigson, P.S. (1990). Effect of taste context and ambient context changes on successive negative contrast. *Animal Learning & Behavior*, 18, 271–6.

Flaherty, C. F., & Kaplan, P. (1979). Gustatory contrast in rats. *Chemical Senses and Flavour*, 4, 63–72.

Flaherty, C. F., & Kelly, J. (1973). Effect of deprivation state on successive negative contrast. *Bulletin of the Psychonomic Society*, 1, 365–7.

Flaherty, C. F., Krauss, K. L., & Hill, W. (1994). Performance of Zucker rats in two consummatory contrast paradigms. *Psychobiology*, 22, 167–72.

Flaherty, C. F., Krauss, K. L., Rowan, G. A., & Grigson, P. S. (1994). Selective breeding for negative contrast. *Journal of Experimental Psychology: Animal Behavior Processes*, 20, 3–19.

Flaherty, C. F., & Largen, J. (1975). Within-subjects positive and negative contrast effects. *Journal of Comparative and Physiological Psychology*, 88, 653–64.

Flaherty, C. F., & Lombardi, B. R. (1977). Effect of prior differential taste experience on retention of taste quality. *Bulletin of the Psychonomic Society*, 9, 391–4.

Flaherty, C. F., Lombardi, B. R., Kapust, J., & D'Amato, M. R. (1977). Incentive contrast uninfluenced by extended testing, imipramine, or chlordiazepoxide. *Pharmacology, Biochemistry, & Behavior*, 7, 315–22.

Flaherty, C. F., Lombardi, B. R., Wrightson, J., & Deptula, D. (1980). Conditions under which chlordiazepoxide influence successive gustatory contrast. *Psychopharmacology*, 67, 269–77.

Flaherty, C. F., McCurdy, M., Becker, H., & D'Allesio, J. (1983). Incentive relativity effects reduced by exogenous insulin. *Physiology & Behavior*, 30, 639–42.

Flaherty, C. F., & Meinrath, A. (1979). Influence of scopolamine on sucrose intake under absolute and relative test conditions. *Physiological Psychology*, 7, 412–18.

Flaherty, C. F., Otto, T., Hsu, D., & Coppotelli, C. (1995, March). Lesions of the hippocampus or entorhinal cortex differentially influence instrumental and consummatory behavior. Paper presented at the Eastern Psychological Association, Boston.

Flaherty, C. F., Portugal, P., & Coppotelli, C. (1995, March). Effect of chronic fluoxetine (Prozac) on contrast in consummatory behavior. Paper presented at the Eastern Psychological Association meeting.

Flaherty, C. F., Powell, G., & Hamilton, L. W. (1979). Septal lesion, sex, and incentive shift effects on open field behavior of rats. *Physiology & Behavior*, 22, 903–9.

Flaherty, C. F., Riley, E. P., & Spear, N. E. (1973). Effect of sucrose concentration and goal units on runway behavior in the rat. *Learning & Motivation*, 4, 163–75.

Flaherty, C. F., & Rowan, G. A. (1985). Anticipatory contrast: Within-subjects analysis. *Animal Learning & Behavior*, 13, 2–5.

   (1986). Successive, simultaneous, and anticipatory contrast in the consumption of saccharin solutions. *Journal of Experimental Psychology: Animal Behavior Processes*, 12, 381–93.

   (1988). Effect of intersolution interval, chlordiazepoxide and amphetamine on anticipatory contrast. *Animal Learning & Behavior*, 16, 47–52.

   (1989a). Rats selectively bred to differ in avoidance behavior also differ in response to novelty stress, in glycemic conditioning, and in reward contrast. *Behavioral and Neural Biology*, 51, 145–64.

(1989b). Negative contrast in the consumption of sucrose and quinine-adulterated sucrose solutions. *Journal of the American College of Nutrition, 8,* 47–55.

Flaherty, C. F., Rowan, G. A., Emerich, D., & Walsh, T. (1989). Effects of intra-hippocampal administration of colchicine on incentive contrast and on radial maze performance. *Behavioral Neuroscience, 103,* 319–28.

Flaherty, C. F., & Sepanak, S. J. (1978). Bidirectional contrast, matching, and power functions obtained in sucrose consumption by rats. *Animal Learning & Behavior, 6,* 313–19.

Flaherty, C. F., Troncoso, B., & Deschu, N. (1979). Open field behaviors correlated with reward availability and reward shift in three rat strains. *American Journal of Psychology, 92,* 385–400.

Flaherty, C. F., Turovsky, J., & Krauss, K. L. (1994). Relative hedonic value modulates anticipatory contrast. *Physiology & Behavior, 55,* 1047–54.

Flaherty, C. F., Wrightson, J., Deptula, D., & Duston, C. (1979). Chlordiazepoxide does not influence simultaneous gustatory contrast. *Bulletin of the Psychonomic Society, 14,* 216–18.

Fletcher, F. M. (1940). Effects of quantitative variation of food – incentive on the performance of physical work by chimpanzees. *Comparative Psychology Monographs, 16,* No. 3, 1–46.

Fontana, D. J., & Commissaris, R. L. (1988). Effects of acute and chronic imipramine administration on conflict behavior in the rat: a potential "animal model" for the study of panic disorder? *Psychopharmacology, 95,* 147–50.

Ford, R. D., Rech, R. H., Commissaris, R. L., & Meyer, L. Y. (1979). Effects of acute and chronic interactions of diazepam and d-amphetamine on punished behavior of rats. *Psychopharmacology, 65,* 197–204.

Franchina, J. J., & Brown, T. S. (1971). Reward magnitude shift in effects in rats with hippocampal lesions. *Journal of Comparative and Physiological Psychology, 76,* 365–70.

Freeman, B. J. (1971). Behavioral contrast: Reinforcement frequency or response suppression. *Psychological Bulletin, 75,* 347–56.

Gaffan, D. (1992). Amygdala and the memory of reward. In J. Aggleton (Ed.), *The amygdala: Neurobiological aspects of emotion, memory, and mental dysfunction* (pp. 471–83). New York: Wiley-Liss.

Gallup, G. G., & Altomari, T. S. (1969). Activity as a postsituation measure of frustrative nonreward. *Journal of Comparative and Physiological Psychology, 68,* 382–5.

Gamzu, E., & Schwartz, B. (1973). The maintenance of key pecking by stimulus-contingent and response independent food presentations. *Journal of the Experimental Analysis of Behavior, 19,* 65–72.

Gandelman, R. (1983). Gonadal hormones and sensory function. *Neuroscience and Biobehavioral Reviews, 7,* 1–17.

Gandelman, R., & Trowill, J. A. (1969). Effects of reinforcement shifts upon subsequent saccharin consumption. *Psychonomic Science, 15,* 25.

Gantt, W. H. (1938). The nervous secretion of saliva: The relation of the conditioned reflex to the intensity of the unconditioned stimulus. *American Journal of Physiology, 123,* 74.

Garcia, J., & Hankins, W. G. (1977). On the origin of food aversion paradigms. In L. M. Barker, M. R. Best, & M. Domjan (Eds.), *Learning mechanisms in food selection* (pp. 3–19). Waco: Baylor University Press.

Gardner, C. R. (1985). Pharmacological studies of the role of serotonin in animal models of anxiety. In A. R. Green (Ed.), *Neuropharmacology of serotonin* (pp. 281–325). Oxford: Oxford University Press.

(1986). Recent developments in 5HT-related pharmacology of animal models of anxiety. *Pharmacology, Biochemistry, & Behavior, 24,* 1479–85.

Gavelek, J. R., & McHose, J. H. (1970). Contrast effects in differential delay of reward conditioning. *Journal of Experimental Psychology, 86,* 454–7.

Gee, K. W., Chang, W-C., Brinton, R. E., & McEwen, B. S. (1987). GABA-dependant modulation of the Cl⁻ ionophore by steroids in the rat brain. *European Journal of Pharmacology, 136,* 419–23.

Geller, I., Bachman, E., & Seifter, J. (1963). Effects of reserpine and morphine on behavior suppressed by punishment. *Life Sciences, 4*, 226–31.

Geller, I. & Seifter, J. (1960). Effects of meprobamate, barbiturates, d-amphetamine and promazine on experimentally-induced conflict in the rat. *Psychopharmacologia, 1*, 482–92.

Gibbon, J., & Church, R. M. (1984). sources of variance in an information processing theory of timing. In H. L. Roitblat, T. G. Bever, & H. S. Terrace (Eds.), *Animal cognition* (pp. 465–88). Hillsdale, NJ: Erlbaum.

Gleitman, H., & Steinman, F. (1964). Depression effect as a function of retention interval before and after shift in reward magnitude. *Journal of Comparative and Physiological Psychology, 57*, 158–60.

Goldberg, M. E., Salama, A. I., Patel, J. B., & Malick, J. B. (1983). Novel non-benzodiazepine anxiolytics. *Neuropharmacology, 22*, 1499–1504.

Goldman, L., Coover, G. D., & Levine, S. (1973). Bidirectional effects of reinforcement shifts on pituitary-adrenal activity. *Physiology & Behavior, 10*, 209–14.

Gonzalez, R. C., & Bitterman, M. E. (1969). Spaced-trials partial reinforcement effect as a function of contrast. *Journal of Comparative and Physiological Psychology, 67*, 94–103.

Gonlazez, R. C., & Champlin, G. (1974). Positive behavioral contrast, negative simultaneous contrast and their relation to frustration in pigeons. *Journal of Comparative and Physiological Psychology, 87*, 173–87.

Gonzalez, R. C., Fernoff, D., & David, F. G. (1973). Contrast, resistance to extinction, and forgetting in rats. *Journal of Comparative and Physiological Psychology, 84*, 562–71.

Gonzalez, R. C., Ferry, M., & Powers, A. S. (1974). The adjustment of goldfish to reduction in magnitude of reward in massed trials. *Animal Learning & Behavior, 2*, 23–6.

Gonzalez, R. C., Gleitman, H,. & Bitterman, M. E. (1962). Some observations on the depression effect. *Journal of Comparative and Physiological Psychology, 55*, 578–81.

Gonzalez, R. C., Holmes, N. K., & Bitterman, M. E. (1967). Resistance to extinction in the goldfish as a function of frequency and amount of reward. *American Journal of Psychology, 80*, 269–75.

Gonzalez, R. C., Potts, A., Pitcoff, K., & Bitterman, M. E. (1972). Runway performance of goldfish as a function of complete and incomplete reduction in amount of reward. *Psychonomic Science, 27*, 305–7.

Gonzalez, R. C., & Powers, A. S. (1973). Simultaneous contrast in goldfish. *Animal Learning & Behavior, 1*, 96–8.

Goodrich, K. P. (1959). Performance in different segments of an instrumental response chain as a function of reinforcement schedule. *Journal of Experimental Psychology, 57*, 57–63.

Goodrich, K. P., & Zaretsky, H. (1962). Running speed as a function of concentration of sucrose during pretraining. *Psychological Reports, 11*, 463–8.

Goomas, D. T. (1981). Multiple shifts in magnitude of reward. *Psychological Reports, 49*, 335–8.

Gordon, W. C., Flaherty, C. F., & Riley, E. P. (1973). Negative contrast as a function of the interval between pre-shift and post-shift training. *Bulletin of the Psychonomic Society, 1*, 25–7.

Gramling, S. E., Fowler, S. C., & Collins, K. R. (1984). Some effects of pimozide on nondeprived rats licking sucrose solutions in an anhedonia paradigm. *Pharmacology, Biochemistry, & Behavior, 21*, 617–24.

Gray, J. A. (1977). Drug effects on fear and frustration: Possible limbic site of action of minor tranquilizers. In L. L. Iversen, S. D. Iversen, & S. H. Snyder (Eds.), *Handbook of psychopharmacology* (Vol. 8, pp. 433–529). New York: Plenum.

   (1982). *The neuropsychology of anxiety: An enquiry into the functions of the septo-hippocampal system*. New York: Oxford University Press.

   (1987). *The psychology of fear and stress*. Cambridge: Cambridge University Press.

   (1990). Brain systems that mediate both emotion and cognition. In J. A. Gray (Ed.), *Psychobiological aspects of relationships between emotion and cognition* (pp. 269–88). Hillsdale, NJ: Erlbaum.

Gray, J. A., Davis, N., Feldon, J., Rawlins, J., & Owens, S. R. (1981). Animal models and anxiety. *Progress in Neuropsychopharmacology, 92*, 491–504.

Gray, J. A., & Smith, P. T. (1969). An arousal-decision model for partial reinforcement and discrimination learning. In R. M. Gilbert & N. S. Sutherland (Eds.), *Animal discrimination learning* (pp. 243–72). London: Academic Press.

Gray, J. A., Whatly, S. A., & Snape, M. (1991). The neuropsychology of anxiety and tolerance for stress. In M. Briley & S. E. File (Eds.), *New concepts in anxiety* (pp. 13–45). Boca Raton: CRC Press.

Green, A.R. (1985). *Neuropharmacology of serotonin*. Oxford: Oxford University Press.

Green, B. G., & Lawless, H. T. (1991). The psychophysics of somatosensory chemoreception in the nose and mouth. In T. V. Getchell, L. M. Bartoshuk, R. L. Doty, & J. B. Snow, Jr. (Eds.), *Smell and taste in health and disease* (pp. 235–53). New York: Raven Press.

Green, S., & Hodges, H. (1991). Animal models of anxiety. In P. Willner (Ed.), *Behavioral models in psychopharmacology: Theoretical, industrial and clinical perspectives* (pp. 21–49). Cambridge: Cambridge University Press.

Grigson, P. S. (1990). A search for the mechanism by which cyproheptadine prevents the occurrence of successive negative contrast. Unpublished doctoral dissertation, Rutgers University.

Grigson, P. S., & Flaherty, C. F. (1991). Cyproheptadine prevents the initial occurrence of successive negative contrast. *Pharmacology, Biochemistry, & Behavior, 40*, 433–42.

Grigson, P. S., & Norgren, R. N. (1994). Effects of lesions of the parabrachial nucleus on negative contrast in consummatory behavior.

Grigson, P. S., Spector, A. C., & Norgren, R. (1993). Microstructural analysis of successive negative contrast in free-feeding and deprived rats. *Physiology & Behavior, 54*, 909–16.

Grindley, G. C. (1929). Experiments on the influence of amount of reward on learning in young chickens. *British Journal of Psychology, 30*, 173–80.

Gross, A. M. (1982). Acting out in children of divorce: An argument for behavioral contrast. *Child and Family Behavioral Therapy, 4*, 87–9.

Gurowitz, E. M., Rosen, A. J., & Tessel, R. E. (1970). Incentive shift performance in cingulectomized rats. *Journal of Comparative and Physiological Psychology, 70*, 476–81.

Gutman, A., Sutterer, J. R., & Brush, F. R. (1975). Positive and negative behavioral contrast in the rat. *Journal of the Experimental Analysis of Behavior, 23*, 377–83.

Haggbloom, S. J. (1979). Effects of a 24–hour intertrial interval on successive differential conditioning and simultaneous negative contrast. *American Journal of Psychology, 92*, 537–46.

Hale, R. L., Johnston, A. L., & Becker, H. C. (1990). Indomethacin does not antagonize the anxiolytic action of ethanol in the elevated plus-maze. *Psychopharmacology, 101*, 203–7.

Halliday, M. S., & Boakes, R. A. (1971). Behavioral contrast and response independent reinforcement. *Journal of the Experimental Analysis of Behavior, 16*, 429–34.

(1974). Behavioral contrast without response-rate reduction. *Journal of the Experimental Analysis of Behavior, 22*, 453–62.

Haltmeyer, G. C., Denenberg, V. H., & Zarrow, M. X. (1967). Modification of plasma corticosterone response as a function of infantile stimulation and electric shock parameters. *Physiology & Behavior, 2*, 61–3.

Hamilton, L. W., & Flaherty, C. F. (1973). Interactive effects of deprivation conditions in the albino rat. *Learning & Motivation, 4*, 148–62.

Hammond, G. R., & Thomas, G. J. (1971). Failure to reactivate the septal syndrome in rats. *Physiology & Behavior, 6*, 599–601.

Handley, S. L., & Mithani, S. (1984a). Effects of alpha– adrenoceptor agonists and antagonists in a maze-exploration model of "fear" motivated behavior. *Nauyn-Schmeideberg Archives of Pharmacology, 327*, 1–5.

(1984b). Effects on punished responding of drugs acting at α_2–adrenoceptors. *British Journal of Pharmacology, 81*, 128P.

Harlow, H. F. (1959). Learning set and error factor theory. In S. Koch (Ed.), *Psychology: A study of a science*, Volume 2. *General systematic formulations, learning, and special processes* (pp. 492–537). New York: McGraw-Hill.

Hart, R. P., & Coover, G. D. (1982). Plasma corticosterone and free fatty acid responses and positive behavioral contrast. *Physiology & Behavior, 29*, 483–8.

Hassin-Herman, A. D., Hemmes, N. S., & Brown, B. L. (1992). Behavioral contrast: Pavlovian effects and anticipatory contrast. *Journal of the Experimental Analysis of Behavior, 57,* 159–75.

Hearst, E., & Jenkins, H. M. (1974). *Sign tracking: The stimulus-reinforcer relation and directed action.* Austin, TX: Monograph of the Psychonomic Society.

Helson, H. (1964) *Adaption-level theory: An experimental and systematic approach to behavior.* New York: Harper & Row.

Hemmes, N. S. (1973). Behavioral contrast in pigeons depends on the operant. *Journal of Comparative and Physiological Psychology, 85,* 171–8.

Henke, P. G. (1972). Amygdalectomy and mixed reinforcement schedule contrast effects. *Psychonomic Science, 28,* 301–2.

(1974). Lesions in the ventromedial hypothalamus and responses to frustrative nonreward. *Physiology & Behavior, 13,* 143–6.

(1976). Septal lesions and aversive nonreward. *Physiology & Behavior, 17,* 483–8.

Henke, P. G., Allen, J. D., & Davison, C. (1972). Effect of lesions of the amygdala on behavioral contrast. *Physiology & Behavior, 8,* 173–6.

Henke, P. G., & Maxwell, D. (1973). Lesions in the amygdala and the frustration effect. *Physiology & Behavior, 10,* 647–50.

Hess, J. L., Denenberg, V. H., Zarrow, M. X., & Pfeiffer, W. D. (1969). Modification of the corticosterone response curves as a function of handling in infancy. *Physiology & Behavior, 4,* 109–11.

Higa, J. J., & McSweeney, F. K. (1987). Behavioral contrast in rats when qualitatively different reinforcers are used. *Behavioral Processes, 15,* 131–42.

Hijzen, T. H., & Slangen, J. L. (1989). Effects of midazolam, DMCM, and lindane on potentiated startle in the rat. *Psychopharmacology, 99,* 362–5.

Hilgard, E. R. (1948). *Theories of learning.* New York: Appleton-Century-Crofts.

(1951). Methods and procedures in the study of learning. In S.S. Stevens (Ed.), *Handbook of experimental psychology* (pp. 517–67). New York: Wiley.

Hinson, J. M., & Staddon, J. E. R. (1978). Behavioral competition: A mechanism for schedule interactions. *Science, 202,* 432–4.

Hodges, H., Green, S., & Glenn, B. (1987). Evidence that the amygdala is involved in benzodiazepine and serotonergic effects on punished responding but not on discrimination. *Psychopharmacology, 92,* 491–504.

Holland, P. C. (1989). Occasion setting with simultaneous compounds in rats. *Journal of Experimental Psychology: Animal Behavior Processes, 15,* 183–93.

Holland, P. C., & Rescorla, R. A. (1979). The effects of two ways of devaluing the unconditioned stimulus after first- and second-order appetitive conditioning. *Journal of Experimental Psychology: Animal Behavior Processes, 5,* 65–78.

Holman, E. W. (1975). Some conditions for the dissociation of consummatory and instrumental behavior in rats. *Learning & Motivation, 6,* 358–66.

Homzie, M. J., & Ross, L. E. (1962). Runway performance following a reduction in the concentration of a liquid reward. *Journal of Comparative and Physiological Psychology, 55,* 1029–33.

Howard, J. L., & Pollard, G. T. (1977). The Geller conflict test: A model of anxiety and a screening procedure for anxiolytics. In I. Hanin & E. Usdin (Eds.), *Animal models of psychiatry and neurology* (pp. 269–78). Oxford: Pergamon.

(1991). Effects of drugs on punished behavior: Preclinical test for anxiolytics. In S. E. File (Ed.), *Psychopharmacology of anxiolytics and antidepressants* (pp. 131–53). New York: Pergamon.

Huang, I-N. (1969). Successive contrast effects as a function of type and magnitude of reward. *Journal of Experimental Psychology, 82,* 64–9.

Hughes, L. F., & Dachowski, L. (1973). The role of reinforcement and nonreinforcement in an operant frustration effect. *Animal Learning & behavior, 1,* 68–72.

Hull, C. L. (1943) *Principles of Behavior.* New York: Appleton-Century-Crofts.

Hull, C. L. (1952). *A behavior system.* New York: Wiley.

Isaacson, R. L. (1982). *The limbic system.* New York: Plenum Press.

Ison, J. R., Daly, H. B., & Glass, D. H. (1967). Amobarbital sodium and the effects of reward and nonreward in the Amsel double runway. *Psychological Reports, 20,* 491–6.

Ison, J. R., Glass, D. H., & Daly, H. B. (1969). Reward magnitude changes following differential conditioning and partial reinforcement. *Journal of Experimental Psychology, 81,* 81–8.

Ison, J. R., & Northman, J. (1968). Amobarbital sodium and instrumental performance changes following an increase in reward magnitude. *Psychonomic Science, 12,* 185–6.

Iverson, L. L., Iverson, S. D., & Snyder, S. H. (Eds.)(1977). *Handbook of psychopharmacology,* Vol. 8, *Drugs, neurotransmitters and behavior* (pp. 433–529). New York: Plenum.

Iversen, S. D. (1983). Animal models of anxiety. In M. R. Trimble (Ed.), *Benzodiazepines Divided* (pp. 87–99). New York: Wiley.

Jaffe, M. L. (1973). The effect of lesions of the ventromedial nucleus of the hypothalamus on behavioral contrast in rats. *Physiological Psychology, 1,* 191–8.

Johnson, D. F., Ackroff, K., Peters, J., & Collier, G. H. (1986). Changes in rats'meal patterns as a function of the caloric density of the diet. *Physiology & Behavior, 36,* 929–36.

Johnston, A. L., & File, S. E. (1986). 5-HT and anxiety: Promises and pitfalls. *Pharmacology, Biochemistry, & Behavior, 24,* 1467–70.

Johnston, A. L., & File, S. E. (1989). Sodium phenobarbitone reverses the anxiogenic effects of compounds acting at three different central sites. *Neuropharmacology, 28,* 83–8.

Kahneman, D., & Tversky, A. (1984). Choices, values, and frames. *American Psychologist, 39,* 341–50.

Karpicke, J. (1978). Directed approach responses and positive conditioned suppression in the rat. *Animal Learning & Behavior, 6,* 216–24.

Kiefer, S. W., & Grijalva, C. V. (1980). Taste reactivity in rats following lesions of the zona incerta or amygdala. *Physiology & Behavior, 25,* 549–54.

Kehne, J. H., Cassella, J. V., & Davis, M. (1988). Anxiolytic effects of buspirone and gepirone in the fear-potentiated startle paradigm. *Psychopharmacology, 94,* 8–13.

Keller, J. V. (1970). Behavioral contrast under multiple delays of reinforcement. *Psychonomic Science, 20,* 257–8.

Keller, K. (1974). The role of elicited responding in behavioral contrast. *Journal of the Experimental Analysis of Behavior, 21,* 249–57.

Kemble, E. D., & Schwartzbaum, J. S. (1969). Reactivity to taste properties of solutions following amygdaloid lesions. *Physiology & Behavior, 4,* 981–5.

Kentridge, R. W., & Aggleton, J. P. (1993). Changes in cis(z)-flupentixol-induced dopamine blockade produce contrast effects in rats. *The Quarterly Journal of Experimental Psychology, 46B,* 113–27.

Kesner, R. P. (1981). The role of the amygdala within an attribute analysis of memory. In Y. Ben-Ari (Ed.), *Amygdaloid complex revisited* (pp. 331-42). Amsterdam: Elsevier.

Kesner, R. P., & Andrus, R. G. (1982). Amygdala stimulation disrupts the magnitude of reinforcement contribution of long-term memory. *Physiological Psychology, 10,* 55–9.

Killeen, P. A. (1972). A yoked-chamber comparison of concurrent and multiple schedules. *Journal of the Experimental Analysis of Behavior, 18,* 13–22.

Kilts, C. D., Commissaris, R. L., Gordon, J. J., & Rech, R. H. (1982). Lack of central 5-hydroxytryptamine influence on the anticonflict activity of diazepam. *Psychopharmacology, 78,* 156–64.

Kilts, C. D., Commissaris, R. L., & Rech, R. H. (1981). Comparison of anti-conflict drug effects in three experimental animal models of anxiety. *Psychopharmacology, 74,* 290–6.

Klinger, E. (1975). Consequences of commitment to and disengagement from incentives. *Psychological Review, 82,* 1–25.

Klinger, E., Barta, S. G., & Kemble, E. D. (1974). Cyclic activity changes during extinction in rats: A potential model of depression. *Animal Learning & Behavior, 2,* 313–16.

Klerman, G. L. (1984). History and development of modern concepts of affective illness. In R. M.

Post & J. C. Ballenger (Eds.), *Neurobiology of mood disorders* (pp. 1–19). Baltimore: Williams and Wilkens.

Knarr, F. A., & Collier, G. (1962). Taste and consummatory activity in amount and gradient of reinforcement functions. *Journal of Experimental Psychology, 63,* 579–88.

Kobre, K. R., & Lipsitt, L. P. (1972). A negative contrast effect in newborns. *Journal of Experimental Child Psychology, 14,* 81–91.

Koch, S. (Ed.) (1959). *Psychology: A study of a science,* Volume 2. *General systematic formulations, learning, and special processes.* New York: McGraw-Hill.

Kodera, T. L., & Rilling, M. (1976). Procedural antecedents of behavioral contrast: A re-examination of errorless learning. *Journal of the Experimental Analysis of Behavior, 25,* 27–42.

Kostowski, W., Plaznik, A., & Stefanski, R. (1989). Intrahippocampal buspirone in animal models of anxiety. *European Journal of Pharmacology, 168,* 393–6.

Kramarcy, N., Mikulka, P., & Freeman, F. (1973). The effects of dorsal hippocampal lesions on reinforcement shifts. *Physiological Psychology, 1,* 248–50.

Krane, R. V., & Ison, J. R. (1971). Positive induction in differential instrumental conditioning: Effect of the interstimulus interval. *Journal of Comparative and Physiological Psychology, 75,* 129–35.

Kruse, H., Theurer, R., Dunn, W., Novick, J., & Shearman, G. T. (1980). Attenuation of conflict-induced suppression by clonidine: indication of anxiolytic activity. *Drug Development Research, 1,* 137–43.

Kshama, D., Hrishikeshava, H. J., Shanbhogue, R., & Munonyedi, U. S. (1990). Modulation of baseline behavior in rats by putative serotonergic agents in three ethoexperimental paradigms. *Behavioral and Neurobiology, 54,* 234–53.

Lal, H., & Emmett-Ogelsby, M. W. (1983). Behavioral analogues of anxiety. *Neuropharmacology, 22,* 1423–41.

Lawless, H. T.(1986). Sensory interactions in mixtures. *Journal of Sensory Studies, 1,* 259–74.

Lawrence, D. H. (1949). Acquired distinctiveness of cues: I. Transfer between discriminations on the basis of familiarity with the stimulus. *Journal of Experimental Psychology, 39,* 770–84.

Lawson, R. (1957). Brightness discrimination performance and secondary strength as a function of primary reward amount. *Journal of Comparative and Physiological Psychology, 50,* 35–9.

Leaf, R. C., & Muller, S. A. (1965). Effects of shock intensity, deprivation, and morphine in a simple approach-avoidance conflict situation. *Psychological Reports, 17,* 819–23.

Leary, R. W. (1958). Homogeneous and heterogeneous reward of monkeys. *Journal of Comparative and Physiological Psychology, 51,* 706–10.

LeDoux, J. E. (1990). Information flow from sensation to emotion: Plasticity in the neural computation of stimulus value. In M. Gabriel & J. Moore (Eds.), *Learning and computational neuroscience: Foundations of adaptive networks* (pp. 3–51). Cambridge, MA: MIT Press.

(1992). Emotion and the amygdala. In J. Aggleton (Ed.), *The amygdala: Neurobiological aspects of emotion, memory, and mental dysfunction* (pp. 339–51). New York: Wiley–Liss.

Lehr, R. (1974). Partial reward and positive contrast effect. *Animal Learning & Behavior, 2,* 221–4.

Levine, S. (1956). A further study of infantile handling and adult avoidance learning. *Journal of Personality, 25,* 70–80.

Levine, S., Haltmeyer, G. C., Karas, G., & Denenberg, V. H. (1967). Physiological and behavioral effects of infantile stimulation. *Physiology & Behavior, 2,* 55–9.

Lister, R. G. (1987). The use of a plus–maze to measure anxiety in the mouse. *Psychopharmacology, 92,* 180–5.

(1991). Ethologically based animal models of anxiety disorders. In S. E. File (Ed.), *Psychopharmacology of anxiolytics and antidepressants* (pp. 155–85). New York: Pergamon.

Locurto, C. M., Norris, J., Cataldo, P. F., & LaPlace, A. (1981). Time allocation and positive conditioned suppression. *Behavior Analysis Letters, 1,* 123–30.

Logan, F. A. (1960). *Incentive.* New Haven, CT: Yale University Press.

Logue, A. W., & King, G. R. (1991). Self-control and impulsiveness in adult humans when food is the reinforcer. *Appetite, 1,* 1–16.

Lombardi, B. R., & Flaherty, C. F. (1978). Apparent disinhibition of successive but not of simultaneous negative contrast. *Animal Learning & Behavior, 6*, 30–42.

Lorge, I., & Sells, S. B. (1936). Representative factors in the rat under "changed incentive technique." *Journal of Genetic Psychology, 49*, 479–480.

Lowes, G., & Bitterman, M. E., (1967). Reward and learning in the goldfish. *Science, 157*, 455–7.

Lucas, G. A., Gawley, D. J.,& Timberlake, W. (1988). Anticipatory contrast as a measure of time horizons in the rat: Some methodological determinants. *Animal Learning & Behavior, 16*, 377–82.

Lucas, G. A., & Timberlake, W. (1992). Negative anticipatory contrast and preference conditioning: Flavor cues support preference conditioning, and environmental cues support contrast. *Journal of Experimental Psychology: Animal Behavior Processes, 18*, 34–40.

Lucas, G. A., Timberlake, W., Gawley, D. J., & Drew, J. (1990). Anticipation of future food: Suppression and facilitation of saccharin intake depending on the delay and type of future food. *Journal of Experimental Psychology: Animal Behavior Processes, 16*, 169–77.

Ludvigson, H. W., & Gay, S. E. (1966). Differential reward conditioning, S^- contrast as a function of the magnitude of S^+. *Psychonomic Science, 5*, 289–90.

(1967). An investigation of differences determining contrast effects in differential reward conditioning. *Journal of Experimental Psychology, 75*, 37–42.

MacCorquodale, K., & Meehl, P. E. (1948). On a distinction between hypothetical constructs and intervening variables. *Psychological Review, 55*, 95–107.

Mackinnon, J. R. (1968). Competing responses in a differential magnitude of reward discrimination. *Psychonomic Science, 12*, 333–4.

Mackintosh, N. J. (1971). Reward and the after-effects of reward in the learning of goldfish. *Journal of Comparative and Physiological Psychology, 76*, 225–32.

Mackintosh, N. J. (1974). *The psychology of animal learning*. London: Academic Press.

(1983). *Conditioning and associative learning*. Oxford: Oxford University Press.

Mackintosh, N. J., Little, L., & Lord, J. (1972). Some determinants of behavioral contrast in pigeons and rats. *Learning & Motivation, 3*, 148–61.

Mackintosh, N. J., & Lord, J. (1973). Simultaneous and successive contrast with delay of reward. *Animal Learning & Behavior, 1*, 283–6.

Majewska, M. D., Harrison, N. L., Schwartz, R. D., Barker, J. L., & Paul, S. M. (1986). Steroid hormone metabolites are barbiturate-like modulators of the GABA receptor. *Science, 232*, 1004–7.

Malone, J. C., Jr. (1976). Local contrast and Pavlovian induction. *Journal of the Experimental Analysis of Behavior, 26*, 425–40.

Malone, J. C., Jr., & Cleary, T. L. (1986). Positive local contrast and S^- duration: Theories of local contrast and a resolution. *Behavioural Processes, 13*, 39–52.

Manabe, K. (1992). Real-time detection of orientation during negative behavioral contrast with key pecking and a turning response. *Journal of the Experimental Analysis of Behavior, 57*, 209–18.

Manabe, K., Kuwata, S., & Kurashige, N. (1992). Time allocation of various activities under multiple schedules in pigeons. *Behavioural Processes, 26*, 113–23.

Mansbach, R. S., & Geyer, M. A. (1988). Blockade of potentiated startle responding in rats by 5-hydroxytryptamine$_{1A}$ receptor ligands. *European Journal of Pharmacology, 156*, 375–83.

Marcucella, H., & MacDonall, J. S. (1977). A molecular analysis of multiple schedule interaction: Negative contrast. *Journal of the Experimental Analysis of Behavior, 28*, 71–82.

Mason, S. T., & Fibiger, H. C. (1979). Current topics. I. Anxiety: The locus coeruleus disconnection. *Life Sciences, 256*, 2141–7.

Mast, V. K., Fagen, J. W., Rovee-Collier, C. K., & Sullivan, M. W. (1980). Immediate and long-term memory for reinforcement context: The development of learned expectancies in early infancy. *Child Development, 51*, 700–7.

Matsumoto, R. T. (1969). Relative reward effects in differential conditioning. *Journal of Comparative and Physiological Psychology, 68*, 589–92.

Maxwell, F. R., Calef, R.S., Murray, D. W., Shepard, J. C., & Norville, R. A. (1976). Positive and negative successive contrast effects following multiple shifts in reward magnitude under high drive and immediate reinforcement. *Animal Learning & Behavior, 4,* 480–4.

McAllister, D. E., McAllister, W. R., Brooks, C. I., & Goldman, J. A. (1972). Magnitude and shift of reward in instrumental aversive learning in rats. *Journal of Comparative and Physiological Psychology, 80,* 490–501.

McCain, G., & Cooney, J. (1975). PCE: I. The effects of three reward magnitude shifts. *Bulletin of the Psychonomic Society, 6,* 523–6.

McCleary, R. A. (1961). Response specificity in the behavioral effects of limbic system lesions in the cat. *Journal of Comparative and Physiological Psychology, 54,* 605–13.

McGaugh, J. L., Introini-Collison, I. B., Cahill, L., Kim, M., & Liang, K. C. (1992). Involvement of the amygdala in neuromodulatory influences on memory storage. In. J. Aggleton (Ed.), *The amygdala: Neurobiological aspects of emotion, memory, and mental dysfunction* (pp. 431–51). New York: Wiley-Liss.

McHose, J. H. (1970). Relative reinforcement effects: S1/S2 and S1/S1 paradigms in instrumental conditioning. *Psychological Review, 77,* 135–46.

McHose, J. H., McHewitt, E. R., & Peters, D. P. (1972). Average reward as a determinant of S⁻ performance in differential conditioning. *Psychonomic Science, 29,* 129–32.

McHose, J. H., & Moore, J. N. (1976). Expectancy, salience, and habit: A noncontextual interpretation of the effects of changes in the conditions of reinforcement on simple instrumental responses. *Psychological Review, 83,* 292–307.

McHose, J. H., & Peters, D. P. (1973). Differential instrumental conditioning as a function of percentage and amount of positive stimulus reward. *Journal of Experimental Psychology, 100,* 413–15.

  (1975). Partial reward, the negative contrast effect, and incentive averaging. *Animal Learning & Behavior, 3,* 239–44.

McLean, A. P. (1992). Contrast and reallocation of extraneous reinforcers between multiple schedule components. *Journal of the Experimental Analysis of Behavior, 58,* 497–511.

McLean, A. P., & White, K. G. (1983). Temporal constraint on choice: Sensitivity and bias in multiple schedules. *Journal of the Experimental Analysis of Behavior, 39,* 405–26.

McMillan, D. E. (1973). Drugs and punished responding: IV. Effects of propranolol, ethclorynol, and chloralhydrate. *Research Communications in Chemical Pathology and Pharmacology, 1,* 167–74.

McSweeney, F. K. (1975). Matching and contrast on several concurrent-press schedules. *Journal of the Experimental Analysis of Behavior, 23,* 193–8.

  (1978). Negative behavioral contrast on multiple treadle-press schedules. *Journal of the Experimental Analysis of Behavior, 29,* 463–73.

  (1982). Positive and negative contrast as a function of component duration for key pecking and treadle pressing. *Journal of the Experimental Analysis of Behavior, 37,* 281–93.

  (1983). Positive behavioral contrast when pigeons press treadles during multiple schedules. *Journal of the Experimental Analysis of Behavior, 39,* 149–56.

  (1987). Suppression by reinforcement: A model for multiple-schedule behavioral contrast. *Behavioural Processes, 15,* 191–209.

McSweeney, F. K., Ettinger, R. H., & Norman, W. D. (1981). Three versions of the additive theories of behavioral contrast. *Journal of the Experimental Analysis of Behavior, 36,* 285–97.

McSweeney, F. K., & Melville, C. L. (1988). Positive contrast as a function of component duration using a within-session procedure. *Behavioural Processes, 16,* 21–41.

  (1993). Behavioral contrast for key pecking as a function of component duration when only one component varies. *Journal of the Experimental Analysis of Behavior, 60,* 331–43.

McSweeney, F. K., & Melville, C. (1991). Behavioral contrast as a function of component duration for lever pressing using a within-session procedure. *Animal Learning & Behavior, 19,* 71–80.

McSweeney, F. K., & Norman, W. D. (1979). Defining behavioral contrast for multiple schedules. *Journal of the Experimental Analysis of Behavior, 32,* 457–61.

Meinrath, A. B., & Flaherty, C. F. (1987). Preweanling handling influences open-field behavior, but not negative contrast or sucrose "neophobia." *Animal Learning & Behavior, 15*, 83–92.

Meiselman, H. L. (1971). Effect of presentation procedure on taste intensity functions. *Perception and Psychophysics, 10*, 15–18.

Mellgren, R. L. (1971a). Positive contrast in the rat as a function of number of preshift trials in the runway. *Journal of Comparative and Physiological Psychology, 77*, 329–36.

(1971b). Shift in magnitude of reward after minimal acquisition. *Psychonomic Science, 23*, 243–4.

(1972). Positive and negative contrast effects using delayed reinforcement. *Learning and Motivation, 3*, 185–93.

Mellgren, R. L., & Dyck, D. G. (1974). Reward magnitude and differential conditioning: Effects of sequential variables in acquisition and extinction. *Journal of Comparative and Physiological Psychology, 86*, 1141–8.

Mellgren, R. L., Seybert, J. A., Wrather, D. M., & Dyck, D. G. (1973). Preshift reward magnitude and positive contrast in the rat. *American Journal of Psychology, 86*, 383–7.

Mellgren, R. L., Wrather, D. M., & Dyck, D. G. (1972). Differential conditioning and contrast effects in rats. *Journal of Comparative and Physiological Psychology, 80*, 478–83.

Miczek, K. A. (1973). Effects of scopolamine, amphetamine, and benzodiazepines on conditioned suppression. *Pharmacology, Biochemistry, & Behavior, 1*, 401–11.

Mikulka, P. J., Lehr, R., & Pavlik, W. B. (1967). Effect of reinforcement schedules on reward shifts. *Journal of Experimental Psychology, 74*, 57–61.

Miller, I. J., Jr., & Bartoshuk, L. M. (1991). Taste perception, taste bud distribution, and spatial relationships. In T. V. Getchell, L. M. Bartoshuk, R. L. Doty, & J. B. Snow, Jr. (Eds.), *Smell and taste in health and disease* (pp. 205–33). New York: Raven Press.

Miller, N. E. (1959). Liberalization of basic S-R concepts: Extensions to conflict behavior, motivation, and social learning. In S. Koch (Ed.), *Psychology: A study of a science*, Volume 2. *General systematic formulations, learning, and special processes* (pp. 196–292). New York: McGraw-Hill.

Miller, N. E., & Barry, H., III (1960). Motivational effects of drugs: Methods which illustrate some general problems in psychopharmacology. *Psychopharmacology, 1*, 169–99.

Miller, R. R., & Grahame, N. J. (1991). Expression of Learning. In L. Dachowski & C. F. Flaherty (Eds.), *Current topics in animal learning: Brain, emotion & cognition* (pp. 95–117). Hillsdale, NJ: Erlbaum.

Mohler, H., & Okada, T. (1977). Benzodiazepine receptors: demonstration in the central nervous system. *Science, 198*, 849–851.

Morales, A., Torres, M. D. C., Megias, J. L., Candido, A., & Maldonado, A. (1992). Effect of diazepam on successive negative contrast in one-way avoidance learning. *Pharmacology, Biochemistry, & Behavior, 43*, 153–7.

Moret, C. (1985). Pharmacology of the serotonin autoreceptor. In A. R. Green (Ed.), *Neuropharmacology of serotonin* (pp. 21–49). Oxford: Oxford University Press.

Morgan, C. L. (1894). *Introduction to Comparative Psychology*. London: Walter Scott, Ltd. Reprint: Lanham, MD: University Publications of America, 1977.

Morrow, A. L., Suzdak, P. D., & Paul, S. M. (1988). Benzodiazepine, barbiturate, ethanol and hypnotic steroid hormone modulation of GABA-mediated chloride ion transport in rat brain synatoneurosomes. In G. Biggio & E. Costa (Eds.), *Chloride channels and their modulation by neurotransmitters and drugs* (pp. 247–61). New York: Raven Press.

Morse, W. H. (1964). Effect of amobarbital and chlorpromazine on punished behavior in the pigeon. *Psychopharmacologia, 6*, 286–94.

Moser, P. C. (1989). An evaluation of the elevated plus-maze test using the novel anxiolytic buspirone. *Psychopharmacology, 99*, 48–53.

Moser, P. C., Tricklebank, M. D., Middlemiss, D. N., Mir, A. K., Hibert, M. F., & Fozard, J. R. (1990). Characterization of MDL 73005EF as a 5–HT_{1A} selective ligand and its effects in animal models of anxiety: Comparison with buspirone, 8–OH–DPAT and diazepam. *British Journal of Pharmacology, 99*, 343–9.

Moskowitz, H. R. (1973). Models of sweetness additivity. *Journal of Experimental Psychology*, *99*, 88–98.

Mowrer, O. H. (1960). *Learning theory and behavior*. New York: Wiley.

Murphy, H. M., & Brown, T. S. (1970). Effects of hippocampal lesions on simple and preferential consummatory behavior in the rat. *Journal of Comparative and Physiological Psychology*, *72*, 404–15.

Nachman, M., & Ashe, J. H. (1974). Effects of basolateral amygdala lesions on neophobia, learned taste aversions, and sodium appetite in rats. *Journal of Comparative Physiology*, *87*, 622–43.

Nation, J. R., Mellgren, R. L., & Wrather, D. M. (1975). Contrast effects with shifts in punishment level. *Bulletin of the Psychonomic Society*, *5*, 167–9.

Nation, J. R., Wrather, D. M., & Mellgren, R. L. (1974). Contrast effects in escape conditioning of rats. *Journal of Comparative and Physiological Psychology*, *86*, 69–73.

Nevin, J. (1973). Stimulus control. In J. A. Nevin & G. S. Reynolds (Eds.), *The study of behavior: learning, motivation, emotion, and instinct* (pp. 144–52). Glenview, Il: Scott, Foresman and Co.

Nevin, J. A., & Shettleworth, S. J. (1966). An analysis of contrast effects in multiple schedules. *Journal of the Experimental Analysis of Behavior*, *9*, 305–15.

Nevin, J. A., Smith, L. D., & Roberts, J. (1987). Does contingent reinforcement strengthen operant behavior? *Journal of the Experimental Analysis of Behavior*, *48*, 17–33.

New York Times (1984, November 24), p. 4.

New York Times (1986, August 14), p. B9.

New York Times (1987, January 11).

New York Times (1987, July 21), p. 1.

New York Times (1989, March 3), p. A29.

Norgren, R. (1984). Central neural mechanisms of taste. In J. M. Brookhart & V. P. Mountcastle (Eds.), *Handbook of physiology: The nervous system.* (pp. 1087–91). Baltimore: Williams & Wilkins.

Ogren, S., & Fuxe, K. (1985). Effects of antidepressant drugs on serotonin receptor mechanisms. In A. R. Green (Eds.), *Neuropharmacology of serotonin* (pp. 131–80). Oxford: Oxford University Press.

Padilla, A. M. (1971). Analysis of incentive and behavioral contrast in the rat. *Journal of Comparative and Physiological Psychology*, *75*, 464–70.

Panksepp, J., & Trowill, J. (1971). Positive and negative contrast in licking with shifts in sucrose concentration as a function of food deprivation. *Learning & Motivation*, *2*, 49–57.

Papini, M. R., & Ishida, M. (1994). Role of magnitude of reinforcement in spaced-trial instrumental learning in turtles (*Geoclemys reevesii*). *Quarterly Journal of Experimental Psychology*, *47B*, 1–13.

Papini, M. R., Mustaca, A. E., & Bitterman, M. E. (1988). Successive negative contrast in the consummatory responding of didelphid marsupials. *Animal Learning & Behavior*, *16*, 53–7.

Pavlov, I. (1927). *Conditioned reflexes*. London: Oxford University Press.

Pellow, S. (1986). Anxiolytic and anxiogenic drug effects in a novel test of anxiety: Are exploratory models of anxiety in rodents valid? *Methods and Findings in Experimental Clinical Pharmacology*, *8*, 557–65.

Pellow, S., Chopin, P., File, S. E., & Briley, M. (1985). Validation of open:closed arm entries in an elevated plus-maze as a measure of anxiety in the rat. *Journal of Neuroscience Methods*, *14*, 149–67.

Pellow, S., Johnston, A. L., & File, S. E. (1987). Selective agonists and antagonists for 5–hydroxytryptamine receptor subtypes, and interactions with yohimbine and FG-7142 using the elevated plus-maze test in the rat. *Journal of Pharmacology*, *39*, 917–28.

Pert, A., & Bitterman, M. E. (1970). Reward and learning in the turtle. *Learning & Motivation*, *1*, 121–8.

Pert, A., & Gonzalez, R. C. (1974). Behavior of the turtle (*Chrysemys picta picta*) in simultaneous, successive, and behavioral contrast situations. *Journal of Comparative and Physiological Psychology*, *87*, 526–38.

Peters, D. P., & McHose, J. H. (1974). Effects of varied preshift reward magnitude on successive negative contrast effects in rats. *Journal of Comparative and Physiological Psychology*, 86, 85–95.

Peters, J. A., Kirkness, E. F., Callachan, H., Lambert, J. J., & Turner, A. J. (1988). Modulation of the GABA receptor by depressant barbiturates and pregnane steroids. *British Journal of Pharmacology*, 94, 1257–69.

Petersen, E. N., & Lassen, J. B. (1981). A water lick paradigm using drug experienced rats. *Psychopharmacology*, 75, 236–9.

Phillips, A. G., & LePiane, F. G. (1986). Effects of pimozide on positive and negative incentive contrast with rewarding brain stimulation. *Pharmacology, Biochemistry, & Behavior*, 24, 1577–82.

Pich, E. M., & Samanin, R. (1986). Disinhibitory effect of buspirone and low doses of sulpiride and haloperidol in two experimental anxiety models in rats: Possible role of dopamine. *Psychopharmacology*, 89, 125–30.

Pinel, J. P., & Rovner, L. I. (1977). Saccharin elation effect. *Bulletin of the Psychonomic Society*, 9, 275–8.

Poling, A., Urbain, C., & Thompson, T. (1977). Effects of d-amphetamine and chlordiazepoxide on positive conditioned suppression. *Pharmacology, Biochemistry, & Behavior*, 7, 233–7.

Pollard, G. T., & Howard, J. L. (1979). The Geller–Seifter conflict paradigm with incremental shock. *Psychopharmacology*, 62, 117–21.

Porter, J. H., Johnson, D. N., & Jackson, J. Y. (1985). Anxiolytic testing of buspirone in rodents. *Society for Neuroscience Abstracts*, No. 126.11.

Porter, J. J., Madison, H. L., & Senkowski, P. C. (1968). Runway performance and competing responses as a function of drive level and method of drive measurement. *Journal of Experimental Psychology*, 78, 281–4.

Portugal, P., Coppotelli, C., & Flaherty, C. F. (1995). Effect of chronic fluexetine (Prozac) on anticipatory and successive negative contrast. Eastern Psychological Association, Boston, March.

Premack, D., & Hillix, W. A. (1962). Evidence for shift effects in the consummatory response. *Journal of Experimental Psychology*, 63, 284–8.

Purdy, R. H., Morrow, A. L., Moore, P. H., Jr., & Paul, S. M. (1991). Stress-induced elevations in gamma-amino-butyric acid type A receptor-active steroids in the rat brain. *Proceedings of the National Academy of Sciences*, 88, 4553–7.

Rabin, J. S. (1975). Effects of varying sucrose reinforcers and amobarbital sodium on positive contrast in rats. *Animal Learning & Behavior*, 3, 290–4.

Rabiner, D. L., Kling, J. W., & Spraguer, P. A. (1988). Modulation of taste-induced drinking: The effects of concentration shifts and drinking interruptions. *Animal Learning & Behavior*, 16, 365–76.

Rachlin, H. (1973). Contrast and matching. *Psychological Review*, 80, 217–234.

Rashotte, M. E. (1979). Reward training: Contrast effects. In M. E. Bitterman, V. M. LoLordo, J. B. Overmier & M. E. Rashotte (Eds.), *Animal learning: Survey and analysis* (pp. 195–239). New York: Plenum.

Raymond, B., Aderman, M., & Wolach, A. H. (1972). Incentive shifts in the goldfish. *Journal of Comparative and Physiological Psychology*, 78, 10–13.

Rescorla, R. A. (1985). Associative learning: Some consequences of contiguity. In N. M. Weinberger, J. L. McGaugh & G. Lynch (Eds.), *Memory systems of the brain: Animal and human cognitive processes* (pp. 211–30). New York: Guilford Press.

(1992). Hierarchical Associative relations in Pavlovian conditioning and instrumental training. *Current Directions in Psychological Science*, 1, 66–70.

Reynolds, G. A. (1961). An analysis of interactions in a multiple schedule. *Journal of the Experimental Analysis of Behavior*, 4, 107–17.

Riblet, L. A., Taylor, D. P., Eison, M. S., & Stanton, H. C. (1982). Pharmacology and neurochemistry of buspirone. *Journal of Clinical Psychiatry*, 43, 11–16.

Ridgers, A., & Gray, J. A. (1973). Influence of amylobarbitone on operant depression and elation effects in the rat. *Psychopharmacologia*, 32, 265–70.

Riley, E. A., & Dunlap, W. P. (1979). Successive negative contrast as a function of deprivation condition following shifts in sucrose concentration. *American Journal of Psychology, 92*, 59–70.

Roberts, W. A. (1966). The effects in magnitude of reward on runway performance in immature and adult rats. *Psychonomic Science, 5*, 37–8.

Roberts, W. A., & Pixley, L. (1965). The effect of chlorpromazine on the depression effect. *Psychonomic Science, 3*, 407–8.

Robichaud, R. C., Sledge, K. L., Heffner, M. A., & Goldberg, M. E. (1973). Propranolol and chlordiazepoxide on experimentally-induced conflict and shuttlebox performance in rodents. *Psychopharmacologia, 32*, 157–60.

Rogers, P. J. (1985). Returning "cafeteria-fed" rats to a chow diet: Negative contrast and effects of obesity on feeding behavior. *Physiology & Behavior, 35*, 493–9.

Rolls, E. T. (1992). Neurophysiology and functions of the primate amygdala. In J. Aggleton (Ed.), *The amygdala: Neurobiological aspects of emotion, memory, and mental dysfunction* (pp. 143–65). New York: Wiley-Liss.

Rosen, A. J. (1966). Incentive shift performance as a function of magnitude of sucrose rewards. *Journal of Comparative and Physiological Psychology, 62*, 487–90.

Rosen, A. J., Glass, D. H., & Ison, J. R. (1967). Amobarbital sodium and instrumental performance changes following reward reduction. *Psychonomic Science, 9*, 129–30.

Rosen, A. J., & Ison, J. R. (1965). Runway performance following changes in sucrose rewards. *Psychonomic Science, 2*, 335–6.

Rosen, A. J., & Tessel, R. E. (1970). Chlorpromazine, chlordiazepoxide and incentive shift performance in the rat. *Journal of Comparative and Physiological Psychology, 72*, 257–62.

Rovee-Collier, C. K., & Capatides, J. B. (1979). Positive behavioral contrast in 3-month-old infants on multiple conjugate reinforcement schedules. *Journal of the Experimental Analysis of Behavior, 32*, 15–27.

Rovee-Collier, C. K., Sullivan, M. W., Enright, M., Lucas, D., & Fagen, J. W. (1980). Reactivation of infant memory. *Science, 208*, 1159–61.

Rowan, G. A., & Flaherty, C. F. (1987). Effect of morphine on negative contrast in consummatory behavior. *Psychopharmacology, 93*, 51–8.

  (1991). Consummatory contrast effects in Maudsley reactive and nonreactive rats. *Journal of Comparative Psychology, 105*, 115–24.

Royall, D. R., & Klemm, W. R. (1981). Dopaminergic mediation of reward: Evidence gained using a natural reinforcer in a behavioral contrast paradigm. *Neuroscience Letters, 21*, 223–9.

Royce, J. R., Poley, W., & Yeudall, L. T. (1973). Behavior-genetic analysis of mouse emotionality: I. Factor analysis. *Journal of Comparative and Physiological Psychology, 83*, 36–47.

Salinas, J., Packard, M. G., & McGaugh, J. L. (1993). Amygdala modulates memory for changes in reward magnitude: Reversible post-training inactivation with lidocaine attenuates the response to a reduction in reward. *Behavioral Brain Research, 59*, 153–9.

Satinder, K. P. (1981). Ontogeny and independence of genetically selected behaviors in rats: Avoidance response and open field. *Journal of Comparative and Physiological Psychology, 95*, 175–87.

Savage, R., & Eysenck, H. (1964). The definition and measurement of emotionality. In H. Eysenck (Ed.), *Experiments in motivation* (pp. 292–314). Oxford: Pergamon.

Scheel-Kreuger, J., & Petersen, E. N. (1982). Anticonflict effect of the benzodiazepines mediated by a GABAergic mechanism in the amygdala. *European Journal of Pharmacology, 82*, 115–16.

Schmajuk, N. A., Segura, E. T., & Ruidiaz, A. C. (1981). Reward downshift in the toad. *Behavioral and Neural Biology, 33*, 519–23.

Schrier, A. M., (1958). Comparison of two methods of investigating the effect of amount of reward on performance. *Journal of Comparative and Physiological Psychology, 51*, 725–31.

  (1965). Response rates of monkeys (*Macaca mulatta*) under varying conditions of sucrose reinforcement. *Journal of Comparative and Physiological Psychology, 59*, 378–84.

  (1967). Effects of an upward shift in amount of reinforcer on runway performance in rats. *Journal of Comparative and Physiological Psychology, 64*, 490–2.

(1969). Effect of reinforcement context on rate-concentration functions for monkeys. *Psychological Reports, 24*, 23–29.

Schrier, A.M. & Harlow, H.F. (1956). Effect of amount of incentive on discrimination learning by monkeys. *Journal of Comparative and Physiological Psychology, 49*, 117–22.

Schwartz, B. (1975). Discriminative stimulus location as a determinant of positive and negative contrast in the pigeon. *Journal of the Experimental Analysis of Behavior, 23*, 167–76.

Schwartz, B., & Gamzu, E. (1977). Pavlovian control of operant behavior: An analysis of autoshaping and its implications for operant conditioning. In W. K. Honig & J. E. R. Staddon (Eds.), *Handbook of operant behavior* (pp. 53–97). Englewood Cliffs, NJ: Prentice-Hall.

Schulkin, J., McEwen, B. S., & Gold, P. W. (1994). Allostasis, amygdala, and anticipatory angst. *Neuroscience and Biobehavioral Reviews, 18*, 385–96.

Scull, J. (1973). The Amsel frustration effect. *Psychological Review, 79*, 352–61.

Scull, J., Davies, K., & Amsel, A. (1970). *Journal of Comparative and Physiological Psychology, 71*, 478–83.

Sepinwall, J. (1985). Behavioral effects of antianxiety agents: Possible mechanisms of action. In L. S. Seiden & R. L. Balster (Eds.), *Behavioral pharmacology: The current status* (pp. 181–203). New York: Alan R. Liss.

Sepinwall, J., & Cook, L. (1978). Behavioral pharmacology of antianxiety drugs. In L. L. Iversen, S. D. Iversen & S. H. Snyder (Eds.), *Handbook of psychopharmacology* (pp. 345–93). New York: Plenum.

Sepinwall, J., & Cook, L. (1980). Relationship of gamma-aminobutyric acid (GABA) to antianxiety effects of benzodiazepines. *Brain Research Bulletin, 5*, 839–48.

Sepinwall, J., Grodsky, F. S., Sullivan, J. W., & Cook, L. (1973). Effects of propranolol and chlordiazepoxide on conflict behavior in rats. *Psychopharmacologia, 31*, 375–82.

Seybert, J. A., & Mellgren, R. L. (1972). Positive contrast: Control of ceiling effect using a long runway. *Psychological Reports, 31*, 14.

Seybert, J. A., Mellgren, R. L., & Jobe, J. B. (1973). Sequential effects on resistance to extinction at widely spaced trials. *Journal of Experimental Psychology, 101*, 151–4.

Sgro, J. A., Glotfelty, R. A., & Podlesni, J. A. (1969). Contrast effects in delay of reward in a double alleyway. *Psychonomic Science, 16*, 29–31.

Shanab, M. E., & Biller, J. D. (1972). Positive contrast in the runway obtained following a shift in both delay and magnitude of reward. *Learning & Motivation, 3*, 179–84.

Shanab, M. E., & Cavallaro, G. (1975). Positive contrast obtained in rats following a shift in schedule, delay, and magnitude of reward. *Bulletin of the Psychonomic Society, 5*, 109–12.

Shanab, M. E., Domino, J., & Ralph, L. (1978). The effects of repeated shifts in magnitude of food reward upon the barpress rate in the rat. *Bulletin of the Psychonomic Society, 12*, 29–31.

Shanab, M. E., & Ferrell, H. J. (1970). Positive contrast in the Lashley maze under different drive conditions. *Psychonomic Science, 20*, 31–2.

Shanab, M. E., France, J., & Young, T. (1975). Negative contrast effect obtained with downshifts in magnitude but not concentration of solid sucrose reward. *Bulletin of the Psychonomic Society, 5*, 429–32.

(1976). Positive and negative contrast effects obtained following shifts in liquid sucrose reward in thirsty rats. *Animal Learning & Behavior, 4*, 9–12.

Shanab, M. E., & McCuistion, S. (1970). Effects of shifts in magnitude and delay of reinforcement upon runway performance in the rat. *Psychonomic Science, 21*, 264–6.

Shanab, M. E., Sanders, R., & Premack, D. (1969). Positive contrast in the runway obtained with delay of reward. *Science, 164*, 724–5.

Shanab, M. E., & Spencer, R. E. (1978). Positive and negative contrast effects obtained following shifts in delayed water reward. *Bulletin of the Psychonomic Society, 12*, 199–202.

Shanab, M. E., & White, R. (1972). Positive contrast obtained with punishment. *Journal of General Psychology, 86*, 247–51.

Shephard, R. N. (1987). Toward a universal law of generalization for psychological science. *Science, 237*, 1317–23.

Sills, M. A., Wolfe, B. B., & Frazier, A. (1984). Determination of selective and nonselective compounds for the $5-HT_{1A}$ and $5-HT_{1B}$ receptor subtypes in rat frontal cortex. *Journal of*

Pharmacology and Experimental Therapeutics, 231, 480–7.

Simmons, R. (1924). The relative effectiveness of certain incentives in animal learning. *Comparative Psychology Monographs, 11*, #7, 1–79.

Skinner, B. F. (1938). *The behavior of organisms*. New York: Appleton-Century-Crofts.

Soderpalm, B., & Engel, J. A. (1988). Biphasic effects of clonidine on conflict behavior: Involvement of different alpha-adrenoceptors. *Pharmacology, Biochemistry & Behavior, 30*, 471–7.

Solomon, R. L., & Corbit, J. D. (1974). An opponent process theory of motivation: Temporal dynamics of affect. *Psychological Review, 81*, 119–45.

Soubrie, P. (1986). Reconciling the role of central serotonin neurons in human and animal behavior. *Behavior and Brain Science, 9*, 319–64.

Spear, N. E. (1965). Replication report: Absence of a successive contrast effect on instrumental running behavior after a shift in sucrose concentration. *Psychological Reports, 16*, 393–4.

(1967). Retention of reinforcer magnitude. *Psychological Review, 74*, 216–34.

(1968). Contrast effects of reinforcer magnitude and within-subject effects of other reinforcement conditions. Empirical and theoretical problems in the analysis of shifts in reinforcement parameters. Paper presented at the Midwestern Psychological Association meetings, Chicago.

Spear, N. E., & Hill, W. F. (1965). Adjustment to new reward: Simultaneous and successive-contrast effects. *Journal of Experimental Psychology, 70*, 510–19.

Spear, N. E., & Pavlik, W. B. (1966). Percentage of reinforcement and reward magnitude effects in a T-maze between and within subjects. *Journal of Experimental Psychology, 71*, 521–8.

Spear, N. E., & Riccio, D. C. (1994). *Memory: Phenomena and Principles*. Boston: Allyn & Bacon.

Spear, N. E., & Spitzner, J. H. (1966). Simultaneous and successive contrast effects of reward magnitude in selective learning. *Psychological Monographs, 80* (10, Whole No. 618).

Spence, K. W. (1937). The differential response of animals to stimuli differing within a single dimension. *Psychological Review, 44*, 430–44.

(1951). Theoretical interpretations of learning. In S. S. Stevens (Ed.), *Handbook of experimental psychology* (pp. 690–729). New York: Wiley.

(1956). *Behavior theory and conditioning*. New Haven: Yale University Press.

Spencer, H. (1870). *Principles of Psychology,* 2nd Ed. London: Longman (Cited in Boakes, 1984).

Spencer, R. E., & Shanab, M. E. (1979). Contrast effects as a function of delay and shifts in magnitude of water reward in thirsty rats. *Bulletin of the Psychonomic Society, 13*, 93–6.

Staddon, J. E. R. (1982). Behavioral competition, contrast, and matching. In M. L. Commons, R. J. Herrnstein & H. Rachlin (Eds.), *Quantitative analysis of behavior:* Vol. 2. *Matching and maximizing accounts* (pp. 243–61). Cambridge, MA: Ballinger.

Staddon, J. E. R., & Simmelhag, V. L. (1971). The "superstition" experiment: A re-examination of its implications for the principles of adaptive behavior. *Psychological Review, 78*, 3–43.

Stanton, M., & Amsel, A. (1980). Adjustment to reward reduction (but no negative contrast) in rats, 11, 14, and 16 days of age. *Journal of Comparative and Physiological Psychology, 94*, 446–58.

Stanton, M., Lobaugh, N., & Amsel, A. (1984). Age of first appearance of simultaneous and successive negative contrast in infant rats. *Journal of Experimental Psychology: Animal Behavior Processes, 10*, 376–89.

Stein, L., Wise, C. D., & Beluzzi, J. D. (1975). Effects of benzodiazepines on central serotonergic mechanisms. In E. Costa & P. Greengard (Eds.), *Mechanism of action of benzodiazepines* (pp. 29–44). New York: Raven Press.

Stevens, S. S. (1969). Sensory scales of taste intensity. *Perception and Psychophysics, 6*, 302–7.

Suarez, S. D., & Gallup, G. G. (1981). An ethological analysis of open-field behavior in rats and mice. *Learning & Motivation, 12*, 342–63.

Taylor, D. P., Eison, A. S., Eison, M. S., Riblet, L. A., Temple, D. L., & Vander Maelen, C. P. (1984). Biochemistry and pharmacology of the anxioselective drug buspirone. *Clinical Neuropharmacology, 7*, Suppl. 1, 886.

Taus, S. E., & Hearst, E. (1972). Effects of intertrial (blackout) duration on response to a positive stimulus. *Psychonomic Science, 19*, 265–6.

Terrace, H. S. (1966a). Stimulus control. In W. K. Honig (Ed.), *Operant behavior: Areas of research and application* (pp. 271–344). New York: Appleton-Century-Crofts.

(1966b). Behavioral contrast and the peak shift: Effects of extended discrimination training. *Journal of the Experimental Analysis of Behavior, 9*, 613–17.

(1966c). Discrimination learning and inhibition. *Science, 154*, 1677–80.

(1968). Discrimination learning, the peak shift, and behavioral contrast. *Journal of the Experimental Analysis of Behavior, 11*, 727–41.

Thiebot, M. H. (1986). Are serotonergic neurons involved in the control of anxiety and in the anxiolytic activity of benzodiazepines? *Pharmacology, Biochemistry, & Behavior, 24*, 1471–7.

Thomas, L. (1983). *Late night thoughts on listening to Mahler's Ninth symphony.* New York: Viking.

Thorndike, E. L. (1911). *Animal intelligence: Experimental studies.* New York: Macmillan.

Timberlake, W. (1983). Rat's response to a moving object related to food or water: A behavior-systems analysis. *Animal Learning & Behavior, 11*, 309–20.

Timberlake, W., & Engle, M. (1995). Decremental carryover of sucrose ingestion in rats in the negative anticipatory contrast procedure. *Journal of Experimental Psychology: Animal Behavior Processes, 21*, 304–17.

Timberlake, W., Gawley, D. J., & Lucas, G. A., (1987). Time horizons in rats foraging for food in temporally separated patches. *Journal of Experimental Psychology; Animal Behavior Processes, 13*, 302–9.

Timberlake, W., & Grant, D. L. (1975). Auto-shaping in rats to the presence of another rat predicting food. *Science, 190*, 690–2.

Tinklepaugh, O. L. (1928). An experimental study of representative factors in monkeys. *Journal of Comparative Psychology, 8*, 197–236.

Tolman, E. C. (1932). *Purposive behavior in animals and men.* New York: Century.

(1959). Principles of purposive behavior. In S. Koch (Ed.), *Psychology: A study of a science, Volume 2. General systematic formulations, learning, and special processes* (pp. 92–157). New York: McGraw-Hill.

Tombaugh, T. N., Szostak, C., Voorneveld, P., & Tombaugh, J. W. (1982). Failure to obtain functional equivalence between dopamine receptor blockade and extinction: Evidence supporting a sensory-motor conditioning hypothesis. *Pharmacology, Biochemistry, & Behavior, 16*, 67–72.

Tomie, A. (1994). Spatial conjunction of reward cue and instrumental response manipulandum (CAM) induces excessive, compulsive, and cyclic patterns of instrumental performance. Unpublished paper, Rutgers University, New Brunswick, NJ.

Torres, M. D. C., Morales, A., Megias, J. L., Candido, A., & Maldonado, A. (1994). Flumazenil antagonizes the effect of diazepam on negative contrast in one-way avoidance learning. *Behavioral Pharmacology, 5*, 637-41.

Treit, D. (1985). Animal models for the study of anti-anxiety agents: A review. *Neuroscience and Biobehavioral Reviews, 9*, 203–22.

Turner, D. M., Ransom, R. W., Yang, S-J., & Olsen, R. W. (1989). Steroid anesthetics and naturally occurring analogs modulate the gamma-amino-butyric acid receptor complex at a site distinct from the barbiturates. *Journal of Pharmacology and Experimental Therapeutics, 248*, 960–6.

Valle, F. P. (1990). Evidence for a calorically costly negative consummatory contrast in rats. *Animal Learning & Behavior, 18*, 387–92.

Vieth, A., & Rilling, M. (1972). Comparison of time-out and extinction as determinants of behavioral contrast: An analysis of sequential effects. *Psychonomic Science, 27*, 281–2.

Vogel, J. R., Beer, B., & Clody, D. E. (1971). A simple and reliable conflict procedure for testing antianxiety agents. *Psychopharmacologia, 21*, 1–7.

Vogel, J. R., Mikulka, P. J., & Spear, N. E. (1968). Effects of shifts in sucrose and saccharin concentrations on licking behavior in the rat. *Journal of Comparative and Physiological Psychology, 66*, 661–6.

Vogel, J. R., & Principi, K. (1971). Effects of chlordiazepoxide on depressed performance after reward reduction. *Psychopharmacologia, 21*, 8–12.

Waddington, K. D., & Heinrich, B. (1981). Patterns of movement and floral choice by foraging bees. In A. C. Kamil & T. D. Sargent (Eds.), *Foraging behavior: Ecological, ethological, and psychological approaches*. New York: Garland STPM Press.

Wagner, A. R. (1959). The role of reinforcement and nonreinforcement in an "apparent frustration effect." *Journal of Experimental Psychology, 57*, 130–6.

(1969). Frustrative non-reward: A variety of punishment? In B. A. Campbell & R. M. Church (Eds.), *Punishment and Aversive Behavior* (pp. 157–81). New York: Appleton-Century-Crofts.

Watson, J. B. (1913). Psychology as the behaviorist views it. *Psychological Review, 20*, 158–77.

(1917). The effect of delayed feeding upon reaction. *Psychobiology, 1*, 51–9.

Weinberg, J., Smotherman, W. P., & Levine, S. (1978). Early handling effects on neophobia and conditioned taste aversion. *Physiology & Behavior, 20*, 589–96.

Weinstein, L. (1970a). Negative incentive contrast effects with saccharin vs. sucrose and partial reinforcement. *Psychonomic Science, 21*, 276–8.

(1970b). Negative incentive contrast with sucrose. *Psychonomic Science, 19*, 13–14.

Weinstock, R. B. (1971). Preacquisition exploration of the runway in the determination of contrast effects in the rat. *Journal of Comparative and Physiological Psychology, 75*, 107–15.

Weissman, B. A., Barrett, J. E., Brady, L. S., Witkin, J. M., Mendelson, W. B., Paul, S. M., & Skolnick, P. (1984). Behavioral and neurochemical studies on the anticonflict actions of buspirone. *Drug Development Research, 4*, 83–93.

Whitaker-Azmitia, P. M., & Peroutka, S. J. (1990). The neuropharmacology of serotonin. *Annals of the New York Academy of Sciences, 600*.

White, K. G. (1978). Behavioral contrast as differential time allocation. *Journal of the Experimental Analysis of Behavior, 29*, 151–60.

White, K. G., Pipe, M., & McLean, A. P. (1984). Stimulus and reinforcer relativity in multiple schedules: Local and dimensional effects on sensitivity to reinforcement. *Journal of the Experimental Analysis of Behavior, 41*, 69–81.

Wilkie, D. M. (1972). Variable-time reinforcement in multiple and concurrent schedules. *Journal of the Experimental Analysis of Behavior, 17*, 59–66.

Williams, B. A., (1974). The role of local interactions in behavioral contrast. *Bulletin of the Psychonomic Society, 4*, 543–5.

(1976). Behavioral contrast as a function of the temporal location of reinforcement. *Journal of the Experimental Analysis of Behavior, 26*, 57–64.

(1979). Contrast, component duration, and the following schedule of reinforcement. *Journal of Experimental Psychology: Animal Behavior Processes, 5*, 379–96.

(1980). Contrast, signaled reinforcement, and the relative law of effect. *American Journal of Psychology, 93*, 617–29.

(1981). The following schedule of reinforcement as a fundamental determinant of steady state contrast in multiple schedules. *Journal of the Experimental Analysis of Behavior, 35*, 293–310.

(1983). Another look at contrast in multiple schedules. *Journal of the Experimental Analysis of Behavior, 39*, 345–84.

(1988). Component transitions and anticipatory contrast. *Bulletin of the Psychonomic Society, 26*, 269–72.

(1989). Component duration effects in multiple schedules. *Animal Learning & Behavior, 17*, 223–33.

(1990). Pavlovian contingencies and anticipatory contrast. *Animal Learning & Behavior, 18*, 44–50.

(1991). Behavioral contrast and reinforcement value. *Animal Learning & Behavior, 19*, 337–44.

(1992a). Competition between stimulus-reinforcer contingencies and anticipatory contrast. *Journal of the Experimental Analysis of Behavior, 58*, 287–302.

(1992b). Inverse relations between preference and contrast. *Journal of the Experimental Analysis of Behavior, 58*, 303–12.

Williams, B. A. & Wixted, J. T. (1986). An equation for behavioral contrast. *Journal of the Experimental Analysis of Behavior, 45*, 47–62.

(1994). Shortcomings of the behavioral competition theory of contrast: Reanalysis of McLean (1992). *Journal of the Experimental Analysis of Behavior, 61*, 107–12.

Willner, P. (Ed.)(1991). *Behavioral models in psychopharmacology: Theoretical, industrial, and clinical perspectives*. Cambridge: Cambridge University Press.

Wilton, R. N., & Clements, R. O. (1972). A failure to demonstrate behavioral contrast when the S⁺ and S⁻ components of a discrimination schedule are separated by about 23 hours. *Psychonomic Science, 28,* 137–9.

Wilton, R. N., & Gay, R. A. (1969). Behavioral contrast in one component of a multiple schedule as a function of the reinforcement conditions operating in the following component. *Journal of the Experimental Analysis of Behavior, 12,* 239–46.

Wise, C. D., Berger, B. D., & Stein, L. (1973). Evidence of alpha-noradrenergic reward receptors and serotonergic punishment receptors in the rat brain. *Biological Psychiatry, 6,* 3–21.

Wise, R. A. (1982). Neuroleptics and operant behavior: The anhedonia hypothesis. *Behavioral and Brain Sciences, 5,* 39–87.

Witkin, J. M., & Barrett, J. E. (1986). Interaction of buspirone and dopaminergic agents on punished behavior of pigeons. *Pharmacology, Biochemistry, & Behavior, 24,* 751–6.

Wolach, A. H., & Latta, K. (1974). Reward magnitude shifts in turtles (*Pseudemys scripta elegans*). *Psychological Record, 24,* 237–41.

Wolach, A. H., Raymond, B., & Hurst, J. W. (1973). Reward magnitude shifts with goldfish. *Psychological Record, 23,* 371–6.

Wolach, A. H., & Seres, M. (1971). Changes in running speed after incentive shifts. *Psychonomic Science, 23,* 238–40.

Wolfe, J. B., & Kaplon, M. D. (1941). Effect of amount of reward and consummative activity on learning in chickens. *Journal of Comparative Psychology, 31,* 353–61.

Woods, P. J. (1967). Performance changes in escape conditioning following shifts in the magnitude of reinforcement. *Journal of Experimental Psychology, 75,* 487–91.

Woodworth, R. S. (1938). *Experimental psychology*. New York: Holt.

Woodworth, R. S., & Schlossberg, H. (1954). *Experimental psychology*. New York: Holt.

Wookey, P. E., & Strongman, K. T. (1974). Reward shift and general activity in the rat. *British Journal of Psychology, 65,* 103–10.

Yarczower, M. (1970). Behavioral contrast and inhibitive stimulus control. *Psychonomic Science, 18,* 1–3.

Yerkes, R. M., & Dodson, J. D. (1908). Relation of strength of stimulus to rapidity of habit formation. *Journal of Comparative Neurophysiology and Psychology, 18,* 459–82.

Young, R., Urbancic, A., Emrey, T. A., Hall, P. C., & Metcalf, G. (1987). Behavioral effects of several new anxiolytics and putative anxiolytics. *European Journal of Pharmacology, 143,* 361–87.

Zeaman, D. (1949). Response latency as a function of the amount of reinforcement. *Journal of Experimental Psychology, 39,* 466–83.

Author Index

Subject Index